W0018859

# XTP: The Xpress Transfer Protocol

# XTP: The Xpress Transfer Protocol

W. Timothy Strayer

Bert J. Dempsey

Alfred C. Weaver

ADDISON-WESLEY PUBLISHING COMPANY, INC.

Reading, Massachusetts   Menlo Park, California   New York   Don Mills, Ontario
Wokingham, England   Amsterdam   Bonn   Paris   Milan   Madrid   Sydney   Singapore   Tokyo
Seoul   Taipei   Mexico City   San Juan

Many of the designations used by manufacturers and sellers to distinguish their products are claimed as trademarks. Where those designations appear in this book and Addison-Wesley was aware of a trademark claim, the designations have been printed with initial capital letters.

The program and applications presented in this book have been included for their instructional value. They have been tested with care, but are not guaranteed for any particular purpose. The publisher does not offer any warranties or any representations, nor does it accept any liabilities with respect to the programs or applications.

Protocol Engine® is a registered trademark of Protocol Engines, Inc.
SBus® is a registered trademark of Sun Microsystems, Inc.
UNIX® is a registered trademark of UNIX System Laboratories, Inc.

The publisher offers discounts on this book when ordered in quantity for special sales.
For more information please contact:
>  Corporate & Professional Publishing Group
>  Addison-Wesley Publishing Company
>  One Jacob Way
>  Reading, Massachusetts 01867

**Library of Congress Cataloging-in-Publication Data**

Strayer, W. Timothy
>  XTP: The Xpress transfer protocol / W. Timothy Strayer, Bert J. Dempsey, Alfred C. Weaver.
>  p. cm.
>  Includes bibliographical references (p. ) and index.
>  ISBN 0-201-56351-7
>  1. Xpress Transfer Protocol (Computer network protocol)
>  I. Dempsey, Bert J. II. Weaver, Alfred Charles. III. Title.
>  TK5105.5.S79 1992                                            92-5580
>  004.6′2--dc20                                                 CIP

Copyright © 1992 by Addison-Wesley Publishing Company, Inc.

Cover design by Simone R. Payment and C. Shane Sykes

All rights reserved. No part of this publication may be reproduced, stored in a retrieval system, or transmitted, in any form or by any means, electronic, mechanical, photocopying, recording, or otherwise, without the prior written permission of the publisher. Printed in the United States of America. Published simultaneously in Canada.

0-201-56351-7
1 2 3 4 5 6 7 8 9 10 MU 9695949392
First printing, July 1992

# **Dedications**

To my parents, Kathryn and Bill,
and my brothers, David and Steffen,
for their love and support in all that I do.
—Tim Strayer

For the other Bert J.,
the one Geneva B.,
and my incomparable Molly C.
—Bert Dempsey

To the memory of my father, Charles F. Weaver,
who provided me with a lifetime of love, support,
and encouragement.
—Alf Weaver

# Table of Contents

# Preface

In the mid-1970s Ethernet was a protocol specification on paper; today it is a single chip inside the vast majority of networked workstations and PC clusters. Later, other MAC protocols followed the same evolution from software implementations of the state machines to firmware assistance to chipsets on board-level products. Until recently, the siliconization of local area network protocols was limited to medium access control, even though higher layer protocols had been around for over twenty years.

The confluence of certain technological advancements—the maturation of VLSI techniques, the improvements in network hardware capabilities, the shift in application demands on network services—have driven the siliconization process into higher layer network protocols. An international group of researchers, led by Greg Chesson at Protocol Engines Inc., has developed a new *transfer* layer (the integration of the traditional *transport* and *network* layers) communications protocol specifically designed to meet the needs of modern, distributed computing systems. This is the *Xpress Transfer Protocol*.[1]

To some extent, the design of XTP has been motivated by the desire to exploit the same performance advantages gained by the silicon implementations of MAC protocols. Yet XTP is more than just a transport and network layer protocol suite placed in a silicon package. The design incorporates ideas found in several extant communications protocols and also provides new services useful to current and emerging distributed applications. XTP provides these services with a number of orthogonal protocol options from which the XTP user selects the configuration that supports the user's needs. This design reflects a clear separation of policy from mechanism.

XTP is specifically designed for implementation in hardware as the *Protocol Engine*. The Protocol Engine attacks the problem of reducing the overall communications subsystem overhead through hardware-assisted buffer management, data copying, and protocol processing. When coupled with a commercial FDDI network, the Protocol Engine will be able to process packets at the same speed as their arrival from the network medium. Thus, the Protocol Engine promises to provide transport and network layer services at rates of 100 Mbits/sec in the near future, and gigabit/sec speeds as the hardware technology matures.

We have been involved in the on-going design and evaluation of XTP since its inception in 1987. Our research group, the Computer Networks Laboratory at the Uni-

---

[1] **The XTP Protocol Definition is in the public domain and is available on request from Protocol Engines Inc., 1900 State Street, Suite D, Santa Barbara, California 93101, U.S.A., or by electronic mail at Internet address *xtp-request@pei.com*.**

versity of Virginia, has participated in the Protocol Engines Inc.'s Technical Advisory Board and has implemented versions of XTP culminating with the now-current version 3.6. Our experience with XTP ranges over a number of different platforms (e.g., Intel 80x86, Motorola 680x0, SUN SPARCstation, RS/6000), operating systems (e.g., DOS, pSOS+, UNIX, AIX), and local area networks (Ethernet, Token Ring, and FDDI).

The purpose of this book is to explain the origin, features, functionality, advantages, structure, operation, and uses of the Xpress Transfer Protocol. The book is intended to serve as a professional reference for scientists, engineers, and engineering managers who specify, design, install, or supervise computer communications networks. In addition, the book should prove interesting to researchers and advanced students of communications protocols since it discusses the relevant concerns and issues of protocol design at the transport and network layers. It provides a comprehensive survey of some of the most important transport protocols developed during the last fifteen years, and also discusses group communication concepts as an introduction to how a transport protocol can support a reliable multicast paradigm. Finally, the book gives a detailed description of XTP's internal design and operation, with explanation on the motivation behind key design decisions.

Over the past four years the XTP project has evolved from abstract ideas to software implementations in experimental environments to a mature protocol ready for silicon. We feel fortunate to have had an active role in this not-so-easy birth of a new networking technology.

W. Timothy Strayer
Bert J. Dempsey
Alfred C. Weaver

University of Virginia
March 1992

# Acknowledgements

We would like to thank our friends and colleagues in the Computer Networks Laboratory, Department of Computer Science, University of Virginia, who have worked with us since 1987 in developing, analyzing, implementing, and evaluating XTP. We are especially indebted to Robert Simoncic, John Fenton, and Alex Colvin, the primary designers of our XTP implementations at the University of Virginia. We also recognize many fruitful and engaging conversations with James McNabb and Timothy Hartrick during this period.

We thank our reviewers who gave the manuscript a thoughtful reading and thereby improved the final product. We gratefully acknowledge the pioneering work of Greg Chesson and Larry Green, the driving forces behind XTP and the Protocol Engine project.

# Foreword

Networking protocols are like houseguests—a small number of them seems like a crowd. So what would possess someone to create a new protocol when most computer systems already have a full house, and why should anyone write a book about it? Answers to these and other questions can be found in **XTP: The Xpress Transfer Protocol** by Strayer, Dempsey, and Weaver.

The majority of networking books are like accounting texts, but with less charisma. They catalog facts and procedures, bits and bytes, but rarely discuss the circumstances or reasoning behind a design. Not so for this book about XTP. The authors devote roughly one-third of the pages and four of the nine chapters to background information about XTP and other protocols. These background chapters keep the rest of the book from becoming another numbing recitation. Along the way the book provides answers to the question of "why design a new protocol?"

In the first chapter the authors begin by describing several aspects of network evolution and argue for a corresponding evolution in protocol techniques. They characterize XTP as a natural outgrowth of changing technical environments. The second and third chapters compare the design philosophies in XTP to the design philosophies found in other well-known protocols and in the formal models of OSI. These chapters bring together a diversity of networking concepts that are usually separated in the literature. This creates an audience for the book beyond the specialists who may be interested in only XTP.

The basics of XTP are presented as successive refinements in chapters four, five, and six, and the issues of addressing and multicast are discussed in chapters seven and eight. XTP frame formats and procedures are introduced in chapter four and then discussed in increasing detail in later chapters. This style of presentation is slightly unusual among protocol reference works, which usually strive for more terse, compact, and formal descriptions. However, it makes the book more accessible for a reader who either is studying network protocols for the first time or is already familiar with the area and wants an introduction to XTP.

Cross-pollination of protocol designs can blur the distinctions between protocols that evolve over time and borrow from the same sources. XTP can claim some uniqueness in its design and methodology—it is a first attempt to include VLSI implementation issues as well as operating system and media considerations. It will probably not be the last attempt. The authors make these points in greater detail than previous XTP-related publications. They also point out that the XTP design does not pretend to be completely unique; it borrows freely from other designs.

The authors are well-qualified to discuss network protocols and real-time systems. Together with their colleagues in the Computer Networks Laboratory at the University of Virginia they have produced several notable systems since the laboratory was formed in 1980. These include a real-time executive, a distributed control system, network performance monitors, and implementations of XTP on several platforms.

Experienced designers and implementors seldom take the time to write a useful book—normally there is a race to build the next great system. In that sense we are fortunate that a book about XTP has been produced by experts who have actually implemented XTP and have been involved in its design. We are also fortunate that the book is about more than just XTP. By embedding the XTP discussion in a larger framework of technology trends, the book records a broad segment of the current state of the art. This book will be a welcome and useful addition to the bookshelves of students and protocol designers, as well as implementors of XTP.

Greg Chesson

# List of Figures

**Chapter 6**

**Chapter 7**

# List of Tables

# 1
# Foundations of the
# Xpress Transfer Protocol

Computer networking technology has seen enormous growth over the past thirty years. In the 1960s, "networking" was synonymous with the telephone network, and communications speeds of hundreds of bits per second were common when using telephone modems; packet radio technology increased the data communications rate to thousands of bits per second. In the 1970s a new concept was introduced: the local area network (LAN). In particular, Ethernet brought transmission speeds of 10 million bits per second (Mbit/sec). In the 1980s, LAN and MAN (metropolitan area network) speeds increased to the order of 100 million bits per second, and we expect to see deployment of wide area network (WAN) gigabit per second networks in the 1990s. Advanced research agencies are thinking aloud about terabit technologies early in the next decade.

How will this seemingly unlimited bandwidth be used? The explosive growth in Internet attachments—recently estimated at 20% per month—suggests that higher connectivity will be a major factor. More people are using electronic mail, file transfer, and remote login than ever before. This increased connectivity supports Bill Wulf's view of a *collaboratory* [WULF88], in which the computer network provides the infrastructure for advanced research in all scientific disciplines.

As more bandwidth becomes available, new applications quickly make use of it. Super-high-resolution displays used for scientific visualization (nuclear reactions, molecular modeling), medical imaging and remote diagnostics (CAT scans, magnetic resonance imagery), and computer-to-computer communication of terabit databases (weather modeling, earth observing satellites) are examples of current and emerging applications that require enormous bandwidth. Yet increasing the bandwidth available to the user only solves part of the problem—many applications must also have low latency. These applications include control systems on ships (navigation, weapons systems), airframes (engine and flight controls), and space vehicles (sensor data acquisition, telemetry), among other time-constrained applications. With the advent of multimedia applications such as teleconferencing, the need for simultaneous high bandwidth and low latency is evident.

In addition, the fundamental nature of computing systems is changing. No longer confined to an individual processor, applications are *distributed* across a multiplicity of computers, thereby making the communications network a critical factor in the overall systems architecture. For a particular system, the choice of communication protocols ultimately controls both the *functionality* of the communications services offered to the applications as well as the *performance* observed by the users of the services. As the link between the raw medium interface and the services available to the application, the transport and network protocols are crucial elements in modern networks.

To be advantageous, any new protocol for modern distributed systems must address the issues of both functionality and performance. With regard to functionality, the protocol should not only provide the traditional connection-oriented services but should support such new ideas as transactions, user-defined service reliability, multi-peer communications, and latency control. With regard to performance, the design of the protocol should permit a wide range of implementation options—from all software to all hardware—so that system designers can balance performance and economics. While the protocol must be invariant, its implementations should scale gracefully from megabit to gigabit media. In other words, the protocol's internal design complexity must not prohibit a high-performance, all-hardware implementation.

# 1.1  Why *Any* New Protocol?

The communications industry has already developed several transport and network protocols, so why change? The motivation for change arises from taking a hard look at the state of the art below, above, and within the data transport service. Looking at the technology below, data rates are higher and bit error rates are lower, thus increasing the ever-widening disparity between the bandwidth available on the medium and the band-width actually available to the transport user. Looking above, distributed applications now treat the network as a "virtual backplane bus" that interconnects the system's components, thereby requiring expanded services from the transport provider. Looking within, a protocol that encourages a range of implementations—software, hardware, or some combination—allows a system designer to balance cost and performance, while holding the protocol itself constant.

## 1.1.1 Changes Below

The recent rise in network signaling speeds has not been accompanied by equivalent gains in the fraction of network bandwidth that is actually available to the application program. For example, where are the applications that—when throughput is measured at the interface to the transport protocol—see a tenfold increase when using Fiber Distributed Data Interface (FDDI) rather than Ethernet?

This disparity between bandwidth *available* and bandwidth *delivered* can be traced in part to the tremendous increase in data transmission rates, the increase in volume of data in transit due to longer data pipelines, and the dramatic decrease in bit error rates on the medium; all of these characterize modern communication systems.

High data rates have at least four effects. First, higher transmission speeds imply shorter per-byte processing times. The processing of a byte at the medium access control (MAC) layer, which is allowed 800 nsec on an Ethernet, is shortened to 80 nsec on FDDI and to 8 nsec on a 1 gigabit per second (Gbit/sec) network. In the same way that implementations of MAC layer protocols have turned to specialized hardware, transport protocols must permit a hardware assistance if processing at media speeds is to be attained.

Second, as gigabit WANs introduce the situation where propagation times exceed transmission times, protocol designers must rethink the traditional notion of handshaking for connection setup. For transaction-oriented applications, it does not make sense for the connection setup and teardown overhead to take longer than the actual data request and response. A more efficient, transaction-oriented paradigm is required.

Third, when data rates were slow and processing was (relatively) fast, designers and implementors built protocols that "packed" the bits of a message in an effort to reduce transmitted packet size. Now the network and the processors are both fast, and preserving this philosophy only burdens the processor without creating any significant gain for the network. To achieve high throughput and low latency simultaneously, protocol design must allow for quick parsing and rapid decision making.

Finally, high data rates imply that there are more bits in the pipeline between users. For example, on a coast-to-coast fiber optic link operating at one Gbit/sec, there can be 20 million bits in transit on a single connection. The designers of protocols originally developed to operate over 56 kilobit per second (Kbit/sec) telephone lines never conceived of having this much data outstanding at one time. Having large volumes of data in transit requires a rethinking of such fundamental transport mechanisms as retransmission strategy, buffer allocation policy, flow control, and rate control. Additionally, it is insufficient for these policies to be applied only end-to-end; intermediate routers must participate in these decisions if they are to be effective.

Low bit error rates are a beneficial result of the move toward fiber optic networks. The two most widely known transport protocols, the Transmission Control Protocol (TCP) and the ISO Transport Protocol class 4 (TP4), were designed for an era when network transmission bandwidth was low and error rates were high. This was a time when copper wire or radio transmission was the medium available, and bit error rates were on the order of $10^{-5}$. But as we enter the 1990s, fiber optic technology is rapidly replacing copper—the long-distance telephone carriers are installing fiber optic lines as fast as they can, the fiber optic FDDI LAN is rapidly gaining consumer acceptance, and all new LAN designs for use on ships, aircraft, and space vehicles specify fiber optic media.

The bit error rate characteristics of fiber optic channels (on the order of $10^{-12}$ or better) are so different from that of other media that a fundamental paradigm shift for protocol designers is occurring. Rather than assuming that the underlying network is basically unreliable and that much protocol effort need be expended for error detection and repair, it is now more realistic to assume that the physical transmission of data is basically reliable. On fiber optic networks, for example, data loss due to buffer overruns is more likely by orders of magnitude than data loss due to corruption on the medium.

## 1.1.2 Changes Above

When data transmission rates were low, the natural reaction of system designers was to limit their use of the network. But now that data rates are high and getting higher, designers increasingly assume that network bandwidth, no longer a scarce resource, may be used with impunity. There seems to be a sense of "the network's there; let's use it!"

Networked applications are no longer foreign to system designers. Perhaps it is the influence of the ubiquitous Internet, but for whatever reason, once a designer has used a system with worldwide connectivity, there is extreme reluctance to engineer stand-alone, unconnected systems. This desire for connectivity naturally adds to the volume of traffic networks must carry.

Once relegated to file transfer and electronic mail, or used simply as a means to share common but expensive peripherals, networks must now supply a plethora of new user services. In a sense, the network has become the "virtual backplane" for distributed applications. Networks may be called upon to support process synchronization, transaction processing, multiple priority messages, reliable one-to-many transmission, both unacknowledged and reliable datagrams, as well as traditional connection-oriented services.

## 1.1.3 Changes Within

Requiring the transport layer simultaneously to support increased functionality and increased performance is a major challenge for a next-generation transport layer design. Achieving this goal will require a restructuring of the way communications services are provided.

Network subsystem processing[1] can always be done the conventional way—by making the host support both protocol processing and the application programs—and this approach is acceptable if neither activity represents a system bottleneck. However, for those applications that do not wish to share the computational power of their host, an alternative is to move some of the network processing overhead onto a separate front-end processor.

Given that many of the functions associated with data transfer are independent, off-host processing provides opportunities for parallelism. The host interface, protocol parsing, network interface, and internal buffer control are all potentially parallel pro-

---

[1] By "network subsystem processing" we mean not only traditional protocol processing but also data movement, buffer management, operating system and application interfacing, and device handling.

cesses. While a particular packet would be handled serially, the processes themselves can be operating in parallel. While one packet is being received from the network, another can be undergoing protocol parsing, while yet another is being transmitted across the backplane to the host. New communications architectures can exploit this parallelism.

Of course, off-host processing is not a guaranteed win. Even if protocol processing were infinitely fast, there are a number of other factors that limit overall system performance. Among them are

- the speed of the backplane bus,
- the front-end's contention for the backplane bus,
- the number of data copies required to move information between the host and the protocol processor,
- the number of hardware interrupts generated by packet processing,
- the choice of a shared memory versus a message passing architecture between the host and the front-end,
- the efficiency of the host's operating system, and
- the subtle interactions that sometimes emerge when using a "device driver" to control a peripheral (the protocol processor).

In addition, one can not discount the elusive factor of quality of implementation. A skillful implementation of a less powerful protocol may nevertheless outperform a naive implementation of a more powerful one. Given these uncertainties, the best a protocol designer can do is to ensure that the protocol's intrinsic design does not unduly restrict the range and style of implementation options.

## 1.1.4 Repair or Replace?

How does one provide transport and network layer services in the 1990s, when there is a simultaneous need for richer services and more efficient execution? The two basic choices are

1. select the best match from among all extant protocols, then modify that protocol as much as necessary to add the required new features, and rely on skillful implementation to improve efficiency, or
2. start with a clean sheet of paper, design a new protocol with all the required features, and make execution efficiency an inherent part of the design process.

The design group for the Protocol Engine Project [CHES87] believed that the modifications required to any extant protocol would be so significant and so numerous that it would be tantamount to designing a new protocol anyway. Thus, the design group chose the second option, and the result of that collective effort is called the *Xpress Transfer Protocol*.

# 1.2   Why *This* New Protocol?

The Xpress Transfer Protocol is notable for several reasons:

- It is designed to accommodate the reality of modern systems: high data rates, densely packed bitpipes, low bit error rates. While XTP itself is not dependent upon any particular underlying medium, it is poised to reap the benefits of modern, fast, fiber optic networks.

- The protocol is itself *programmable* in the sense that the transmitter can select the options that govern the data exchange. Said another way, XTP provides *mechanisms*; the user selects *policy*.

- XTP preserves individual features found to be useful in other extant protocols (see Chapter 3), while at the same time combining and extending these features to support modern distributed processing applications.

- XTP's transfer layer architecture integrates network routing with transport processing. The end-systems can be more tightly coordinated because the intermediate nodes participate in rate control.

- The protocol supports "parametric addressing." Without introducing (yet another) network addressing plan, XTP will operate with any of a dozen different addressing schemes, including Internet addresses and ISO 8348 network addresses.

- For all its power, XTP still retains a basic finite state machine design. When implemented in silicon as the Protocol Engine, XTP will perform all its transfer layer duties and still deliver packets to the host at the same rate that they arrive from the network.

As a result, XTP features both functional and performance advantages over traditional protocols. XTP provides new services to support modern distributed applications and is explicitly designed for high throughput, low latency implementations.

## 1.2.1 Functional Enhancements

### Data Pipeline Size

Protocols that use a relatively small sequence number and/or sliding window space restrict the number of bytes that can be in the data transmission pipeline. This will prove inadequate for the forthcoming gigabit networks of the 1990s. XTP anticipated this situation by providing a full 32-bit sequence number space and sliding window (i.e., up to four gigabytes outstanding on each connection). Also, XTP transitions gracefully to 64-bit sequence numbers for future terabit networks.

## Rate Control

XTP allows parametric control over both the rate of data transmission and the amount of data transmitted at one time. The *rate* parameter allows a receiver to specify a maximum rate at which the transmitter may emit data; this helps synchronize not only the transmitter and receiver but, properly used, the intermediate nodes as well. The *burst* parameter allows the user to specify the maximum amount of data that the receiver can handle effectively; this augments flow control in avoiding buffer starvation. In addition, routers may participate in rate control, so that a connection can be optimized not only for the end-systems but also for the particular route being used. Rate control protects the network while permitting more effective communications end-to-end.

## Priorities

A well-known problem with traditional transport protocols is that they are not very responsive to user data of varying importance. This is particularly crucial for real-time systems. Thus, XTP provides a powerful discrimination mechanism (the *sort* field) at the transport layer. Users optionally encode a 32-bit *sort* value to indicate a message's priority in a space of over 4 billion possibilities. Within the XTP delivery subsystem, including both end-systems and intermediate routers, the *sort* value of incoming packets is used to influence intraprotocol scheduling. At each transmission opportunity, a node selects its most important packet and operates on it; this provides discrimination among competing packets with a granularity of one packet's transmission time.

## Out-of-band Data

It is occasionally useful to send information *about* the data stream without embedding it *within* the data stream itself. This so-called out-of-band channel is useful for passing control information about the state of the end-user processes, or for passing semantic information about the data itself, or for event sequencing via timestamps. XTP accomplishes out-of-band transmission by permitting each packet to carry eight bytes of *tagged* data. XTP delivers the tagged data to the end user, along with a flag indicating its presence, but XTP itself does not interpret tagged data.

## No-error Mode

Some applications do not require retransmission of lost data. If subsequent data will soon be available, it may be preferable to ignore lost data rather than retransmit "stale" data. This is accomplished with XTP's *no-error mode*, which suspends the normal retransmission scheme. Correctly received data is properly sequenced, but gaps in the data are not retransmitted.

## Policy Vs. Mechanism

XTP's provision for no-error mode is a good example of an important underlying philosophy—the separation of *policy* from *mechanism*. XTP attempts to provide a rich set of mechanisms, but avoids implementing specific, pre-established policies. XTP recognizes that only the user has sufficient knowledge concerning the application to truly optimize the parameters of a data exchange.

## Multicast

XTP provides a powerful mechanism for group communication. A multicast transmitter may address an arbitrarily large receiver group, replacing $n$ unicast transmissions with a single multicast transmission. Since this is a transport layer multicast (not a datalink multicast or broadcast), it is reliable end-to-end, providing flow-, rate-, and error-controlled transmission of arbitrary messages to arbitrary-sized groups. The potential applications of multicast (e.g., distributed databases, multimedia workstations, teleconferencing, sensor data distribution) are so numerous that multicast may prove to be XTP's single most important asset.

# 1.2.2 Performance Enhancements

## Header/Trailer Protocol

Classical transport protocols (e.g., TCP, TP4) are *header* protocols in that all control information is prepended to the data packet. This means that the transport checksum must be in the header, which in turn implies that the whole packet must be processed to compute the checksum before transmission can begin. Thus, every byte of every packet must be handled at least twice—once to checksum it and once to transmit it. While control information in XTP is in the header, the data checksum is in the trailer. This allows the transport checksum to be calculated by a hardware checksum unit and to be appended to the data "on-the-fly," thereby eliminating one sequential pass through the data.

## Fixed-length Fields

Classical transport protocols permit variable length headers, which means that the options flags change position within the header depending upon the particular options chosen. To promote efficiency, XTP fixes the length of the header and trailer and the position of all flags within the header.

## Efficient Connection Setup and Teardown

Reliable transmission in TP4 requires the exchange of six packets: two to request and confirm a connection, two to send and acknowledge data, and two to release and confirm the closure of the connection. XTP achieves the same reliability with the exchange of only two packets. This implicit connection setup is not required, however, and the more conventional open handshakes can easily be mimicked. Moreover, unlike TP4 or TCP, XTP's connection close mechanisms enable the implementation of a variety of connection close semantics for the pair of simplex data streams that make up an XTP connection. The connection release paradigms supported include, for example, bidirectional graceful close in which the two data streams are independently closed (reliable transaction), unidirectional graceful close with the initiating side forcing the close of the reverse stream, unidirectional graceful close (acknowledged datagram), and forced terminations (aborts).

## Address Translation

Connection establishment ultimately requires the resolution of a network address into a connection identifier. Resolution of addressing information can be a significant component of per-packet processing overhead. To minimize this overhead, XTP has evolved a key-based scheme. The initial XTP packet that sets up an XTP association contains an *Address Segment* and an *address format* field. Through a hashing function, initial addresses are resolved into a 32-bit *key* field, and subsequent packets can be identified by a table lookup on that field. Furthermore, XTP does not introduce (yet another) network addressing plan; XTP can operate with any of a dozen extant network addressing plans, including the Internet Protocol (IP) and the ISO 8348 addressing scheme.

## Routing

XTP's transfer layer architecture enables efficiencies in end-to-end data delivery. Path establishment is accomplished at the same time, with the same packet used for connection setup. After path establishment, special packet types are provided for path maintenance, independent of the packet exchanges required by the connection. The "cut-through" routing employed in XTP is specifically designed for compatibility with emerging gigabit networks and ATM (Asynchronous Transfer Mode) switches. In addition, the packet format is invariant regardless of whether routing is performed by switched media or traditional network layer routing.

## Retransmission

In a reliable service, error detection results in retransmission. TCP and TP4 both use a go-back-*n* retransmission scheme in which the transmission window is reset and begins anew with the lost byte (TCP) or packet (TP4). This scheme may redeliver information that has already been correctly received. XTP implements go-back-*n*, but in addition permits a potentially more efficient scheme called *selective retransmission*. Receivers can provide a vector indicating what *spans* of information have been correctly received, and the sender can then retransmit only the *gaps*.

## Acknowledgement Control

TCP and TP4 provide automatic acknowledgements for information received correctly; this reflects the designer's underlying assumption that the network frequently loses packets and thus positive acknowledgement is a virtue. XTP allows the transmitter to decide whether and when acknowledgements are desirable. Within XTP, the transmitter is in control. Receivers do what they are asked to do, when they are asked to do it, but in general they do not automatically provide information that is not requested.

## Alignment

Data alignment may seem to be a simple notion, but its use pays big dividends. XTP aligns its fields on 4-byte boundaries. Rather than aligning nonaligned data, which would involve copying, XTP uses an *offset* field and a *length* field to identify the beginning and end of user data in a frame that may be physically longer. Since data copying is a very time-consuming operation, mechanisms that avoid it are advantageous.

## VLSI Implementation

XTP retains a basic finite state machine design. VLSI engineers are working to produce a hardware implementation of XTP that will mate initially with a commercial FDDI chipset. The resulting Protocol Engine will be able to deliver back-to-back packets to the host at the same rate at which they arrive from the network. Future connections to gigabit networks are also envisioned.

# 1.3   History of XTP

The leader of the XTP effort is Greg Chesson, Chief Scientist of the Research and Development Division of Silicon Graphics, Inc. (SGI) and a co-founder of Protocol Engines Inc. Chesson's work in the late 1970s and early 1980s in helping develop the Datakit network at Bell Telephone Laboratories convinced him that conventional transport protocols were too ponderous, and that a new approach was desirable. This opinion was reinforced by his own experience in trying to use existing operating systems, protocols, and networks (UNIX, TCP/IP, and Ethernet in this case) to support visualization, distributed computing, and multimedia applications. In this environment Chesson measured that, compared to the 10 Mbit/sec signaling rate of Ethernet, the application program saw an effective throughput of about 1.2 Mbit/sec [CHES87]. The primary causes for the low throughput were observed to be (1) the sharing of the CPU between the application program and the protocol processing, (2) the multiplicity of interactions with the operating system (generated by the application, the protocol suite, and the network interface) resulting in many context swaps, and (3) the inflexibility of the protocol suite in providing any service other than a reliable byte stream. Chesson concluded that improvements were needed in the fundamental communications services provided, as well as their performance.

Larry Green (then the co-chairman of the Station Management subcommittee for the ANSI X3T9.5 committee that developed FDDI) observed that conventional transport protocols were delivering only a small fraction of FDDI's 100 Mbit/sec data rate to their hosts. Liba Svobodova at IBM Zurich Research Laboratories and Tim Strayer *et al.* at the University of Virginia were publishing performance measurements that confirmed that commercial implementations of the TCP and TP4 protocols were delivering only a small portion of the network's bandwidth to the transport user [SVOB89], [STRA88]. These experiments reinforced Chesson's observation that the reasons for the low throughput were complex, involving not only the protocol design itself but also its interactions with the operating system and network interface.

Recalling his Datakit experience with *lightweight* protocols, Chesson embarked on a project to develop a new solution to the data delivery problem. From the beginning he realized that any practical solution to the problem would have to touch on several protocol issues simultaneously. The protocol's services would have to encompass more possibilities than just traditional, connection-oriented transport; the protocol's packets would have to be easy to parse; the protocol's implementation would have to minimize interactions with the operating system; and finally, the protocol's algorithms would have to be designed for hardware assistance.

Chesson and Green co-founded Protocol Engines Inc. (PEI) in 1987 to pursue the challenge of a high-speed transport protocol implemented in silicon. PEI established a Technical Advisory Board (TAB) in 1987 whose for-profit corporate members[2] represented potential users of a VLSI Protocol Engine; universities, government agencies, and not-for-profit institutions[3] joined the TAB as Research Affiliate (RAF) members. PEI sponsored six meetings annually (beginning in February 1988) to discuss the protocol design. The TAB/RAF quickly became an international group as both researchers and implementors from Canada, France, Germany, Sweden, and the United Kingdom joined those from the United States.

In those early days, the TAB set four objectives for itself:

1. to understand the data transport problem in a fundamental way, by examining what functionality and performance must be provided in a modern, distributed computing system,

2. to devise a transfer layer protocol that could meet those objectives,

3. to make the design public in support of open systems, and to solicit the comments, suggestions, and recommendations of the larger protocol design and implementation community, and

4. to implement the protocol first in software (to facilitate research, testing, and debugging) and then in hardware (to enhance performance).

---

[2.] **By the end of 1991, TAB membership included: AMD, Artel/NASA, Boeing, Concurrent, Crosfield Electronics, DY-4, E-Systems, IBM, Intel, Intergraph, Interphase, Linotype-Hell AG, Lockheed, Northrop, SBE, Scitex, Unisys, Xerox.**

[3.] **By the end of 1991, RAF membership included: Admiralty Research Establishment, Bowman Gray School of Medicine, Concordia University, Electronics & Telecomm Research Institute, Laboratoire de Genie Informatique, Johns Hopkins University, National Center for Supercomputer Applications, Naval Ocean Systems Center, Naval Surface Warfare Center, Superconducting Supercollider Lab, Technical University of Aachen, University of Karlsruhe, University of Kentucky, University of Massachusetts, University of Melbourne, University of Virginia.**

To address the first objective, the TAB studied an array of applications including networks of engineering workstations, real-time weapons control systems on ships, real-time aerodynamic control of aircraft in flight, data management services for NASA's Space Station, and multimedia teleconferencing. The group considered not only the extant topologies of LANs, MANs, and WANs but also the impact of emerging gigabit networks and ATM switches. From these studies, two main conclusions were drawn: (1) modern, complex applications tended to be distributed, and (2) the two traditional transport services, connection-oriented and connectionless (datagram), were inadequate for these new applications. If a new protocol was to be designed, then it needed to support new mechanisms, including transactions, reliable datagrams, multicast, and message priorities.

The second objective, defining the protocol, was achieved by publishing a series of XTP Protocol Definitions, starting with a set of "white papers" in 1987 and leading to the current XTP version 3.6 (January 1992, [PEI92]). Each new revision of the protocol reflected the lessons learned from studying and implementing the previous version. The Protocol Engine chipset design follows the XTP 3.6 Definition.

The third objective, making the protocol design public, was easily accomplished. All the Definitions and all their supporting documents have always been available from PEI. The Xpress Transfer Protocol is in the public domain.

The software implementations (objective four) proved to be an invaluable part of the protocol design process. Implementations at PEI and at several research and industrial sites contributed to the fundamental understanding of the data transfer process, as well as to the development of effective mechanisms to handle the new services such as multicast. The hardware implementation is currently underway.

One group of supporters of the XTP effort has been the designers of the U.S. Navy's SAFENET II (Survivable Adaptable Fiber Optic Embedded Network II) specification [SAFE92]. SAFENET II specifies an all fiber optic shipboard network based on the commercial FDDI standard. As shown in Figure 1.1, it also mandates a dual set of protocols for communications—a suite of ISO protocols selected to encourage interoperability among diverse vendors of heterogeneous components, and the Xpress Transfer Protocol to handle time-constrained applications. SAFENET's adoption of XTP as its transport and network layers on the *lightweight* side of the communications architecture is a major vote of confidence in the XTP project.

Standardization is a slow process, and one which has only recently begun. In 1991 the American National Standards Institute (ANSI) approved a study project for a High Speed Transport Protocol (HSTP), and the results of that effort were submitted to ISO SC6 (International Standardization Organization, subcommittee 6) in February 1992. This group agreed to initiate a new project entitled "Enhanced Communications Functions and Facilities for OSI Lower Layers." These enhancements include:

- very high data throughput capability for operation over high speed transmission facilities (e.g., ATM, FDDI, and Broadband-ISDN)
- multicast operation to support multipeer applications

- selectable error control procedures
- quality of service selection and management
- out-of-band signaling and synchronization
- efficient operation

While the results of the HSTP effort within ISO will certainly not be XTP as we know it now, it seems clear that HSTP will at least embody many of the defining concepts within XTP.  Since the ISO effort is likely to extend until at least 1995, we expect XTP 3.6 and its implementation within the *Protocol Engine* to be viable for several years to come.

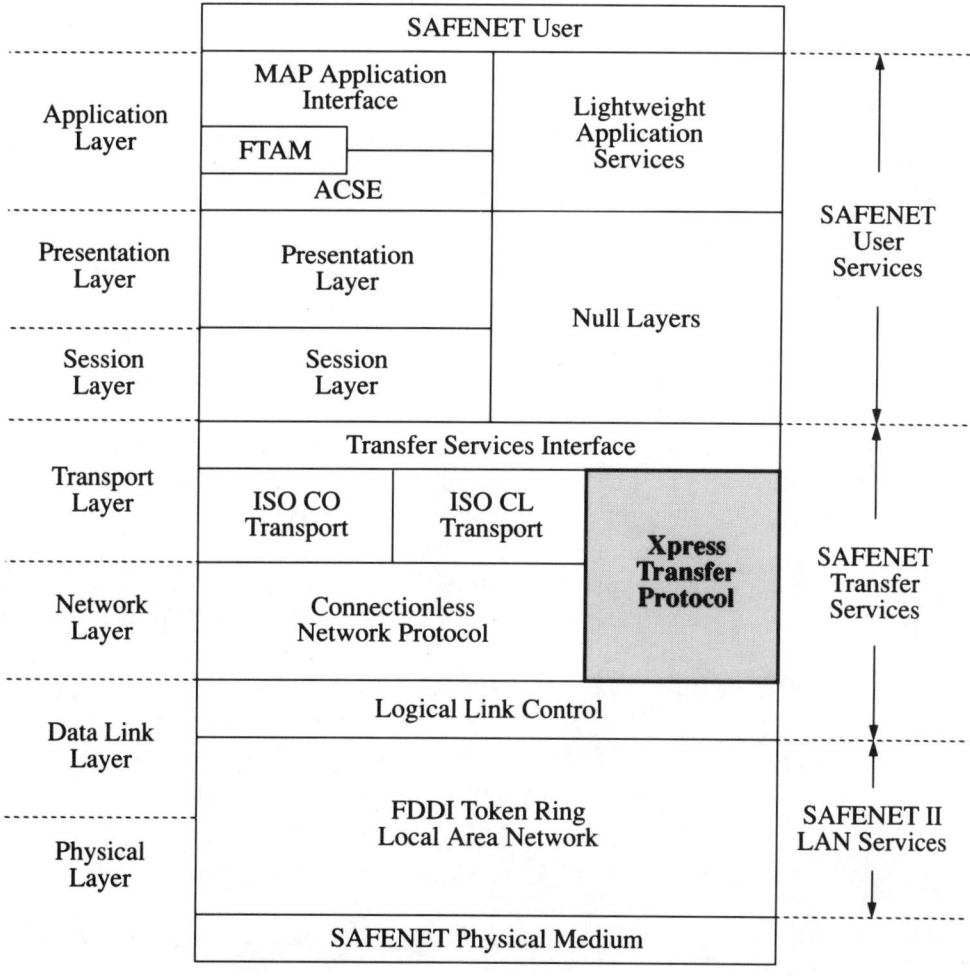

**Figure 1.1 — SAFENET II Communications Architecture**

# 1.4   Organization of Book

The rest of this book is organized as follows.

Chapter 2 reviews the required basic network concepts and terminology. It explains the services provided by the network and transport layers and examines the design choices at these layers. The chapter then offers an architectural overview of XTP and XTP's model of communications.

Chapter 3 surveys the transport protocols and service definitions that most influenced XTP, identifying the lessons learned and the ideas extracted from each. The list of influential protocols covers most of the important conventional and experimental transport protocols from the past fifteen years.

Chapter 4 begins the discussion of the internal workings of the Xpress Transfer Protocol itself. It discusses how packet exchanges are used to implement protocol procedures. The protocol procedures include establishing, maintaining, and terminating XTP duplex connections (*associations*); managing the paths used by associations; controlling data flow and rate; and detecting and correcting errors.

Chapter 5 presents the packet structures used in XTP and describes in detail the components used to build XTP packets—the Header, the Trailer, the Control Segment, and the Information Segment.

Chapter 6 shows how various packet formats are constructed and which fields within the packets are used for particular packet formats. The discussion in Chapter 6 builds on the field-level presentation in Chapter 5 in order to explain both the role of and the legal syntax for each packet format within the protocol.

Chapter 7 describes addressing and encapsulation. This chapter explains how *parametric addressing* is used within XTP to thread a path through intermediate switching nodes between XTP endpoints. Encapsulation specifies how an XTP packet is placed within the frame of an underlying data delivery service.

Chapter 8 contains a general discussion of the growing importance of group communication within distributed applications, followed by an examination of the mechanisms provided by XTP for group communication. In particular, XTP provides a novel multicast mechanism that can be operated with either reliable or unreliable semantics.

Chapter 9 looks ahead to the implementation of XTP in silicon by showing the preliminary design and layout of the Protocol Engine PE1000 chipset. This set of chips, including a MAC interface, a host interface, a buffer controller, and a control processor, implements the various protocol functions in a pipelined manner.

## References

[CHES87]        Chesson, G., "The Protocol Engine Project," *UNIX Review*, Vol. 5, No. 9 (September 1987).

[PEI92]         Protocol Engines Inc., "Xpress Transfer Protocol Definition," Revision 3.6, January 1992.

[SAFE92]        "Survivable Adaptable Fiber Optic Embedded Network II (SAFENET II)," Military Handbook (Draft), 10 January 1992.

[STRA88]        Strayer, W. T., and Weaver, A. C., "Performance Measurement of Data Transfer Services in MAP," *IEEE Network*, Vol. 2, No. 3, pp. 75–81 (May 1988).

[SVOB89]        Svobodova, L., "Measured Performance of Transport Service in LANs," *Computer Networks and ISDN Systems*, Vol. 18, No. 1, pp. 31–45 (1989/90).

[WULF88]        Wulf, W. A., "The National Collaboratory—A White Paper," National Science Foundation, December 1988.

# Network Concepts and
# the XTP Architectural Model

Constructing data communication systems is an inherently complex task involving a large number of hardware and software components. A common approach to network architecture design has been to divide the functionality needed for system interconnection among separate modules. The International Standardization Organization (ISO) has adopted a framework for separating the data communication functions necessary for systems interconnection: the widely recognized Open System Interconnect (OSI) Reference Model. Viewed as a generalized network architecture, the OSI Reference Model provides the context for understanding the Xpress Transfer Protocol's placement and role in a communications subsystem.[1]

In this chapter we begin with a review of the OSI Reference Model itself. We then examine the protocol functions internal to and the services provided by the two layers of the OSI Reference Model that XTP subsumes, *network* and *transport*. This summary of the protocol functions in these layers brings out the set of fundamental issues in moving data across a network that XTP (and any transfer layer protocol) addresses. The following section outlines the basic services that XTP requires from its underlying data delivery provider, typically a data link layer service.

The last half of the chapter discusses fundamental concepts underlying XTP-based communication and outlines the conceptual skeleton of XTP protocol processing. It is not surprising that XTP contains protocol mechanisms and services that do not fit cleanly into the OSI Reference Model view of networking. The primary motivation behind the XTP effort was the realization that next-generation protocol suites are needed to respond to changes in the underlying network hardware and changes in application requirements that have taken place over the past decade.

## 2.1   Network Concepts

In this section we present a number of networking concepts that provide the framework for discussing XTP. After a brief review of the OSI protocol stack's components, we

---

[1] It should be remembered that the OSI Reference Model represents only one effort in constructing a framework for computer communication. The OSI Reference Model is not sacred; it is under

look at Layers 3 and 4 in the OSI Reference Model.[2] We overview the types of data delivery services needed by transport layer users, the internal functions of the transport layer necessary to support these services, the services of the network layer provided to the transport layer entities that use it, and the protocol functions found in the network layer.

## 2.1.1 The OSI Reference Model

The International Standardization Organization's Open Systems Interconnect Reference Model [ISO7498] is a seven-layer architecture for data communication protocol suites, as shown in Figure 2.1. The OSI definition of a *system* is intentionally broad enough to cover both simple systems (e.g., terminal-to-computer interconnection) and complex systems (e.g., the interconnection of two heterogeneous computer networks). When used as a generalized network architecture, the OSI Reference Model facilitates the task of defining standards for linking heterogeneous computers by providing a canonical division of protocol functionality. As such, the OSI Reference Model has proved valuable in its role as a conceptual and functional framework for coordinating the development of protocol standards.

The OSI Reference Model encapsulates a set of communication functions within each layer. Each layer provides a set of services to the next higher layer and requests a set of services from the next lower layer. Layer interaction takes place on well-defined boundaries through small numbers of service primitives. These primitives abstract the details of the more primitive tasks being performed in the service-providing layer. The layered structure of the OSI Reference Model is summarized in Table 2.1.

The *physical layer* is primarily concerned with the electrical and mechanical characteristics of the signaling media used to transform binary information into signals that the medium propagates. The *data link layer* is concerned with utilizing the serial bit stream services provided by the physical layer to provide data communication services along a single network link. For networks using physical broadcast channels, notably local area networks (LANs), the data link layer is subdivided into the medium access control (MAC) and the logical link control (LLC) sublayers. The MAC assembles data into data units, or *frames*, with address and error-detection fields, and provides unreliable data delivery service, including contention for the broadcast channel, across a single physical multidrop segment of the network. The LLC multiplexes several logical links onto the one physical network and may enhance the frame delivery service of the MAC.

---

on-going review, and other (successful) network architectures exist. The OSI Reference Model has, however, become the most well known layering effort, and for that reason it is most appropriate for our purposes here.

[2.] While the OSI Reference Model does not number the seven layers, conventionally the layers are numbered from bottom (Layer 1) to top (Layer 7).

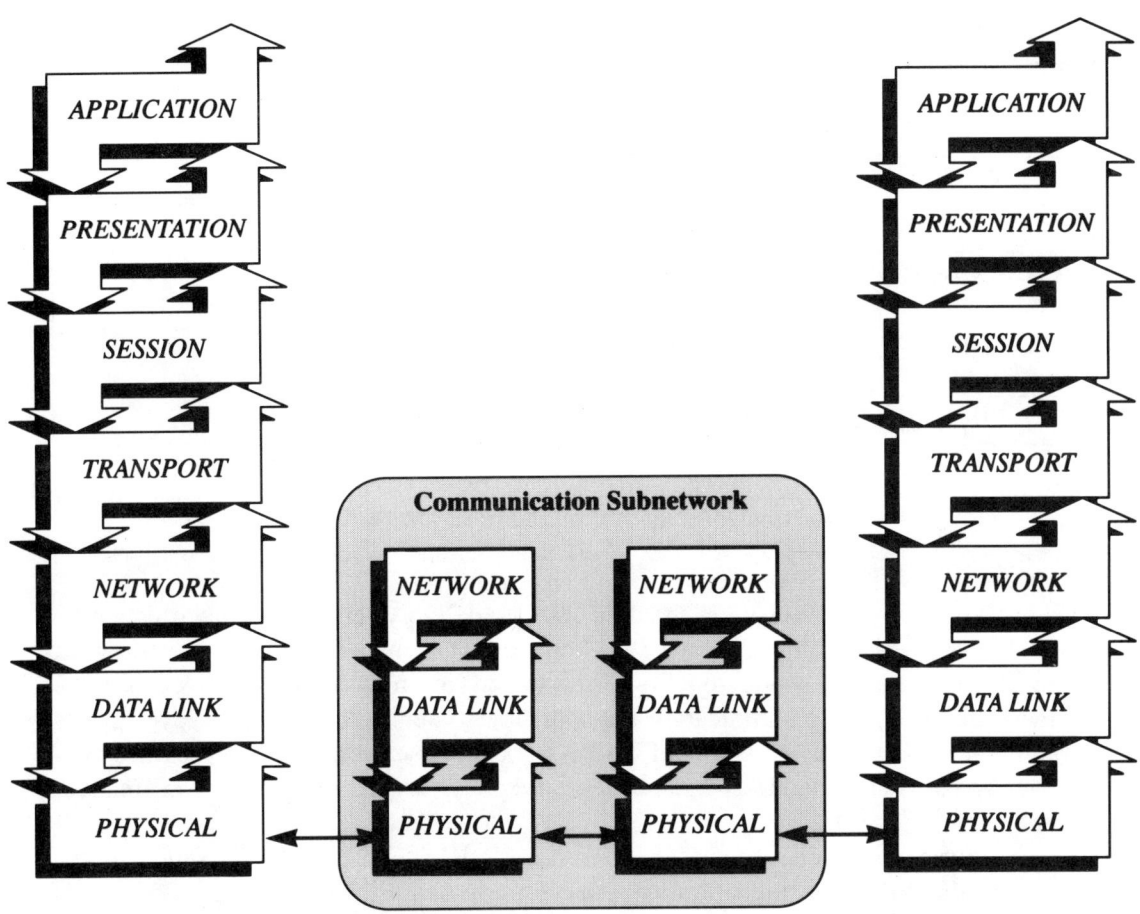

**Figure 2.1 — The OSI Reference Model**

The *network layer* provides the routing and relaying of network layer data units across multiple network segments and multiple networks. Network layer entities reside both at end-nodes and at *intermediate nodes* (or *switches*) internal to the subnetwork. Network layer design issues include all functions related to routing and relaying packets within a network and between different networks (*internetworking*).

The fundamental duty of an intermediate node in a packet-switching network is to route packets. A switch examines a packet's network address to determine whether its destination is on the local segment or on a remote segment of the network. If the destination is remote, the packet is forwarded on the appropriate outgoing data link. By transparently performing routing and relaying, the network layer protects the transport layer from the details of network topology and subnetwork division. Instead, the network layer user can use the abstraction of a unified network in which any peer user can be reached by knowing its global address.

| OSI Layer | | Layer Functions |
|---|---|---|
| 7 — Application | | Application-specific services |
| 6 — Presentation | | Data compatibility between heterogeneous systems |
| 5 — Session | | Dialogue maintenance |
| 4 — Transport | | Reliable end-to-end data transfer |
| 3 — Network | | Routing between network segments |
| 2 — Data Link | LLC | Multiplexing users through access points |
| | MAC | Basic framing and delivery service |
| 1 — Physical | | Digital-to-signal translation for transmission |

**Table 2.1 — The Functionality of the Layers of the OSI Reference Model**

The *transport layer* enhances the network data delivery service by providing a general, reliable message transfer service between end-systems. The goal of the transport layer is to enhance the service quality of the underlying network data delivery service to meet the needs of communicating transport layer users. The transport layer masks from the transport user the details of the network layer service and thus provides end-to-end services that are entirely independent of the underlying interconnection architecture.

The lower four layers of the OSI Reference Model shield the upper layers from the details of the communication facility. Above the transport layer, reliable end-to-end data delivery is no longer a concern since it is a service provided by the underlying layers. Thus the focus in the upper layers of the OSI Reference Model is on user requirements for data exchange services and specific application needs. Using the reliable data delivery services of the transport layer, the *session layer* provides the means for organizing, synchronizing, and managing dialogues between end-nodes. The *presentation layer* is responsible for ensuring that end-systems can communicate successfully, regardless of their internal representations of data. The *application layer* provides services, both of general utility and application-dependent, at the boundary between the open systems communication environment and the application processes that use that environment.

## 2.1.2 Data Transfer Models

Two natural models exist for data transfer across a network: *connection-oriented* and *connectionless*. A connection-oriented service emulates a telephone call. The calling party dials the number of the called party and the called party answers. After the connection is established, conversation flows in both directions. When all the data has been sent, the connection is closed. A connectionless service, on the other hand, follows the postal system model. Each message carries the full destination address, and each message is handled independently of all other messages. Since it is the network and the transport layers that are primarily responsible for the data transfer services over a network, the connection-oriented and connectionless models are generally applied to one or the other or both of these layers.

Whether a connection-oriented or connectionless service is most appropriate depends upon the type of data delivery service needed. Setting up a connection across the network may be too expensive if only a small amount of data is to be sent. For large transfers, on the other hand, a connection may be appropriate due to certain qualities and efficiencies in data transfer over a connection which are not inherently present in a connectionless model. Proper sequencing is an example. Under connectionless service, messages sent to the same destination may not arrive in the same order as they were sent. In contrast, a connection may be thought of as a first-in first-out data pipe from the data sender to the data receiver, since correct sequencing of data is "built-in" to the transfer model.

The OSI Reference Model was originally connection-oriented; that is, each layer offered a connection-oriented service to the layer above. Over time, however, the connectionless approach was adopted as well. In particular, the connection-oriented service model for transport layer protocols (which has remained the dominant paradigm in extant transport layer protocols) was supplemented with a connectionless service. At the network layer, connection-oriented and connectionless approaches, both of which have received wide use, are allowed.

In practice there is a tight coupling between the transport and network layers. From the debates over the use of the connection-oriented versus the connectionless model, two architectures for the network/transport layer tandem have emerged. More accurately, perhaps, the communications world has divided into two tribes over the issue.

The CLIBs (ConnectionLess Is Better) argue that a simple network layer service is best. They argue that the transport layer must ultimately provide end-to-end reliability and data flow management. By trying to construct a reliable network layer service, designers run the risk of creating a network service that is not trusted enough by the users. If that were to occur, then users will duplicate the reliability mechanisms at the transport layer. The CLIBs' position leads to a connectionless network layer protocol with a connection-oriented or connectionless transport layer protocol, e.g., TCP [DARPA81c] and UDP [DARPA80] over IP [DARPA81a] that are found in many UNIX environments.

The PAPs (Phones Are Perfect) argue that the network layer service should provide a reliable, connection-oriented service. Transport layer entities at the network end-nodes are then not burdened with providing reliability; they need to provide only a few basic services over this reliable data delivery service. The number of internal network nodes (where the primary functions of the network layer are performed) are usually far fewer than the network's end-nodes. In the case of a public data network, the difference could be orders of magnitude. Hence, in the PAPs' vision, the complexity of the network should be focused in the relatively few internal nodes, and the users allowed to connect simple transport layer users to the reliable network service. In network architectures where the boundary between the host and the subnetwork is at the boundary between the transport and network layers, the PAP architecture means that the bulk of complexity has been "pushed into the network."

## 2.1.3 Services and Service Access

Figure 2.2 shows the general relationship between the users of services and the providers of services for the transport and network layers. The Application Services represent types of service that transport layer users desire. The OSI Reference Model suggests that a transport layer user is typically a session layer entity. However, many applications find their natural interface to the communications subsystem to be at the transport layer, although, as Andrew Tanenbaum has said, "it is considered in poor taste to point this out publicly" [TANE88]. In any case the Transport Layer Service Interface is a set of transport layer service primitives, which may include both connection-oriented and connectionless primitives, that must be used to implement Application Services.

A connection-based service can offer either *reliable* or *unreliable data delivery*. Reliable connections ensure that all data transmitted by one transport layer user will arrive at the intended transport layer user free from bit errors, in-sequence, and free of any duplication. File transfer and reliable byte streams are examples of application services that may require a reliable connection. Unreliable connections provide a connection-oriented paradigm without the overhead of ensuring complete data integrity. Some applications, such as digital image transfer, may require that a channel be maintained, but not require that the channel provide error-free delivery. Unreliable byte streams and isochronous streams are candidates for unreliable connections.

Application Services that employ connectionless mode service providers either do not require the robust set of functionality provided with a connection-oriented service, or they take it upon themselves to provide the needed functionality. For example, an application process that wishes to send a single message to a remote process may not want to pay the overhead inherent in a connection-oriented data transfer service. Instead, a datagram application service is chosen. If assured delivery of the datagram is required, a return message may serve as the application level acknowledgement. In the same way, a request/response application service may be built upon connectionless mode primitives.

The Transport Layer Service Interface is very important since the Application Services are implemented through transport layer service primitives. The set of service primitives available determines the protocol features that can be manipulated by the layer's user, the manner in which notions of grade of service are conveyed to the Transport Layer Service Provider, and, perhaps most important, the data transfer syntaxes that can be supported. Protocol functionality that can not be exploited through the service interface is of little use. Similarly, the transport layer (as a network layer ser-

Application Services

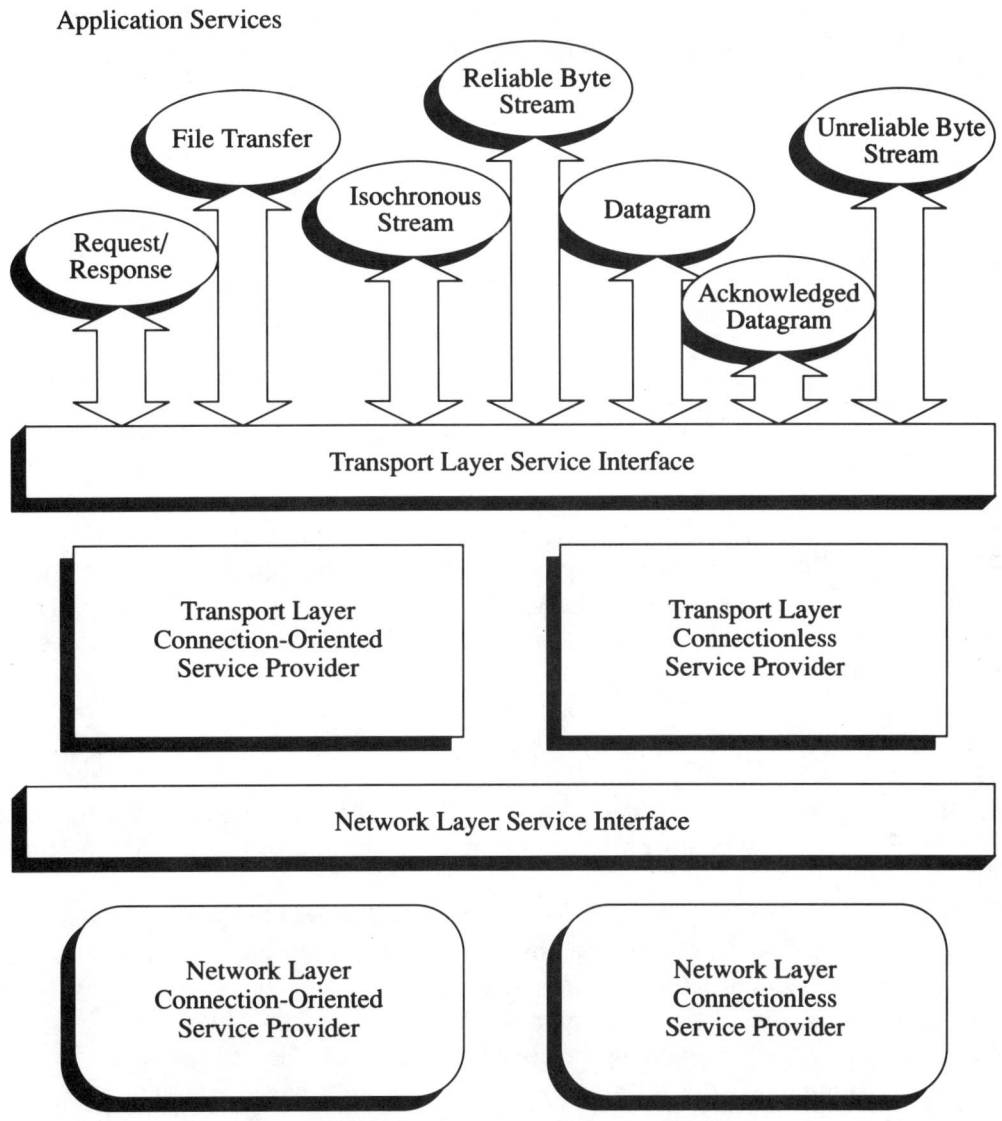

**Figure 2.2 — Transport and Network Layer Service Providers**

vice user) must employ a Network Layer Service Provider. The Network Layer Service Interface encapsulates into primitives those protocol features available from the network layer. As with the transport layer, the Network Layer Service Provider may offer a connection-oriented or a connectionless service.

At any layer boundary in the OSI Reference Model there are two notions of service selection. First, given that there may be multiple service providers within the service-provider layer, the user can select a particular service provider (protocol) within that layer. Service primitives are parametrized to access different entry points, or *service access points* (SAPs), through which the service providers in a layer are reached. Second, having selected a service provider, a user has available a menu of grade-of-service parameters that can be conveyed through service primitives to the service provider. Examples include reliability, performance, and delay characteristics of the transfer, priority policies, and data security. Within the ISO Transport Protocol [ISO8073], the term Transport Layer Quality of Service (QOS) refers to a set of well-defined parameters available at the Transport Layer Service Interface.

## 2.1.4 Transport Layer

As noted above, the transport layer is responsible for enhancing the services of the underlying protocol layers to provide a general messaging service to the transport layer user. At the transport layer, the amount and complexity of protocol processing depends upon two factors: the data transfer service being provided, and the nature of the underlying network layer service. In many ways, the scenario that places the greatest responsibility on the transport layer protocol is that of providing end-to-end reliable data delivery over an unreliable underlying network layer service. This requirement has driven the development of the full suite of transport layer protocol functions discussed in this section.

In general, a transport layer protocol specifies the exchange of information in the form of data and control information. A *packet* is the basic transport information exchange unit. A packet may carry control information in its header and trailer fields, and either data or control information within its middle part. Each of the functions listed above relies upon control information in some form, either in header and trailer fields or in *control packets*.

The choice between a connectionless or a connection-oriented service model at the Application Services level can be supported in theory by any combination of connection-based or connectionless service providers in the transport and network layers. In practice, however, some combinations make more sense than others. For example, using a connectionless transport service over a connection-oriented network layer service would require a network layer connection per transport layer datagram, which is a very inefficient use of network resources.

In this section we examine a connection-oriented transport layer approach. The discussion remains fully general since the functionality of a connectionless transport service is subsumed by that of a connection-oriented approach capable of providing reliable data delivery. Protocol functions found in such transport systems include:

- addressing
- segmentation and reassembly
- connection establishment and termination
- flow and rate control
- error control
- special data transfer services

## Addressing

The transport layer service user passes the transport layer service provider the addressing information necessary to identify a destination transport layer service user. This target user must be specified by (1) a user identification, (2) a transport entity identification, and (3) an end-system identification. The user identification uniquely identifies this transport layer service user among all others also using this service provider. This identifier is typically called a *port*, a *socket*, or, in the ISO world, a *transport service access point* (TSAP). If there is more than one transport layer service provider, then the selection of a particular one is specified by the transport entity identification. The end-system identification uniquely identifies an end-system within the entire network. The network layer service provider uses this identifier, or network layer address, in delivering this packet to the proper end-system.

There are four ways that an initiating transport user can know the address of the destination transport user. First, the address may be known *a priori*, either from some outside source or hard-coded at system start-up time. Second, the address may be well known, as is the case with many application services. Third, the address may be retrieved by some name server or other directory service provider; in this way names are associated with addresses to facilitate target user mobility and reduce addressing complexity. Finally, a well-known address may be used so that on each connection request the process listening on that address immediately spawns another process that starts a new conversation on another address. This prevents tying up the well-known address, and allows others to access its application service.

## Segmentation and Reassembly

The transport layer provides general message transfer services by segmenting arbitrarily large Transport Service Data Units (TSDUs) into multiple smaller Transport Protocol Data Units (TPDUs) suitable for use by the network layer. At the remote transport peer, these TPDUs are reassembled into the original TSDU. In traditional connection-oriented models, the transmitter assigns an integer, called a *sequence number*, either to each user data byte or to each TPDU (depending upon the particular transport protocol in use) in such a way that the receiver may correctly reassemble the original message. Segmentation and reassembly are transparent to the transport layer user.

## Connection Establishment and Termination

Connection management techniques must include the ability to establish and release connections. Connection establishment and release can be based on either *hand-shaking* or *implicit management techniques*. Handshaking involves the exchange of state information between the endpoints of the connection. Figure 2.3 illustrates the three-way handshake that opens an ISO Transport Protocol class 4 (TP4) connection. The initiating transport service user issues a T_Connect.request command, which causes a Connection Request (CR) TPDU to be sent. This CR-TPDU contains various connection service parameters based on default values and service parameters passed

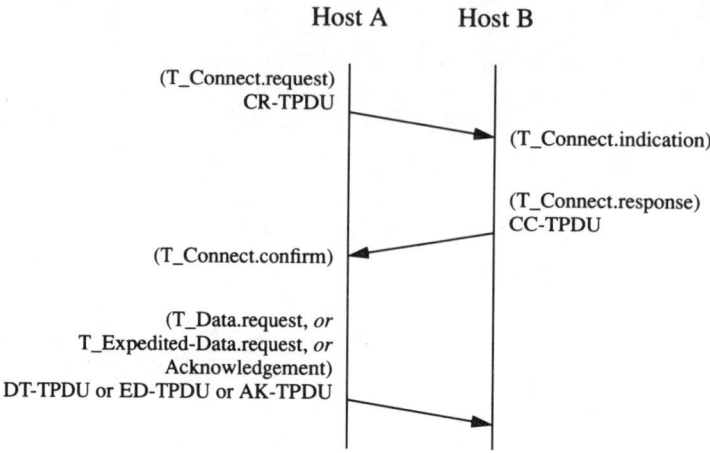

**Figure 2.3 — TP4 Connection Establishment Handshake**

through the user interface. The destination transport service user is informed of this connection request by a T_Connect.indication, at which time the user may issue a T_Connect.response command, causing a Connection Confirm (CC) TPDU to be sent back to the initiator. This CC-TPDU completes the negotiation of service parameters. The initiator must then respond with a Data (DT) TPDU, an Expedited Data (ED) TPDU, or an Acknowledgement (AK) TPDU, in order to complete the connection setup phase.

Implicit connection management takes the form of *on-demand* connection setup and *timer-based* connection management and connection release. On-demand connection setup refers to the establishment of connection state information at the remote endpoint upon the arrival of the first TPDU from the initiating endpoint. Timer-based techniques use timers instead of explicit handshaking to correctly manage the state at connection endpoints. The Delta-t protocol (see Chapter 3) is known for its pioneering work in the use of implicit connections.

An important aspect of the connection establishment and termination procedures is the handling of connection identifiers and connection establishment packets such that spurious connections can not be established or active connections disturbed by packets that have been delayed at intermediate nodes within the network. If a connection initiator retransmits a connection establishment packet, for instance, then two connections may be established where one was intended.

The termination of a connection can be either *graceful* or *abrupt*. A *graceful close* is a connection termination such that all data sent on the connection is guaranteed to be delivered before the connection is terminated. This requires handshaking procedures, which are similar to those shown in Figure 2.3 for connection establishment. Abrupt termination semantics provides no such guarantee; the connection is simply abandoned immediately.

## Flow and Rate Control

Mismatches between a transmitter's ability to deliver data to the network service and the receiving peer's ability to process and buffer that data can severely degrade communication efficiency. Even worse, when the transmitter reacts to the lack of progress by repeatedly retransmitting the data, the problem is exacerbated. The resulting congestion at switching nodes in the network can compromise the entire network's performance. To protect both end-nodes and the network, the transport layer implements functions that constrain the sending side of a connection. There are two types of constraint: *flow control* and *rate control*.

End-to-end flow control links the transmission rate afforded to the transmitter to the buffer resources available for the connection at the receiver. Two common techniques for providing flow control are a fixed *sliding window* and a *credit scheme*. Both techniques depend upon feedback from the receiver to dictate the maximum amount of unacknowledged data at the transmitter.

A sliding window of packet-based sequence numbers is kept at both the transmitter and the receiver. At the receiver this window represents the sequence numbers of those data packets that may be accepted; any data packet arriving with a sequence number outside of the window must be discarded. The window is always a fixed size, and simply slides as data packets are acknowledged. Figure 2.4 illustrates the sliding window

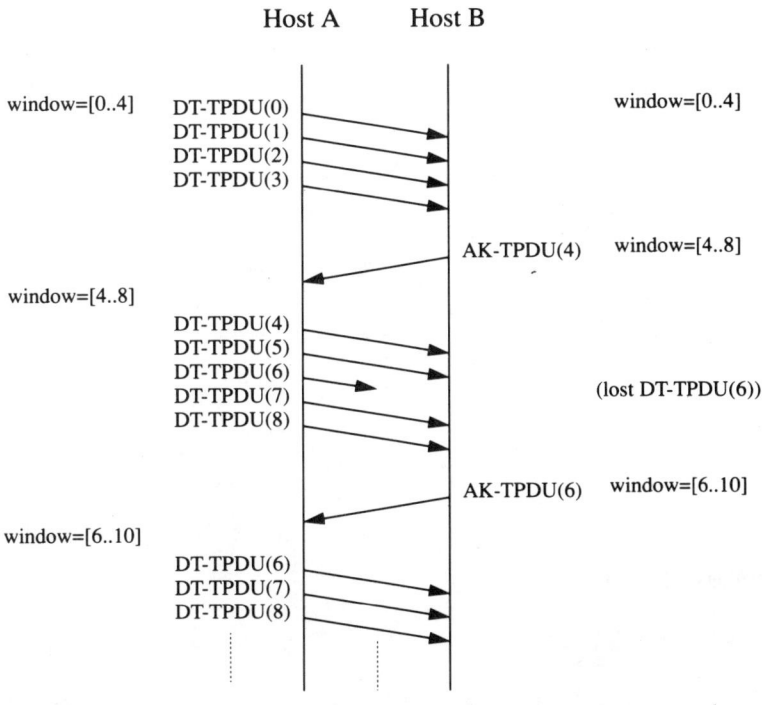

**Figure 2.4 — Sliding Window Flow Control**

flow control scheme. Here the window size is set to 5, and the window initially contains sequence numbers 0 through 4, so the transmitter may send up to five packets. It sends packets numbered 0 through 3. The receiver advances its window with each arriving packet until the lower edge is 4. The receiver then acknowledges the receipt of these four packets, allowing the transmitter to *slide* its window to sequence numbers 4 through 8. Notice that the window only slides over two sequence numbers when the packet with sequence number 6 is lost.

The credit scheme also uses a sliding window, but the window is now of variable size. The size is controlled by a *credit* parameter in the acknowledgement packets; the credit value is used to determine the upper edge of the window while the sequence number of the acknowledgement packet is used to set the lower edge. Figure 2.5 illustrates a situation where the credit is initially 5, hence the window is 0 through 4. After data packets are sent, the acknowledgement packet sent back to the transmitter instructs the transmitter to advance the lower edge of the window to 4 and narrow the window size to 3 (from the *credit* parameter). Hence the window becomes sequence numbers 4 through 6. Three data packets are sent, but the receiver becomes inundated. It responds with an acknowledgement packet containing a credit of 0, effectively closing the window. The transmitter must wait for the receiver to open the window again, and it does eventually with a new credit of 5.

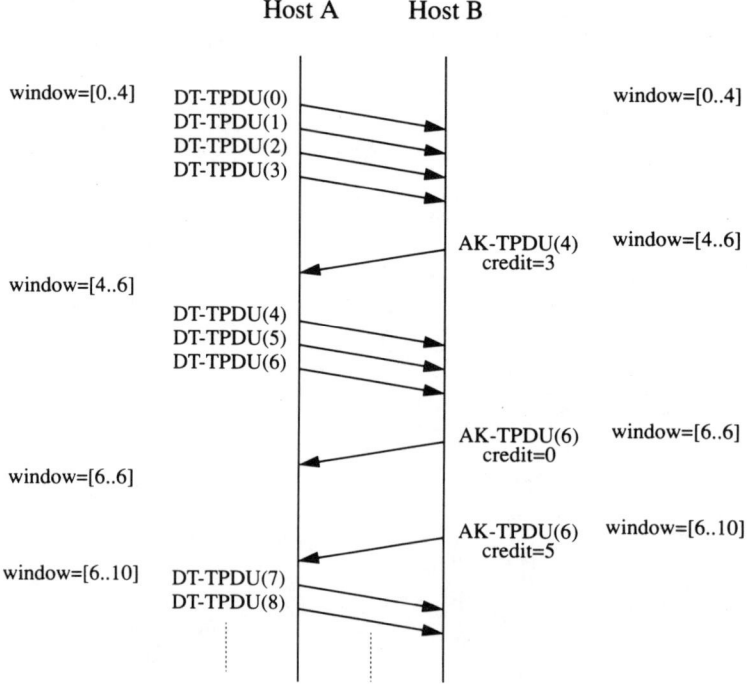

**Figure 2.5 — Credit in Flow Control**

Rate control addresses a similar, but independent, issue concerning transmission constraint: the rate at which the transmitting transport entity is allowed to submit data to the underlying data delivery service. Rate control is desirable since a receiver may drop data not because it has run out of buffer space (i.e., a flow control problem) but because it can not process data as quickly as the transmitter sends it. Rate control is concerned with the size of a burst of data and the number of bursts per unit time. Since processing these bursts of data is not simply a problem for the end-nodes but rather a problem for each processing node along the path between the end-nodes, the size and rate of these bursts should be determined by each of the processing nodes and not just by the end-systems alone.

Most extant transport layer protocols rely on flow control to provide both flow and (hopefully) rate control between the transport layer entities. Flow control parameters, in this case, are adjusted to try to minimize packet loss, whether the loss is caused by problems with end-node buffers or with intermediate node processing. Problems at intermediate nodes are discovered (1) by monitoring the number and frequency of retransmissions, (2) by explicit feedback from the network layer entities, or (3) by heuristics within the protocol such as using roundtrip times to estimate network congestion. Typically, an indication of a problem is only available once the problem has developed.

## Error Control

A reliable data delivery service requires that the user's data be delivered intact, properly sequenced at the destination transport peer, and without duplication. In order to support this service abstraction, the transport layer protocol must have mechanisms to detect bit errors, force packet reordering when necessary, and identify packet loss that may be caused by the underlying data delivery service. A variety of error control functions are used in transport layer connections.

The assignment of sequence numbers to user data, in addition to enabling in-order reassembly of user messages at the destination endpoint, also handles duplication detection. When the duplicate packet arrives while the connection is still active, the sequence number of the duplicate packet is compared against a list (possibly in the form of the window) of valid sequence numbers. Duplicates detected in this way are usually discarded. A duplicate packet that arrives after its connection has been terminated must be detected using connection management procedures in order to avoid the consequences of inadvertently establishing a new connection or disturbing an active one.

An end-to-end data integrity check provides the mechanism for detecting bit errors within a packet. For performance reasons, performing data integrity checks is usually optional. The data integrity check used at the transport layer is typically a *checksum*, which involves summing over the entire length of data in the message. A checksum can be conducted over the message before segmentation or over each constituent packet after segmentation.

Connection endpoints must ensure correct delivery of all data. *Acknowledgements* are messages indicating reception of some part of the data at the receiving side of the connection. *Negative acknowledgements* work in a similar way, indicating that the data was *not* received. Acknowledgements can be sent as control information; in this case they may be tightly coupled with other control algorithms such as flow control and synchronization of the communicating endpoints. Alternatively, acknowledgements can be implicit, as with the expiration of a timer at a connection endpoint.

Data lost or delivered with errors is recovered through retransmissions from the transmitter. The two most widely known schemes for triggering retransmissions are positive acknowledgement with retransmission (PAR) and automatic repeat request (ARQ). Under PAR, if a timer associated with transmit buffers expires before an acknowledgement arrives at the transmitter, the transmitter resends those buffers. With ARQ, the transmitting side of the connection bases retransmissions on explicit control packets from the receiver.

A *selective retransmission* policy is possible if (1) the receiving side of the connection can buffer out-of-order data and (2) acknowledgements can indicate the gaps in the receiver's buffers. If selective retransmission is chosen, the transmitter only resends the user data corresponding to the reported gaps. A simple retransmission policy, go-back-*n*, causes the transmitter to return to the first gap in the data stream and retransmit all data from that point. Go-back-*n* requires less protocol processing and may be more appropriate than selective retransmission in certain networking environments.

## Special Data Transfer Services

Transport layer connections may provide certain special data transfer functions. For example, an urgent data delivery service is sometimes offered. Urgent messages may be given preference in protocol processing at both ends of the connection, be exempt from flow control, and/or be placed ahead of other messages in the delivery queue at the remote peer. Data transfer services that are responsive to user-specified performance requirements may be available, as with the Quality of Service parameters in the ISO Transport Protocol. In order to provide a user with a specified throughput requirement, for instance, such a service may allocate to a connection such resources as buffer space and processor time proportional to the throughput expected.

# 2.1.5 Network Layer

The network layer is responsible for providing interconnection of network layer users (e.g., transport layer entities) such that the users are shielded from the details of the number and characteristics of *subnetworks*[3] separating them. The collection of all attached subnetworks constitutes an *internetwork*; the network layer provides transparent interconnection of all network layer service users attached to the internetwork. To accomplish this, a number of issues must be addressed, including a global addressing scheme to identify users in the internetwork, and a method for routing information

---

[3.] **We use the term *subnetwork* to emphasize that a single autonomous network may be only one of many such autonomous networks among which connectivity exists.**

between users in a way that accounts for any differences between network segments and changing network conditions.

Network layer service providers reside in the general case in both *end-nodes* (or *hosts* or *end-systems*) and *intermediate switching nodes* (or *routers* or *gateways* or *packet-switching nodes* or *switches*). End-nodes are the machines on which application programs are run. Intermediate switching nodes represent machines that are internal to the network and perform routing and other network management functions.

The central question in designing the network layer service is how to organize the routing functionality within subnetworks and between subnetworks. As indicated in Section 2.1.2, this issue has divided network layer designers into two camps, the CLIBs advocating a connectionless approach and the PAPs advocating a connection-oriented approach.

The CLIBs argue against attempting to provide a reliable service within the subnetwork. They argue that since the transport layer protocols in the host must be ultimately responsible for end-to-end reliability the network layer should be kept as simple and flexible as possible. Control over reliability issues is properly left in the end-systems, and pushing mechanisms for reliability into the subnetwork leads to unwanted overhead for some users. The CLIBs also point out the danger that some users of the network service will not fully trust its reliability mechanisms and so duplicate them at higher layers, namely in the transport layer. These arguments lead to a connectionless approach, which views the subnetwork as a simple packet delivery service used by "intelligent" end-systems. The subnetwork is not a "black box," and network layer entities in the end-systems may have knowledge of and participate to some degree in the routing and network management procedures implemented in the intermediate nodes.

The PAPs, on the other hand, focus on reducing the complexity of the transport services in the end-nodes by providing reliable connections in the network layer. The transport service need not be burdened with the complexities of end-to-end reliability since this functionality is "built in" to the subnetwork to which it connects. The subnetwork contains the "intelligence" of the end-to-end data delivery service to which relatively simple hosts can attach.

The trade-offs between the CLIB and PAP approaches are well documented. Virtual circuits are efficient in that, after the circuit is set up, the routing decision for each packet on that circuit has already been determined at every participating switch. Datagram subnetworks perform the forwarding decision for each packet based on its full destination address. This implies that each datagram must carry its global internetwork address. The primary advantage of making routing decisions on a per-packet basis is the resulting flexibility and robustness. When a switching node or a link fails or becomes overloaded, datagram subnetworks can begin routing packets along alternative routes as soon as the failure or overload is detected. No intervention by the end-nodes need take place. Connection-oriented routing, on the other hand, is more vulnerable and less flexible to changes in subnetwork conditions. All the virtual circuits that pass through a failed switch are lost, and new circuits must be established before the communications carried on these circuits can resume.

*Congestion control* refers to preventing and reacting to overloading that can occur at intermediate switching nodes due to dynamic load. Congestion control is important to avoid degradation and even collapse of the network service. Since resources such as buffer space have been allocated at circuit setup time, virtual circuit subnetworks are less susceptible to congestion problems than are datagram subnetworks. The latter tend to implement mechanisms that react to congestion control problems once they develop at a node. Reserving buffers for virtual circuits, in contrast, can be used to manage potential congestion problems before they arise, at the price of possibly dedicating buffers to a circuit that does not use them.

Connectionless network service is appropriate for both connection-oriented and connectionless transport service. On the other hand, network layer virtual circuits are not well suited to support a transport layer connectionless service. A subnetwork organized around virtual circuits forces the network layer user to incur the overhead of connection establishment and maintenance even if this is not appropriate.

Two widely used network layer protocols embody the two approaches to network layer organization: the Internet Protocol (IP) [DARPA81a] and the CCITT X.25 Packet Layer Protocol standard [CCITT84]. In the IP approach to routing, hosts are responsible for sending IP datagrams to a local gateway. The packet then travels from gateway to gateway before being delivered to its destination host by the final gateway. In addition, hosts and gateways send and respond to network status messages. In contrast, X.25, which derives from the common carrier data networks, defines an interface between the user's end-system and an internal network node that serves as that end-system's access node to the subnetwork. The X.25 module in the end-system requests and uses end-to-end virtual circuits across the subnetwork; the actions necessary to set up and maintain these reliable virtual circuits are completely opaque to the end-system.

The X.25 Packet Layer Protocol represents the network layer protocol within the X.25 standards. It is the most widely used protocol for the connection-oriented network layer service provider in the OSI Reference Model. The X.25 standards define the interface between the user's data communications equipment called the Data Terminal Equipment (DTE) and that of the common carrier called the Data Circuit-terminating Equipment (DCE). This is shown in Figure 2.6. Connections are established between DTEs through their respective DCEs. The X.25 standard does not specify the manner in which packets are relayed through the packet-switched network, termed a *cloud*, separating DCEs.

The Internet Protocol has shown the versatility and scalability of a connectionless approach since it has been successfully used since the early 1980s to interconnect an increasingly large number of diverse networks across the United States in the ARPA Internet. The IP software modules residing in packet-switching nodes relay IP datagrams from gateway to gateway until the destination host is reached, as shown in Figure 2.7. Routing is based on the *global addressing* information carried in each IP datagram. Because global addresses are hierarchical in nature, gateways can base routing decisions on only part of the destination address, namely the destination network, as opposed to the full address, which identifies the destination host. This approach significantly reduces the size of routing information at a gateway since the

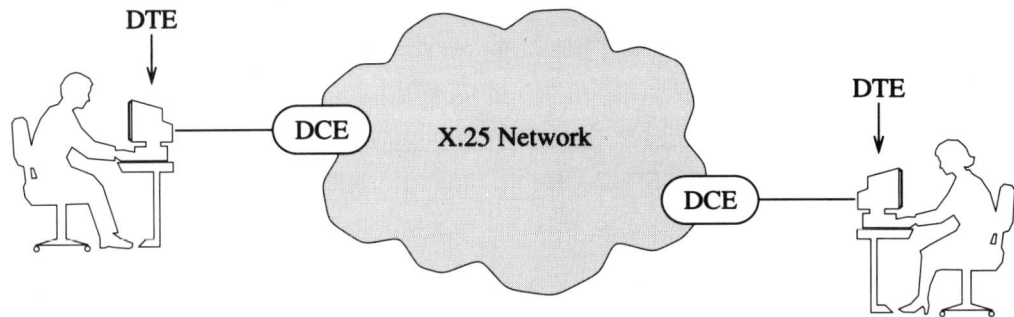

**Figure 2.6 — The X.25 Internetwork Structure**

number of ARPA Internet hosts is a couple of orders of magnitude larger than the number of networks.

A number of auxiliary protocols have been developed for the ARPA Internet to supplement IP routing functionality. The Internet Control Message Protocol (ICMP) [DARPA81b], for instance, is a required part of any IP software module. It provides a general mechanism for both debugging network problems and for internal error-correction coordination between IP modules. IP modules at gateways and hosts generate ICMP messages relating to local observations about network status, suspicious events, and error conditions in order to inform other IP modules. Another example is the Address Resolution Protocol (ARP) [PLUM82], which maps Internet addresses to physical addresses. This protocol is used to determine dynamically (rather than through static tables) the binding between an Internet address and the local machine address.

A connectionless approach to the organization of the network layer offers two types of service primitives: (1) sending or receiving a datagram (possibly with service selection options) and (2) network status inquiries such as timestamped packets. In the ARPA Internet, the IP protocol provides the former, and the latter is largely handled using the ICMP protocol. The service interface for the connection-oriented approach, on the other hand, looks much like that for connection-oriented transport services. Connection management primitives allow the establishment and termination of network layer connections while data transfer primitives send and receive data over established connections.

Network layer protocol functions—independent of the connection-oriented versus connectionless debate—can be categorized as:

- definition of global addressing space
- routing algorithms
- internetworking
- congestion control strategy
- error handling
- fragmentation and reassembly
- special services

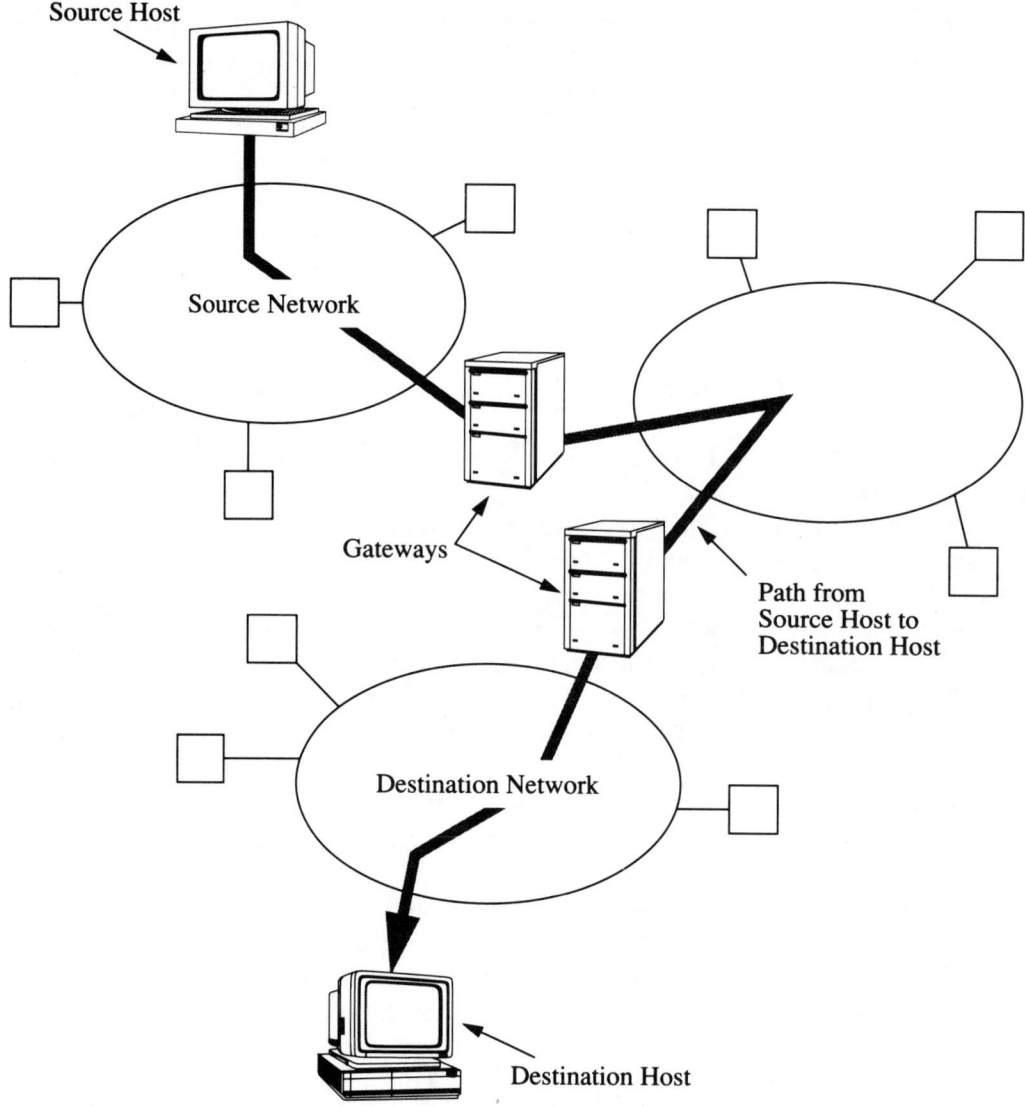

**Figure 2.7 — IP Internetworking Structure**

## Definition of Global Addressing Space

It is the responsibility of the network layer to deliver data across one or more subnetworks from source to destination end-systems. Hence, addressing information at the network layer should uniquely identify each end-system in the internetwork. To accomplish this the network layer defines a *global addressing scheme*.

A natural way to organize the global address space is in a hierachical fashion. Logically, the address has two components, *network* and *station*, where the *network* part identifies the destination subnetwork among all subnetworks in the internetwork and the *station* part identifies the destination host attached to that destination subnetwork. Thus, the pair (*network, station*) uniquely identifies the destination end-node.

Such a division allows the internal nodes of the network to focus on routing first to the destination subnetwork (given by the *network* part), and then to the destination end-system (identified by the *station* part). This approach dramatically reduces the amount of routing information that needs to be kept at each router since the number of subnetworks is generally orders of magnitude smaller than the number of hosts. Each router maintains knowledge of hosts on the local segments. Such routing may involve translation between the station name as given in the global address and a local name for the destination host.

## Routing Algorithms

The routing algorithm is the software used to determine the links over which a packet will be forwarded as it travels from the source to the destination host. The simplest form of routing is *static routing* in which packets travel over paths calculated at network setup. While static routing may be sufficient in some small networks, routing algorithms that take into account run-time changes in network topology and load are often necessary. Under *adaptive routing*, each switch has a forwarding database, or *routing table*, that contains information on or derived from network conditions, such as delay characteristics or load estimates for individual network segments.

Adaptive routing schemes can be classified by how they maintain and build their routing tables. *Isolated routing* algorithms make use only of information gleaned from packet traffic through the local switch. *Centralized routing* utilizes global information that is gathered and processed by a single master routing node. The master node communicates periodically with the switches to gather statistics on the network, uses this information to construct the routing tables, and then broadcasts the routing tables to the switches. Centralized routing schemes suffer from the drawback that the master node is a single point of failure for the entire network. Finally, *distributed routing* involves communication between the switches in order to use both local and nonlocal information in routing decisions. Several popular routing algorithms within the ARPA Internet community follow a distributed scheme in which network reachability and status information propagate from neighboring switch to neighboring switch.

Under adaptive routing, packet forwarding algorithms are properly independent of the *router-router protocols* that update routing tables. Under a connection-oriented model, packet forwarding decisions are made on a per-route basis while in the connectionless model they are made on a per-packet basis. Routing tables contain cost metrics for forwarding links, and packets are forwarded over the link with lowest cost. Certain classes of routing policies, however, allow the end-node to dictate some or all of the set of switches that will handle a packet. Thus, although there is obviously an interdependence, the content of routing tables and their use as a forwarding database are decoupled in the general case. Router-router protocols determine only the former.

## Internetworking

When packets must be routed between different subnetworks, special network switching nodes called *internetworking units* (IWUs) must provide packet relaying functions. In this discussion internetworking units refer to network layer relays; network layer relays are necessary when the interconnected subnetworks are using the same protocols above the network layer, and forwarding frames at the data link layer is not feasible.

Internetworking functionality at the network layer must resolve any problems due to differences in the two subnetworks' internal routing protocols, addressing schemes, or maximum packet sizes. The two approaches to internetworking are again a connection-oriented and a connectionless style. CCITT X.75 [ISO10029] is a connection-oriented approach for concatenating X.25 circuits across separate virtual circuit subnetworks. The ISO Connectionless Network Protocol [ISO8473] approach follows very closely along the lines of IP.

In general, the trade-offs between connection-oriented and connectionless internetworking are much the same as between these two approaches for routing within a subnetwork. Datagram approaches are more susceptible to congestion but more robust in the face of congestion or component failure; virtual circuit-based IWUs can control buffer allocation and thus congestion more readily, ensure sequenced and duplicate-free data delivery, and are vulnerable to intermediate node failure. A crucial difference between the two approaches is that the connection-oriented X.75 standards only allow for internetworking between virtual circuit subnetworks. Datagram internetworking, on the other hand, can accommodate both connection-based and connectionless subnetworks.

## Congestion Control Strategy

Internal network nodes need mechanisms to protect the integrity of the network when too many packets are being injected. A number of strategies have been studied. Connection-oriented approaches such as X.25 can ease congestion by allocating buffers at virtual circuit setup time; if buffers are not available at a particular switch, the circuit must either be threaded through some other switch or the circuit establishment fails altogether. In addition, reliable circuits generally provide end-to-end flow control which aids in network congestion control. In networks employing a connectionless mode network layer service, congestion control is typically handled by either discarding packets at overloaded routers, or using *source quench* messages that perform rudimentary flow control by throttling hosts that are injecting too many packets into the network.

Yet, the issue of congestion at intermediate nodes concerns more than just buffer availability; rather, it is the inability of an intermediate node to *process* packets as fast as the packets enter the node. This problem is most acute in packet-switching networks where resources and processing time are less likely to be dedicated in advance. Furthermore, congestion occurs if the network interface hardware can not physically accept packets as fast as they arrive. In general, congestion within these packet-switching intermediate nodes can be reduced by rate control.

Since the rate of packet injection at the sending end-node should be constrained by the rate of packet processing at the slowest intermediate node along the path between the end-nodes, there must be some mechanism for communicating this "weak-link" rate back to the sending end-node. Unfortunately, most network layer protocols do not have an explicit facility for either informing the sending end-node or controlling the rate of injection even if that rate could be known. In this respect, congestion control through controlling packet injection rates is an end-to-end issue, since it involves information from the entire path; on the other hand, it is really the processing rates at each individual switching node that causes the congestion in the first place, and so in some sense congestion control is a hop-to-hop issue. Certainly, cooperation between end-to-end services and the hop-to-hop services supporting them must take place, yet the boundary between the transport and network layers often prevents this cooperation.

## Error Handling

How and where to provide error control is one of the issues that fuels the debate between the CLIBs and the PAPs. If the transport layer service provides robust error detection and recovery, it would be redundant to include such robustness at the network layer. Yet, if the network layer provided those functions, the transport layer complexity could be reduced considerably. At any rate, connection-oriented network service generally provides error detection and recovery procedures similar to those found in connection-oriented transport, i.e., sequence number assignments, acknowledgements, and retransmissions.

The connectionless network service assumes that recovery, if required by the application, will be handled at a higher layer. This service is more interested in removing very old, and potentially dangerous, packets. Given that a packet should be delivered within a finite amount of time, a packet that remains in the network for an excessive period is often there by mistake. These old packets can be detected by using a *time-to-live* field within the packet that sets a maximum lifetime for the packet. An intermediate node that finds a packet whose time-to-live has expired will discard the packet. This prevents network congestion due to errant switches or malformed packets, and reduces the likelihood of problems at the end-system protocol state machine where the arrival of stale control information may place the machine in an unwanted state.

Since network layer packets rely heavily on the addressing information contained within the header, most network layer protocols require a checksum over at least the header. Clearly, a corrupted address renders the packet useless, and in some cases harmful, so each intermediate node along the path verifies the checksum. A packet found in error is immediately discarded. Otherwise, the checksum is recalculated after any packet processing, and the packet is forwarded to the next node. Thus the network layer checksum protects the packet in a hop-to-hop manner; a higher layer checksum will provide end-to-end data (and control information) integrity checks.

Another important component of network layer error handling is providing diagnostic messages. Besides communication relating to router-router protocols that aid in routing table maintenance, network layer switches are often capable of emitting a variety of diagnostic reports. These control messages are sent back to a packet's source when the packet could not be routed or other error conditions are detected. Error reports aid end-systems and internal switching nodes in diagnosing and recovering from problems such as failed nodes, unknown addresses, and invalid virtual circuit identifiers.

## Fragmentation and Reassembly

The size of the largest packet a subnetwork can handle is a characteristic of that subnetwork. When packets are exchanged from one subnetwork to another, entering packets must not exceed the largest packet size, or *maximum transmission unit* (MTU), that can be handled by that subnetwork. If a packet traversing the internetwork encounters a subnetwork whose MTU is smaller than the size of the packet, the intermediate nodes must manage the size mismatch. There are two things that the intermediate nodes may do: (1) discard the packet, or (2) break the packet up into smaller pieces, called *fragments*, whose size can be handled. This second option is called *fragmentation*, and its inverse, the recombining of fragments into the original packet, is called *reassembly*.

In fragmentation, an original packet is broken up into two or more constituent packets. These constituent packets are full-fledged packets in their own right, complete with appropriate addressing and other control information. In addition, information must be included within these constituent packets to allow the fragments to eventually be reassembled into the original packet so that the order of the information within this original packet may be preserved. Furthermore, since these constituent packets may themselves be fragmented, this information must allow all fragments, and fragments of fragments, to be reassembled into the original order.

An alternate strategy is to avoid the extra mechanics of fragmentation altogether by having the end-systems discover the smallest MTU along each route. This minimum MTU may be known *a priori*, or it may be kept as extra information in the routing tables. Keeping this information in routing tables, however, may require disseminating MTU information throughout the entire internetwork, and keeping that information current as routes change. Another technique to discover the minimum MTU is to somehow negotiate this value as a parameter of the data transfer; this negotiation is often included in setting up virtual circuits.

## Special Services

Various optional services may be available to the network layer user within a particular protocol. The IP header, for instance, includes an *options* field for special services relating to security, route recording, timestamping, and data priority. X.25 functionality includes options for reverse charging, enforcement of simplex communication (e.g., do not accept any in-coming calls), and delivery of small urgent messages, which are allowed to by-pass flow control constraints. In addition, X.25 has a *fast select* facility that enables a 128-byte transaction using connection establishment/confirmation packets.

# 2.2   XTP Architecture

Having reviewed the communication functions that the OSI Reference Model places at the network and transport layers, we turn now to XTP.[4] The purpose of this section is to introduce the XTP communications model, outline the conceptual skeleton of the XTP protocol, and to define XTP terminology in an effort to avoid possibly misleading connotations that terms such as *connection* unavoidably bring with them.

## 2.2.1 XTP Transfer Layer Architecture

The Xpress Transfer Protocol is a *transfer layer* protocol—meaning that XTP performs both the transport layer functions discussed above as well as many elements of the network layer.[5] This departure from the transport/network layer duality in the OSI Reference Model is driven by the design goals of XTP and by the direction in which network hardware technology is evolving.

The designers of XTP wished to produce a high-performance protocol that would provide the end-to-end reliability of transport systems, was targeted for siliconization, incorporated new transport functionality, and reflected lessons learned from the implementation and design experience of other transport layer protocols. Given these goals, an immediate observation is that creating a high-performance transport layer protocol is a largely pointless exercise if the underlying network layer service can not be relied upon to match this performance. Particularly striking would be the performance mismatch between a siliconized transport layer and a network layer protocol running in software. In short, in order to have the performance benefits offered by an end-to-end silicon path, the network layer had to be considered in the XTP design.

A number of protocol issues argue for an integration of transport and network layer functions into a single protocol. First, a unified transport and network layer protocol can coordinate end-to-end flow and rate control procedures with those for network congestion control. Increased connectivity and network communication between disparate network hosts make this integration of control algorithms very important. Current transport layer techniques such as estimating network congestion using roundtrip times may prove inadequate. Second, redundant aspects of the transport and network layer functionality (e.g., integrity checks over data and control information) can be handled uniformly under a single, unified protocol mechanism. Finally, problems with transport layer policies being second-guessed or nullified by network layer policies can be eliminated. For example, the priority value carried in each XTP packet reflects not only how it will be treated at XTP end-systems but also how it will be treated by XTP

---

[4.] **The reader is again cautioned that XTP's functionality does not fit cleanly into the OSI Reference Model's view of Layers 3 and 4.**

[5.] **In addition XTP incorporates protocol services such as multicast that were not anticipated by the OSI Reference Model's view of Layers 3 and 4, although on-going work within the standards community will eventually bring changes to the OSI Reference Model. Multipeer communication, in particular, is an active issue.**

switching nodes. The problem of mapping the priority levels of the transport layer onto those of the network layer service is eliminated.

As to the nature of the network service implemented by XTP, the protocol provides a streamlined connection-oriented routing functionality. Careful attention has been paid to performance aspects within the protocol design so that a silicon implementation of an XTP switch can be expected to move packets between network segments at rates near to those of high-speed fiber optic media. For example, XTP address translation is designed such that, in the majority of cases, a single 32-bit value can be used to index into the routing tables. Provision is also made for fast path setup using identifiers for well-known paths, in the flavor of, for instance, X.25 Permanent Virtual Calls.

The XTP designers acknowledge, however, that switching functionality, which the OSI Reference Model designers envisioned as belonging in the network layer, is appearing increasingly often in the lower layers. The success of the IEEE 802.1 work on Layer 2 switches is one example. Another is the standards now emerging for the Asynchronous Transfer Mode (ATM). Greg Chesson observes that "trends in media design are causing a gradual obsolescence of traditional Layer 3 architecture. The reason is that media providing switched virtual circuits such as ATM change the way we think about Layer 3" [CHES91a]. Consequently, the XTP design is crafted such that it can perform switching but is not disturbed when switching is unnecessary due to the presence of switching media.

## 2.2.2 XTP Data Communication Model

We present two views of the XTP data communication model. Figure 2.8 presents the architecture of an XTP host implementation and shows the relationship between the conceptual processes of an XTP implementation and their associated data structures. This "single node view" is provided to show the processes that handle data given to and received from the XTP users. Figure 2.9 depicts a pair of communicating XTP hosts and the network switching nodes between them. This "end-to-end view" is used to introduce important concepts in XTP peer-to-peer communication.

### Single Node View

The architecture of the Xpress Transfer Protocol state machine can be understood in terms of Figure 2.8. This abstraction of the protocol's workings has four processing components: the READER, the RECEIVER, the WRITER, and the SENDER. The RECEIVER and the SENDER processes provide XTP's interface to the network, while the READER and WRITER processes provide XTP's interface to the host. Their set of associated data structures include Control Blocks, Context Records, a Translation Map, Input Queues, and Output Queues.[6]

---

[6.] It should be emphasized that this representation of the protocol architecture is an abstraction intended to aid the reader; none of the entities is part of the XTP Definition nor does this presentation necessarily reflect a wise implementation plan for the protocol.

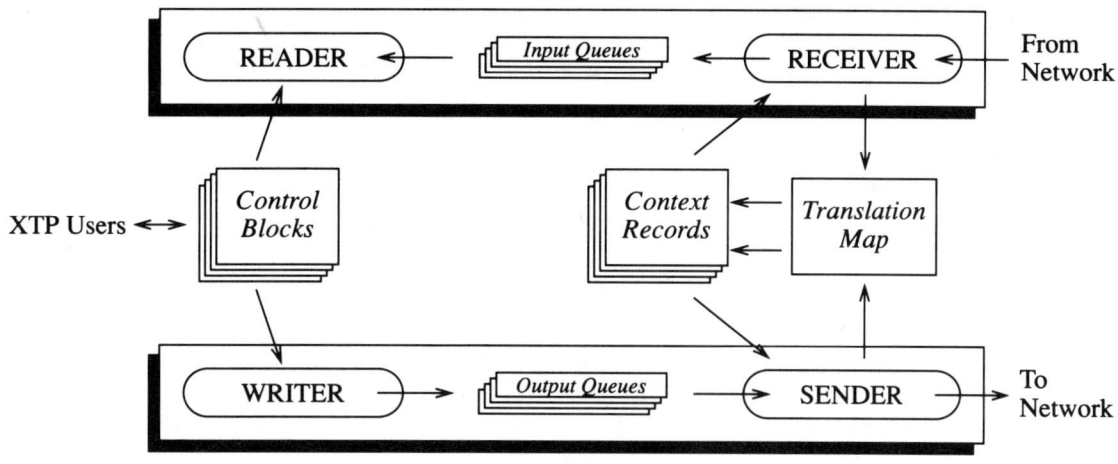

**Figure 2.8 — XTP Host Architecture**

The RECEIVER acts on packets received from the network and places the user data received in the proper Input Queue. This data will be delivered to the XTP user by the READER process. The READER process communicates with the upper-layer software or application resident on the host via some system-dependent data structure, which is represented as a Control Block in Figure 2.8.

An XTP user that wishes to send data to a remote XTP user transfers the data to the WRITER process via Control Block commands. The WRITER accepts data from the host and sorts it into appropriate Output Queues. The SENDER process delivers the

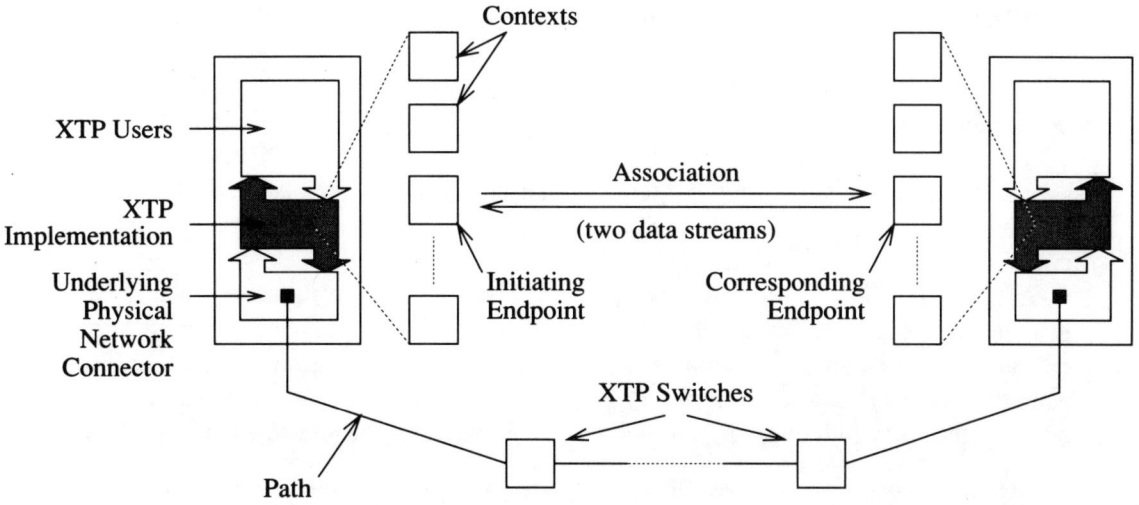

**Figure 2.9 — XTP Peer-to-Peer Communication Model**

contents of these Output Queues to the network, where some data delivery service forwards it to the next XTP implementation along the path between end-systems.

The Context Records are the XTP data structures holding state information about each active XTP endpoint at this XTP host implementation. The SENDER may update certain context variables on outputting a packet belonging to that context. The SENDER also places the values of certain context state variables in outgoing packets so that the packet will reach its intended destination and to communicate the state of the local context to a remote context.

The Context Records are the XTP data structures holding state information about each active XTP connection at this XTP host implementation. The Translation Map is XTP's database for mapping packets to their proper Context Records. Upon output of a packet to the network, the SENDER uses the Translation Map to access the appropriate Context Record both for updating local context variables and placing the values of certain local context variables in the outgoing packet. The RECEIVER uses information in incoming packets to index into the Translation Map and thereby determine the Context Record holding state information relevant to that packet.

## End-to-End View

We now turn our attention to the path that data takes as it is transferred from one endnode to another. Still referring to Figure 2.8, data enters an XTP implementation via the WRITER process and is eventually placed onto the network by the SENDER process. The data traverses some link or series of bridged links until it either comes to the destination host or to a node that will forward it along its path. When the data arrives at the destination host, the RECEIVER accepts the data, queues it, and the READER delivers the data in an appropriate form to the host. Figure 2.9 shows this end-to-end view of XTP data transfer.

When an XTP user wishes to communicate with one or more other XTP users, it does so by establishing an *association*. An association is the collection of all XTP state information, both at XTP end-systems and XTP intermediate nodes, used to effect a duplex data transfer. For a particular association, the state information kept at any one host is called a *context*; the context information is held in a Context Record. For each association, a host has a unique context for that association. We also refer to contexts as active entities since changes in the state variables of the context trigger protocol actions such as forming and sending packets.[7]

A context is also called an *endpoint* because it is a terminus of data flowing between the members of an association. An association is established when an *initiating endpoint* sends an association-establishment packet to a destination host, and that destination host creates a *corresponding endpoint* for the association. An association generally has only two endpoints; however, XTP provides for one-to-many (*multicast*)

---

[7.] **In later discussions we sometimes refer, for brevity, to two hosts communicating. This should always be understood to mean "a context at one host" communicating with "a context at the other host."**

associations as well as one-to-one (*unicast*) associations. A multicast association usually has more than two endpoints.

An association is composed of two distinct flows of data, one in each direction from endpoint to endpoint. (Multicast associations allow data flow only in the one-to-many direction.) These flows are called *data streams*. A data stream is an arbitrarily long, ordered sequence of data transferred from one endpoint to the group of one or more endpoints. The source of the data stream is called the *transmitter*; the set of endpoints that are the destinations of the data stream are called *receivers*. Since unicast associations allow duplex transfers, a unicast endpoint can be both a transmitter and a receiver.

Endpoints of an association do not need to reside on the same local network; an association may span several gateways between networks. These gateways, or intermediate nodes, are called *switches*. XTP switches are designed to emulate the "cut-through switching" used by ATM [GECH89] and other fast packet switches. The ordered set of nodes from one association endpoint to another is called a *path*; a path-establishing packet leaves behind a trail of local forwarding information in the switches that forward it.

Paths are directional. We usually refer to the direction of a path in terms of the direction of data flow of the association using that path. In this way a *forward path* refers to the path used by the forward traffic in an association, and similarly for *reverse paths*. While convenient, this definition of forward path is not formally well defined since paths and associations do not have a one-to-one relationship. XTP enables associations to share paths through a *route sharing* mechanism and thereby to amortize the cost of establishing a path when more than one association exists between a pair of XTP end-nodes.

In order to provide fast Translation Map lookups, XTP forces traffic flowing on the reverse data stream of an association to be forwarded across the same set of switching nodes (in reverse order, of course) as the forward data stream of that association. Thus we may speak of a *dual-path* as the forward and reverse path pair used by some set of associations. Path lifetimes and release mechanisms are independent of the associations that use them; thus an association may have more than one path over the course of the association's lifetime.

## 2.2.3 XTP Data Delivery Service Requirements

XTP requires the underlying data delivery service to provide only a few basic services: data integrity using a hardware cyclic redundancy code (CRC) or equivalent check, a simple framing capability, and a data delivery service between hosts on the same physical network segment. XTP algorithms specifically require source and destination physical addresses, and a length indication from the physical frame.

In a local area network environment, XTP finds sufficient the services offered by, for example, IEEE 802.2 Logical Link Control [IEEE84] Unacknowledged Connec-

tionless Service (Type I). Recall that the IEEE LLC standards specify the upper sublayer of the data link layer (as shown in Table 2.1). The LLC sublayer, in conjunction
with the MAC sublayer, provides link layer functionality over multiple access links, the
most common media type in LAN environments. LLC Type I service provides datagram frame delivery over the local network segment and any other network segments
reachable via link layer switches.

XTP packets must be placed in the protocol data units of the underlying data delivery service. *Encapsulation* is a general technique for defining an interface between
XTP and any underlying service provider that can deliver to XTP the minimum set of
supporting services. Encapsulation of XTP packets into the frames of a number of
well-known LAN standards as well as the Internet Protocol is defined in the XTP Definition (and discussed in Section 7.2).

## References

[CCITT84]      Comité Consultatif International de Télégraphique et Téléphonique, "The X.25
               Packet Layer Protocol," 1984.

[CHES91a]      Chesson, G., "The Evolution of XTP," in **Proceedings of the Third Interna-
               tional Conference on High Speed Networking**, North-Holland, Amsterdam, The
               Netherlands, 1991.

[DARPA80]      Postel, J., ed., "User Datagram Protocol," RFC 768, USC/Information Sciences
               Institute, August 1980.

[DARPA81a]     Postel, J., ed., "Internet Protocol—DARPA Internet Program Protocol Specifica-
               tion," RFC 791, USC/Information Sciences Institute, September 1981.

[DARPA81b]     Postel, J., ed., "Internet Control Message Protocol," RFC 792, USC/Information
               Sciences Institute, September 1981.

[DARPA81c]     Postel, J., ed., "Transmission Control Protocol—DARPA Internet Program Proto-
               col Specification," RFC 793, USC/Information Sciences Institute, September
               1981.

[GECH89]       Gechter, J., and O'Reilly, P., "Conceptual Issues for ATM," *IEEE Network*, Vol. 3,
               No. 1, pp. 14–16 (January 1989).

[IEEE84]       Institute of Electrical and Electronics Engineers, "IEEE Standard 802.2 Logical
               Link Control," 1984.

[ISO7498]      International Organization for Standardization, "Information Processing Sys-
               tems—Open Systems Interconnection—Basic Reference Model," *Draft Interna-
               tional Standard 7498*, October 1984.

[ISO8073]      International Organization for Standardization, "Information Processing Sys-
               tems—Open Systems Interconnection—Transport Protocol Specification," *Draft
               International Standard 8073*, July 1986.

[ISO8473]      International Organization for Standardization, "Information Processing Sys-
               tems—Open Systems Interconnection—Data Communications Protocol for Pro-
               viding the Connectionless-Mode Network Service," *Draft International Standard
               8473*, March 1986.

[ISO10029]       International Organization for Standardization, "Operation of an X.25 Internetwork Unit," *Technical Report 10029*, March 1989.

[PLUM82]         Plummer, D. C., "Ethernet Address Resolution Protocol: Or Converting Network Protocol Addresses to 48-bit Ethernet Address for Transmission on Ethernet Hardware," RFC 826, USC/Information Sciences Institute, November 1982.

[TANE88]         Tanenbaum, A., **Computer Networks**, Second Edition, Prentice Hall, Englewood Cliffs, New Jersey, 1988, p. 370.

# 3
# Influential Protocols

The developments that have motivated and shaped the design of the Xpress Transfer Protocol have come from above and below. Above the transport layer, new application domains such as distributed systems and multimedia workstations demand new services from the communication subsystem. The XTP designers recognized that a single protocol could be expected to handle a wide range of service models—message, stream, transaction, bulk, controlled rate, and multicast—since, at a fundamental level, all these services are concerned with the delivery of bits from a source to one or more sinks. The differences among the service models relate to their fundamental assumption regarding the quantity, reliability, frequency, and destination of data transmissions. XTP was designed so that it can support this multiplicity of data transfer syntaxes.

From below, the transport layer must respond to the dramatic advances in network hardware that has led to the 100 Mbit/sec fiber optic LANs already in place and to gigabit networks on the immediate horizon. These high-speed networks encourage the movement of the hardware/software boundary higher in the protocol stack. In particular, advances in VLSI design make it feasible to put a (streamlined) transfer layer protocol into VLSI, thus allowing for an "end-to-end silicon path."

Within the framework of supporting new user services with a protocol designed for VLSI implementation, the XTP designers set about rethinking from first principles the problem of reliable end-to-end data transfer. While a number of approaches—including some radical departures from conventional designs—were explored in the course of XTP's development, in its final form the transport aspect of XTP may be characterized as containing, in addition to a few truly novel transport mechanisms, many of the well-known transport reliability mechanisms associated with conventional connection-oriented transport protocols. Many of these conventional mechanisms, however, have been substantially re-engineered, both individually and in their interrelationships, in order to achieve the flexibility and orthogonality necessary to support various service models.

While the designers of XTP approached the problem of reliable end-to-end data transfer starting from first principles, XTP was not created in a vacuum. The protocol design process drew explicitly and implicitly on the lessons learned from the experience of other protocol designers and implementors. In this chapter we examine the most significant of these influences.

We start with an examination of two conventional protocols, the Transmission Control Protocol (TCP) and the ISO Transport Protocol class 4 (TP4), which represent the state of the art in standard commercial networks. These protocols offer a set of baseline algorithms and protocol techniques whose power and limitations have been widely studied as the result of years of implementation experience in a wide variety of heterogeneous networks. In addition to proving the engineering soundness behind many conventional transport techniques, the shortcomings inherent to these conventional end-to-end data delivery architectures have spurred experimentation in implementation and protocol design.

The other transport designs that have most influenced XTP are diverse in their intended networking environments (e.g., WANs, real-time LANs, distributed systems), their emphasis on particular service models (e.g., request/response, bulk transfers, universal data transport), and their architectures. The designers of XTP identified and incorporated the best elements from these protocols, which can be briefly characterized as follows:

- **Delta-t** is responsible for pioneering work in hazard-free communication when using implicit connections.
- The **Network Block Transfer** (NETBLT) protocol design includes novel data rate control in order to optimize bulk transfers.
- **GAM-T-103** introduced the concept of a transfer layer architecture.
- The **Versatile Message Transaction Protocol** (VMTP) efficiently supports transactional communication, optimizing its protocol procedures for request/response exchanges.
- The **Datakit** network architecture suggested the value of a simplified, hardware-supported receiver design as embodied in the **Universal Receiver Protocol**.

# 3.1   Conventional Transport

It is instructive to consider the relationship between XTP and the two most widely known standards for reliable transport layer protocols, namely the Transmission Control Protocol [DARPA81c] and the ISO Transport Protocol class 4 [ISO8073]. XTP starts with a different architectural framework (the transfer layer), a wider array of supported service models, different assumptions about the dominant factors in communication overhead, and an orientation toward implementation in silicon instead of in software. Nonetheless, a central part of XTP functionality is that of these conventional transport protocols: providing for a reliable end-to-end messaging service where the underlying data delivery service is assumed to be able to re-order, corrupt, lose, or significantly delay packets in route. We use the term *reliable data delivery* to identify this data delivery service type.

We look at how the conventional transport protocols, TCP and TP4, with their associated wealth of implementation experience, influenced both what was put into and what was left out of the Xpress Transfer Protocol.

## 3.1.1 TCP

During the mid-1970s the Defense Advanced Project Research Agency (DARPA) began development of a set of data communication standards for use within the military. This development was driven by the need to support communication and interoperability among the multi-vendor computer systems in use by the military. By 1977–1978 the development efforts had spawned a set of five military standards. The standard of interest in this section is MIL-STD-1778, the Transmission Control Protocol (TCP), which was designed to work over the unreliable network data delivery service defined in MIL-STD-1777 and known as the Internet Protocol (IP).

TCP is designed to provide reliable data delivery with some auxiliary functionality such as priority data. The protocol does not implement a particular service interface in the sense that the TCP specification does not dictate service interface primitives or service parameters. The interface between application network services (typically provided by operating system network software) and TCP can be characterized as a reliable byte stream over a full-duplex virtual circuit connection. Users view the reliable virtual circuit provided by TCP as a pipe; after a connection is established, bytes are pushed into the pipe and flow out the remote end in the same order. User data is not structured by the transport service (TCP); instead a remote user must understand how to interpret the arriving byte stream.

TCP is a connection-oriented sliding window protocol which uses byte-based sequence numbers, positive acknowledgements, and timer-based retransmission to provide reliable service. Each TCP connection provides full-duplex octet stream communication between the two endpoints of the connection.

## 3.1.2 ISO Transport Protocol

The Open Systems Interconnect architecture has defined five classes of connection-oriented transport protocol service numbered 0 through 4. The differences among these five service classes are related to the type and quality of service required by the Session Layer and, more directly, by the quality of service provided by the network layer. ISO Transport Protocol class 4 (TP4) assumes that the Network Layer provides nothing more than an unreliable datagram delivery service. The network service usually associated with TP4 is the ISO Connectionless Network Protocol (CLNP) which provides services very similar to IP. TP4 mechanisms are a superset of those for the other transport classes.

In the OSI Reference Model the service using the Transport Layer protocol is typically a Session Layer entity, not an entity outside of the communication subsystem (as with TCP). The service interface that TP4 implements is explicitly defined in terms of a small set of parametrized service calls, and TP4 data delivery services roughly match TCP's services. The service interface for TP4 formalizes the notion of *option negotiation*, the user's ability to specify values for the quality-of-service needed when establishing a connection. The reliable data delivery service is message-oriented, not stream-oriented as with TCP.

TCP was well-established at the time of the development of the ISO Transport Protocol standards, and TCP influenced TP4 heavily. Not surprisingly then, TP4 is a connection-oriented sliding window protocol that uses positive acknowledgements and timer-based retransmission. Connections provide full-duplex octet stream communication between their endpoints. However, there are a few important differences in the protocol mechanisms of TCP and TP4. For example, the block-oriented nature of data transfer in TP4 implies that sequence numbers are assigned on the basis of protocol data units (PDUs), not on the basis of bytes, as with TCP. Other significant deviations from TCP's mechanisms are noted in the discussions below.

## 3.1.3 Conventional Mechanisms

In order to highlight the reasoning behind important XTP design decisions, we examine to what extent XTP's mechanisms and control algorithms reflect those employed by TCP and TP4.

### Connection Establishment and Termination

For data transfers that require reliable data delivery, the transport peers must establish and manage the state information necessary to control the transfer. In particular, the connection establishment and termination phases of a data transfer can be considered independent of the actual movement of data. The connection establishment and termination procedures must ensure that no "false connections" can be created and that each packet is mapped to its proper destination. That is, without a careful design, packets delayed and/or duplicated in route to their destination can result in erroneous interpretations of state information at the receiving host, with very unpredictable results.

TCP and TP4 use three-way handshakes to set up and properly initialize the endpoints of a duplex connection. For connection termination TP4 does not define a graceful close since it is assumed that graceful termination will be handled by a higher layer. Thus TP4 uses only a two-way handshake to shut down a connection. TCP, on the other hand, provides a graceful close using a three-way handshake. In order to ensure that both sides close reliably, TCP's closing handshake requires the use of a timer at the endpoint initiating the close procedure so that the endpoint can retain state information long enough to be sure that the final acknowledgement releasing the connection arrived at the remote endpoint.

Connections amortize over the lifetime of a connection the cost of the opening and closing handshaking sequences. Opening and closing handshakes may be overlapped in TCP, but not in TP4. For long-lived connections this cost is reasonable and even negligible, but handshaking schemes are expensive for short-lived connections. This is especially true in TP4 where only a small amount of data can be transferred during the handshakes. While data may be sent in a TCP connection-opening packet, that data can not be reliably delivered to the user until the three-way handshake is complete (i.e., the connection is fully and safely open). Given the importance of request/response communication in many networks, especially distributed systems environments, support for efficient transfers on short-lived connections can not be ignored by next-generation transport protocols.

In recognition of the latency penalty and packet transmission overhead associated with handshaking, some transport protocols, namely Delta-t and later VMTP, use implicit connection setup and timer-based release of state information at the endpoints. By carefully aging state information at the endpoints, the first packet in a communication can safely create a connection upon arriving at its destination. XTP incorporates the ideas behind on-demand connection setup pioneered by these protocols. However, unlike these earlier protocols, XTP retains a connection-oriented approach. (Of course, XTP goes beyond the capabilities of conventional connections, as emphasized in the use of the term *association*.)

XTP uses a mixture of handshaking and timer-based techniques in order to provide a range of association establishment and release semantics. These semantics are designed to efficiently support both long-lived and short-lived associations. Data can be carried in the XTP connection-opening packet and connection identifiers are managed such that the arrival of the connection-opening packet opens the association (on-demand setup). The use of handshakes to close associations, with a variety of semantics including a graceful close, avoids some of the buffer and timer overhead incurred by completely timer-driven connection management schemes (as in Delta-t).

## Flow Control

TCP and TP4 use the credit-based sliding window technique for end-to-end flow control. This technique effectively controls packet loss due to overflowing buffers at the receiver. A well-tuned sliding window also allows the transmitter to keep the pipeline between it and the receiver full and thus to increase the efficiency of the data transfer. XTP's flow control is based on the sliding window technique with credits as well.

Conventional end-to-end flow control does not address the following data-rate problems: (1) packet loss due to a transmitter exceeding the processing capacity of the receiver and (2) packet loss at intermediate nodes due to either insufficient buffer space or too much data sent in a single burst. The first problem, rate control, arises, for example, in LAN communications when a fast receiver overwhelms the network interface of a slower machine with back-to-back packets. TCP and TP4 contain no mechanisms for rate control.

As for the second problem, TCP contains a mechanism for indirectly detecting and thereby reacting to transient congestion at intermediate nodes. Each endpoint in a TCP connection uses estimates of the roundtrip time to the peer host to detect congestion at intermediate nodes. Under the "slow-start" algorithm devised for TCP [JACO88], a node drastically reduces the number of packets that it sends if large increases in the roundtrip time take place. After this initial reduction, the node slowly increases its packet transmission rate back to its previous level. In addition to this TCP mechanism, congested IP routers can send a control message that throttles an end-system. In this way, the IP layer creates backpressure that throttles the data rate of a TCP endpoint.

However, while these mechanisms help reduce the probability of a "congestion collapse" within a TCP/IP internetwork, they are largely reactive and fairly crude. They do not allow the consideration of the intermediate systems' capacities in setting the data-rate constraints at end-systems.

In addition to its window-based flow control mechanism, XTP provides an orthogonal rate control mechanism. Rate and flow control together constrain the transmitter's output such that both conventional end-to-end flow control and the two data-rate problems above are addressed. XTP's formulation of a rate control facility follows the lead of NETBLT, the first protocol to incorporate rate control based on the two parameters of a maximum data transmission rate and a maximum burst size. The sender is constrained to send no more than the number of bytes specified in the burst size over a given interval of time. The length of this interval is derived by dividing the burst size by the maximum transmission rate. This mechanism provides effective rate control with less demanding timer granularity and management than specifying a minimum interpacket gap, the rate control method used in VMTP.

XTP's transfer layer architecture enables the participation of intermediate nodes in the rate control algorithm. Intermediate switching nodes play an active part in setting and adjusting the rate control parameter values at each endpoint of an XTP association. In addition to the negotiation of rate control parameters between endpoints that can take place at any point during an association, XTP switches can independently communicate new rate control settings to the endpoints of the associations that pass through them. Thus, as one of its functions, XTP rate control provides a direct means for dealing with the problem of network congestion at intermediate nodes, a problem difficult to address under the duality of a network/transport layer division of functionality.

## Error Handling

Like the conventional transports, XTP detects errors via sequence numbers, length fields, and checksums. TCP, TP4, and XTP all rely on a length field in the header to indicate the amount of user data present in the packet. XTP follows TCP in using byte-based sequence numbers as the data descriptors, but XTP uses 32-bit descriptors as well as a sliding window of 32 bits. TCP, while using 32-bit descriptors, has a 16-bit sliding window. Transfers across high-bandwidth networks now being deployed will easily involve data of a size necessitating at least 32-bit descriptors and window sizes. In anticipation of the need for even larger descriptors, moreover, the XTP Definition outlines a method for using a field carried in every XTP packet (the *sync* field in the XTP Header) to handle sequence number aliasing problems on very high-speed networks.

Conventional transports provide a single checksum, calculated on a per-packet basis, as the data integrity check over both user data and protocol control information. XTP packets carry two checksums, one over the body of the packet (where user data, if any is present in the packet, is carried) and one over the control information in the packet's header. The data checksum can be turned off for reasons of efficiency. The use of the data checksum is independent of the mandatory checksum over the header, which protects the protocol from corrupted state information.

The data checksum in an XTP packet is carried in the packet's trailer. In contrast to the conventional protocols' placement of the checksum in the packet header, putting the data checksum in the trailer allows the checksum to be computed as a packet is being streamed out onto the network. Placement in the header forces the sequence of calculating the checksum on the buffered data, placement of the checksum in the header, and then outputting the packet onto the network.

As with the conventional transports, error correction in XTP is achieved through retransmission of data. TCP and TP4 adopt a positive acknowledgement with retransmission (PAR) scheme using a go-back-$n$ retransmission algorithm. Under PAR the receiver only acknowledges data received error-free and in-sequence. Retransmissions are triggered by timeouts at the sender for unacknowledged data, and the go-back-$n$ scheme dictates that all data from the point of last acknowledgement be retransmitted. TP4 adds the option of having the receiver generate acknowledgements based on a timer at the receiver, rather than solely on the arrival of packets.

XTP implements a quite different error correction scheme. XTP uses automatic repeat request (ARQ) in which the sender bases retransmission on reports from the receiver. Moreover, error reporting from the receiver in an XTP association is informative enough to allow selective retransmission. In a high-bandwidth network where the number of packets in transit can be very large, using a go-back-$n$ retransmission algorithm can be very inefficient. Since go-back-$n$ retransmission is only a special case of the selective retransmission, XTP defines a retransmission mechanism wherein both selective and go-back-$n$ retransmission policies can be supported. The XTP Definition ensures that nodes supporting selective retransmission and those supporting only go-back-$n$ interoperate.

The problems inherent in the conventional approach to error control are well documented. (In recognition of these deficiencies, proposals have been made for both TCP and TP4 to modify their original error correction schemes.) Obtaining good values for timers proves to be a source of great complexity at the sender, especially in networks in which the roundtrip delay has a high variance [ZHAN86]. XTP addresses this problem directly in separating roundtrip time estimation procedures from data transfer procedures. Roundtrip time estimates can be made at any point and as often as the XTP transmitter deems necessary. In addition, the XTP Definition outlines a method for further reducing the overhead of roundtrip time handshakes.

Retransmission of data based on timer expirations at the sender can be counterproductive if the network is becoming congested. XTP separates the orthogonal actions of data retransmission and synchronization of the communicating endpoints by providing distinct mechanisms for retransmission decisions, estimating network roundtrip time, and synchronizing the state of the XTP endpoints. This decomposition of protocol functions promises to avoid at least some of the difficulties associated with the intermingling of these protocol functions in conventional protocols.

XTP's approach to error correction springs in part from one of its most fundamental design strategies: simplifying the receiver. Experience has shown that, in general, protocols require more processing per packet at the receiver than at the sender, and hence the receiver is the bottleneck in protocol processing [FRAS89]. In high-speed networking, and in particular with XTP's goal of processing packets at the speed of the underlying 100-plus Mbit/sec media, the receiver must not be overburdened if it is not to be overrun by the network. Thus, the XTP receiver operates as a slave to its transmitter, and the XTP design reduces receiver processing requirements wherever possible. The design philosophy of a simplified, hardware-assisted receiver that is driven by the transmitter was taken as a fundamental tenet behind the Universal Receiver Protocol, which grew out of the Datakit network architecture.

With respect to error correction, this principle of a simple receiver manifests itself in having the sender dictate acknowledgement generation at the receiver. With a few exceptions, the XTP receiver is required to issue a control packet only when its transmitter sends a status request command in a packet header. Besides reducing the number of states in the protocol state machine, this master-slave relationship has the significant advantage of enabling the sender to request control packets at synchronization points independent of patterns determined by data acknowledgement.

Another important aspect of the XTP error correction scheme is the ability to run an association in a mode in which error correction is turned off (the "no-error mode"). This service feature is absent from the conventional transports, yet it is clearly useful for some data traffic profiles. Internally, the protocol mechanism for turning off error control is simple to implement: the receiver informs the sender that every packet was received, whether or not it really was. At the sender, control packet processing is exactly the same as in the error-controlled mode of operation. This is an example of how XTP, with its mandate of supporting multiple service models, extends traditional mechanisms so that, with very little protocol overhead, new services can be supported.

## Service Selection/Auxiliary Services

XTP provides a richer set of data delivery services than conventional transports through allowing the user to select a configuration of protocol options that matches the service desired. The XTP user can, for example, independently disable flow, rate, or error control. Perhaps most significantly, XTP defines a multicast association that provides for flow-, rate-, and error-controlled data delivery to a set of receivers. The need for multicast was not anticipated in the initial designs of TCP and TP4. In addition to new data services, XTP also provides auxiliary services similar to those in conventional transports for enhancing the reliable data delivery service.

Each of TP4, TCP, and XTP provides some degree of prioritized communication. A TP4 connection has two sequence number spaces, one for ordinary data and one for expedited data. The protocol semantics dictate that, after sending a packet of expedited data, no other packet may be transmitted until the expedited data packet is acknowledged. TCP has two options related to priority, the *push* flag and the *urgent pointer*. The semantics of the push flag are that the packet with this option set contains data that should be delivered to the user in an expedited, although still in-sequence, fashion. The transmission buffers for the connection are flushed immediately when the push flag is set. The urgent pointer indicates the place in the data stream where data requiring special attention begins. Urgent data may travel in packets carrying ordinary data, as opposed to TP4's expedited data packet type. The TCP definition does not specify what actions a receiver should take to speed processing of urgent data, though presumably some expeditious processing is required.

XTP supports prioritized communication by providing a 32-bit priority field. This field can be used to prioritize an entire data stream, or it can be changed on a per-packet basis. Unlike TP4, an XTP transmitter is not forced to block after outputting a packet of high importance. The 32-bit priority field allows discrimination policies that are more expressive than the conventional priority schemes. Such a wide priority field enables operating system-level priority values, which may even be based on time values, to be directly translated into XTP priority values. Finally, the transfer layer architecture ensures that the processing precedences preserved at switching nodes are the same as those at the end-systems.

XTP also provides a small channel for out-of-band data. Each XTP packet may carry an 8-byte *tag* of data at the beginning of the packet. This tag is in the sequence number space and thus error-controlled in a reliable transfer. Like all user data, the data carried in the tag field is transparent to XTP. Upon reception of a tag, the XTP receiver notifies the user of the tag's appearance in the data stream. Tags thus can serve to mark the data stream or carry management information for the purposes of higher-layer protocols. Like TCP, XTP derives considerable flexibility and simplification from being able to work from the model of user data as an unmarked stream of bytes. The tag feature provides a means for higher-layer protocols to impose application- and protocol-specific structuring on the byte stream with very little overhead for XTP.

## 3.2  Delta-t

Delta-t [WATS83] is a high-performance transport protocol designed to meet the needs of an integrated network and distributed operating system architecture. In the late 1970s the Lawrence Livermore National Laboratories developed LINCS, the Livermore Integrated Network Computing System, to integrate a wide range of heterogeneous computing systems from PCs to supercomputers. The need in this system was for a high-performance transport protocol that could effectively support both the request/response transaction style of communication found in client/server interactions, as well as the stream style communications found in terminal and bulk data transfer interaction. At the time TCP was the only available general purpose transport protocol but, since TCP was designed for long-lived connections, TCP could not efficiently provide request/response interactions without an excessive number of connection management packet exchanges.

It was a design goal of Delta-t, therefore, that the minimum number of packets exchanged for a reliable, *hazard-free* connection be exactly two packets in the usual case, one for data and one for acknowledgement. No other packets are required for connection opening and closing since the arrival of the first packet in a communication opens the connection, and the connection is released by a timeout. It is through timer-based mechanisms that hazards to a connection are avoided, since three-way hand-shakes and unique connection identifiers are not sufficient to prevent certain pathologi-cal situations.

A *connection* in Delta-t is defined to mean the time during which state information is maintained at each communicating endpoint. Connection opening requires that state be reliably instantiated at both ends; connection closing similarly requires that this state be reliably deallocated at each end by some point in time. Logically, there are perma-nent connections between any pair of streams, and these connections exist in a *default* state. The default state is simply the retention of *no* state information. When a sender wishes to establish a connection, it instantiates state information at its end and sends an initial packet. This initial packet causes the receiver to instantiate state information for this connection, and the connection is moved to the active state. This is an *implicit connection setup*. As long as there may be outstanding packets associated with this instantiation of the state information, this state information must be retained to ensure that no packet intended for this connection disturbs or creates another connection. In general, if, by some mechanism, a protocol can ensure this, the connection manage-ment procedures are termed *hazard-free*.

Connection hazards are introduced by lost, duplicate, or out-of-sequence packets. To provide hazard-free connection management, the lifetime of each packet must be bounded and strictly enforced. A common method of bounding a packet's lifetime is by using a *time-to-live* field, the value of which is the amount of time that this packet remains valid. Once a packet's time-to-live becomes zero, it must be discarded. The maximum time-to-live value for any packet in the network is called the *maximum packet lifetime*, or MPL. The state information for a connection, including the "used" error control and connection identifiers, must be aged by an amount of time based on this MPL before the state information can be deallocated and the identifiers reused. In this way the information within a packet may be unambiguously identified, so that either the information can be incorporated into the state of the connection, or the packet can be identified as useless and discarded.

If the information within a packet is not properly identified, that information can erroneously change the state of some existing connection or cause a "false connection" to be established. Watson [WATS81] has shown that all error control identifiers must be aged at least two times the MPL, plus the retransmission interval at the sender, plus the queueing delay at the receiver. In particular, old and new data with the same sequence numbers can be confused if sequence numbers are not properly aged. Similarly, con-nection identifiers must be aged to ensure that a packet containing an identifier for an old connection does not get delivered to a new connection which happens to be reusing the same connection identifier.

The state information at each end of the connection must be retained until no packets associated with this connection could possibly be outstanding. A timer at the receiver is refreshed upon each arriving packet. The value of this timer must be chosen so as to guarantee that all retransmissions and other duplicates will be received while the receiver's state information is still retained. This ensures that stale or other faulty information can be recognized as such. The sender maintains its state information long enough to guarantee that all data sent or retransmitted has had a chance to be acknowledged. If the timers at both ends of the connection are properly maintained, no explicit connection termination packets need be exchanged as the quiescent connection will eventually return to the default state. This is *implicit connection termination*.

Delta-t's self-proclaimed main contribution was to demonstrate how timer mechanisms may be used for safe connection management and, through the use of these timer-based mechanisms, to develop a hazard-free connection-oriented protocol. Experience gained from the development and use of Delta-t provides a general prescription for connection management [WATS89a]. Delta-t's designers entreat future protocol designers to conduct extensive case analyses with respect to hazards, identify where hazards may occur, and ensure that proper mechanisms are used to guard against them.

XTP's procedures for handling error control identifiers, namely its sequence numbers, its connection identifiers (*key* values), and its path identifiers (*route* values), are designed specifically with Delta-t's requirements for hazard-free communication in mind. The sequence number space, which covers $2^{32}$ bytes, is sufficiently wide for the 100-plus Mbit/sec LANs of today, and XTP is designed to transition easily to 64-bit sequence numbers when gigabit/sec networks become commonplace. After being used, a *key* value, which is used to identify an association, and a *route* value, which is used to identify a path between hosts, are required to remain inactive for the period of time proven to be appropriate by Delta-t. With regard to this requirement, the XTP Definition offers explicit guidelines to implementors for ensuring that these values are properly aged.

As in Delta-t, a fully error-controlled XTP association can be established and terminated in as few as two packets. XTP's initial packet, called a FIRST packet, causes state information to be instantiated at the receiving endpoint. Since data can be sent in the FIRST packet, the sender can include in the FIRST packet the user data, a request for the status of the receiver, and notification of the beginning of the association termination handshake. The receiver responds with a control packet that acknowledges the data and completes the termination handshake.

Delta-t allows a connection to remain active after all packets have been sent and received, relying on timers to deallocate the state information. Delta-t keeps the state information to prevent old or duplicate packets from appearing after the connection is terminated, which can result in the creation of a false connection. By contrast, XTP associations are terminated by using an explicit handshake augmented when necessary with a timer; state information is deallocated upon completing the handshake, although the entry in the context lookup database is kept until no hazard due to reappearing packets is possible. Consequently, under certain conditions, XTP avoids the overhead of managing "zombie" contexts.

The Delta-t protocol is specified in [WATS83]. Features and experience with the protocol are given in [WATS89a] and [WATS89b]. Timer-based mechanisms are presented in [WATS81].

# 3.3  NETBLT

The Network Block Transfer (NETBLT) protocol [CLAR87a] is a transport layer protocol specifically designed for efficient transfers of large amounts of data. The algorithms which make up this protocol are optimized to provide high throughput over long-delay channels while retaining good performance in LAN environments. This is done by minimizing network congestion, delays associated with long haul links, and packet loss.

NETBLT's design was driven by several observations about flow control and error recovery algorithms in the conventional transport protocols. Commonly, a "window" of outstanding data is maintained; acknowledgements advance the window and timers detect loss of data. The efficiency of the communication is directly related to the size of the window and how often acknowledgements are sent. Clark, *et al.*, in [CLAR87b], suggest that two major problems in transport protocols are the overloading of windows and the misuse of timers. Windows are used to control the flow of data; changes by the receiver in the sender's window size either enable or throttle the data transmission. Since in general the receiver only generates control packets when its window is filled, lost data delays the window's movement until a timer expiration detects the data loss. Furthermore, a window only expresses the constraint on how much data may be outstanding, not the rate at which that data may be sent.

Since reliable bulk data transfer is concerned with the efficiency of the communication as measured in terms of throughput, the transport protocol providing this reliable data transfer should detect errors as soon as possible. Yet, in order to detect errors quickly, control packets must be exchanged more often, which in itself reduces the efficiency of the communication. NETBLT's solution to providing efficient, yet reliable, communications is to decouple the flow and error control mechanism so that detection of lost packets is not tied to how and when flow control is employed. Selective acknowledgements are used to identify precisely what parts of the data are lost. Since packet loss can be due to congestion and insufficient processing resources, rather than bit errors, the window-based flow control mechanism in NETBLT explicitly incorporates data rate information to reduce this packet loss.

In a NETBLT data transfer, each message is divided by the application process into several large buffers whose maximum size is dependent upon the amount of free memory available to NETBLT. Each buffer is then completely and reliably transferred by first segmenting the buffer into packets, transmitting these packets, and then reassembling the packets into the buffer at the receiver. At the end of a buffer transfer, the receiver requests retransmission of any packets not properly received. Once the buffer is completely delivered, the buffer is released and a new buffer is sent. In this way the buffer acts as the window. This continues until the entire message is transferred.

The transfer is controlled by two levels of flow control. On the first level, the user controls how much data is placed into the data buffer. This buffer size is negotiated prior to the exchange so that both ends are using same-sized buffers. Once the buffer size is established, the buffer is transferred without interruption. To prevent overruns at the receiver or at any intermediate gateway or router, the second level (NETBLT level) of flow control, that based on the data rate, is enforced on bursts of packets. In this rate-based flow control, a *burst size* and a *burst rate* are negotiated at the beginning of each buffer transfer (based on known parameters and the results of the last buffer transfer) so that the transmitter is constrained to transmit a maximum number of packets within a set period of time.

Since the receiver knows the size of the buffer and the rate of the transfer, the receiver can deduce how long it should wait on the buffer transfer before concluding that some data has been lost. The receiver, therefore, instead of the transmitter, maintains the retransmission timer. Any packets not received by the time the timer expires are considered lost. The receiver communicates the reception status by sending a packet acknowledging only those packets that were actually received; the transmitter will retransmit only those packets needed to fill the buffer. This reduces the number of packets required for error recovery, and thus the congestion on the network.

XTP provides the mechanisms for selective acknowledgement and selective retransmission for those applications which may benefit from it—such as bulk data transfers over high-delay networks. An XTP receiver reports gaps in the data so that the transmitter may selectively retransmit the lost data. Since XTP is designed to be useful for many different data transfer profiles, however, XTP does not dictate the use of only selective retransmission for error recovery, but supports go-back-*n* as well.

As with NETBLT, XTP decouples flow and error control by separating the request for reception status from the operation of the window-based flow control mechanism. In NETBLT, the receiver maintains timers and drives the retransmissions; in XTP, however, the sender is responsible for requesting reception status and acting upon it. Thus, normal recovery from lost packets does not rely on timer expirations.

In NETBLT, data is transferred between users with dedicated same-size buffers, so no data is ever lost at the end systems due to insufficient buffer space. XTP provides a similar mode of operation called the *reservation* mode. In reservation mode, the receiving XTP entity must open the flow control window only as wide as dedicated buffers will allow. Consequently, the credit issued from the receiver to the sender reflects precisely the buffer space dedicated for that transfer; no packets can be lost due to lack of buffer space.

NETBLT's major contribution to the design of XTP is its two-parameter rate control algorithm. NETBLT identifies the need to regulate both the rate at which the transmitter submits a burst of packets as well as the size of each burst, based on the receiver's ability to process those bursts. As in NETBLT, an XTP receiver communicates burst and rate values to the transmitter, specifying how fast that transmitter can send packets.

Rate control in XTP, however, is considered a separate issue from flow control. XTP provides a window-based flow control mechanism to manage the buffer space within the communicants. Rate control, conversely, manages the processing capability of each node along the path between the communicants. The rate at which a transmitter should produce packets must be no greater than the rate at which any one node along the path can consume and process those packets. Since XTP is a transfer layer protocol, and thus includes the responsibilities of the network layer, the rate control algorithm incorporates information about the resources in each node along the path, not just the processing capacity of the receiver.

# 3.4   GAM-T-103 Military Real-Time Local Area Network Architecture

In 1987 the French Ministry of Defense published the GAM-T-103 specification [FREN87] for Military Real-Time Local Area Networks (MRT-LANs). This specification formalizes and organizes into an hierarchical framework the services required for military real-time communications. GAM-T-103 was developed as the result of an analysis of the requirements and specific constraints of MRT-LANs, and the applicability of current hierarchical specifications, namely the OSI Reference Model, to meet those requirements and constraints. GAM-T-103 is analogous to the OSI Reference Model in that GAM-T-103 specifies an hierachical layering scheme, but it does not define the specific protocols for data transfer.

There are four layers in the GAM-T-103 model: the USER layer, the TRANSFER layer, the DATALINK layer, and the PHYSICAL layer. GAM-T-103 specifies only the USER-layer/TRANSFER-layer interface and the services of the TRANSFER layer; the other interfaces are not specified in order to allow equipment-dependent optimization. While the contents of the TRANSFER layer are not specified by GAM-T-103, the types of communication and assumptions on those types are given.

The GAM-T-103 designers determined that the OSI Reference Model was inadequate for the real-time LAN environment that GAM-T-103 envisions. Their decision to embrace a *transfer layer* architecture reflects a reassessment of how protocol functionality should be distributed, given the service and performance requirements of real-time LANs. Many of the requirements for the GAM-T-103 environment are shared by current and emerging distributed systems, making the conclusions of the GAM-T-103 project more generally applicable than just the design of military real-time networks. Examples include the importance placed on capabilities for low latency messages, point-to-multipoint and multipoint-to-point traffic, and synchronization.

The XTP designers recognized the value of a transfer layer architecture in achieving a high-performance end-to-end protocol. While the impact of design decisions on implementations' performance is difficult to quantify, it seems clear that an explicit fusion of the transport and network layers during the protocol design process should lead to more streamlined protocol processing than that in designs that handle the two layers independently. While in the past it has been adequate to separate how the network layer delivers a packet from how the transport layer manages the message transfer, as performance demands increase, the interaction between the services of these two layers necessarily becomes more tightly integrated.

In addition to its transfer layer structure, XTP agrees with the GAM-T-103 project in its emphasis on certain data communication functionality called out in the GAM-T-103 service profile. Perhaps the most prominent example is the recognition of the need for group communication. GAM-T-103 defines the semantics for point-to-multipoint (multicast) as well as multipoint-to-point (concentration) topologies. XTP is designed so that multicast is a natural extension to the unicast communication paradigm; that is, group communications are flow-, rate-, and error-controlled using the same facilities as unicast communications.

GAM-T-103 is specified by the document [FREN87], and is described in less formal terms in [COCQ89]. A performance evaluation of protocols based on the GAM-T-103 specification can be found in [MINE89].

## 3.5   Versatile Message Transaction Protocol

The Versatile Message Transaction Protocol (VMTP) [CHER88a] was developed at Stanford University as the communication component within the V Distributed System [CHER88b]. VMTP is the result of the observation that, as distributed systems become more prolific, the use of clusters of workstations and file servers is shifting from predominately file distribution to distributed computation and on-demand paging. Consequently, the required communication services in such an environment rely heavily upon request/response interaction. The designers of VMTP contend that the design of protocols, networks, and network interfaces should be rethought from first principles in the context of this new environment.

Three major areas are recognized by the designers of VMTP as deficiencies with current transport level protocols: performance, naming, and functionality [CHER89]. Current connection-oriented and connectionless transport protocols offer poor response for transaction-oriented communication. A connection costs too much to set up and tear down for each transaction, yet reliability and other features from connection-oriented protocols are essential. Poor performance also results from the loss of data due to resource overruns. For efficiency the window size in window-based flow control is usually large, yet a burst of a whole window may overrun the receiver's buffers. As for naming, the number of service access points is not very large, and the service access point addresses are unique only within a host. This inhibits process migration and the use of mobile hosts. Lastly, current transport protocols suffer from lack of functionality, specifically security, priority, and a multicast and datagram service which share the same naming, transmission, and reception facilities as the "normal" transport service.

VMTP provides transport communication services via a *message transaction model*. A message transaction consists of a request message sent by a client process to one or more server processes, followed by zero or more response messages sent back to the client by the server processes. VMTP contends that connections in the classic sense are redundant since the users of the communication facility will themselves be maintaining a conversation. Therefore, VMTP uses transaction exchanges to facilitate conversations on a higher level. A *conversation* is a sequence of related communication actions; message transactions just provide the information exchange to support conversations.

The simplest conversation for a transaction-based protocol is a transaction itself. A transaction is initiated by a *client entity* sending a *request message* to a *server entity* and terminated by the server sending back a *response message*. The response implicitly acknowledges the receipt of the request. Either the next request, an explicit VMTP-level acknowledgement, or a transaction timeout within VMTP acknowledges the receipt of the response.

In VMTP there are three variants on the basic message transaction which widen its applicability and efficiency. These variations may be combined to provide even more flexibility. A *group message transaction* is a transaction in which the client sends a multicast to a group of server entities; in return, the client may receive multiple responses. A *datagram* transaction occurs when a client sends the request message with an indication that no response is expected. A *forward message session* is a transaction in which a request message may be forwarded to another server which responses directly to the client. This is an optimization of nested remote procedure calls.

Like NETBLT, VMTP attributes significant packet loss to resource overruns. Also like NETBLT, VMTP uses a selective retransmission scheme to recover lost packets. Acknowledgements within VMTP carry a bit mask to reflect which of the packets arrived safely. Rather than using explicit parameters for its rate-based flow control as does NETBLT, VMTP deduces the proper interpacket gap from the patterns of packet loss reflected in the acknowledgement bit mask.

VMTP emphasizes the need for *stable addressing* to ensure that an entity address either retains the same meaning as long as the meaning is valid, or that the address becomes invalid for a period of time sufficient to avoid confusion. This is similar in concept to the aging of error control identifiers in Delta-t; however, by applying this aging to transport layer entity identifiers as well as error control identifiers, process migration is supported since network visible entities have host-independent addresses.

The VMTP effort has argued the need for a different service model for communications within a distributed system. Rather than viewing communications as that between peers, VMTP recognizes that a large part of information exchange follows a client/server model. VMTP provides communications primitives based on a transaction paradigm and which are highly optimized for request/response behavior. To do this, VMTP rejected outright the use of a connection-oriented transport service provider due to the overhead associated with connection management.

Although the way XTP manages its state information resembles a connection-oriented approach, XTP can support transactions very efficiently. Like VMTP, state information is built with the arrival of the first packet in an association. Also like

VMTP, this information is kept as long as data exchanges continue. Since data may be sent with the first packet of the association, XTP can support a transaction in the same number of packet exchanges as VMTP, yet XTP uses exactly the same mechanisms as it would for a long-lived transfer. Satisfying the needs of distributed systems, especially in providing an efficient transaction mechanism, was a major design goal of XTP.

The selective retransmission facility provided by XTP is somewhat similar to the bit-mask selective retransmission scheme in VMTP. While a VMTP packet is acknowledged by a bit position in a bit mask, XTP's selective retransmission scheme uses *spans* (beginning and ending byte sequence numbers of received data) to acknowledge data. While both schemes for selective retransmission allow a single acknowledgement packet to inform the transmitter of the loss of several chunks of data, XTP does not use the selective retransmission information for adjusting the interpacket spacing. Rather, XTP uses explicit rate control parameters to reduce resource overrun errors.

VMTP's stable addressing eases process migration by decoupling transport layer entity identifiers from specific hosts. While XTP does not require stable addressing for its users, it does provide within its parametric addressing facility the ability to have "direct addressing." Within closed systems, direct addressing in XTP enables a user-defined addressing scheme that may incorporate optimizations and local addressing needs. Stable addressing represents such a local addressing need that can be achieved through proper administration of a direct addressing scheme.

VMTP has been the subject of much research and many papers. The protocol specification is given in [CHER88a], and several general protocol overviews are given in [CHER86], [CHER89], and [WILL89a], and experience with VMTP is reported in [NORD89]. Furthermore, as well as providing the primary example of a transaction-based transport layer protocol, VMTP provides the communication support for the V Distributed System [CHER88b], [CHER87], [WILL89b].

## 3.6   Datakit and the Universal Receiver Protocol

Datakit [FRAS83] is a communications architecture designed at Bell Labs in the late 1970s. Although the Datakit network supports circuit-switched communication, it resembles packet-switching in its internal mechanisms. The Datakit architecture specifies functionality that maps to the lower four layers of the OSI Reference Model. The Universal Receiver Protocol (URP) [FRAS89b] grew out of the Datakit end-to-end protocol development effort.

The focus of the Datakit project was to develop a very general data transport architecture. The designers of Datakit saw the need for ubiquitous interconnection for telecommunications devices. In analogy to the power distribution system, users want a "telecommunications socket" into which their devices plug for communication services. This idea would only be useful if the communication service available at the socket can be made reasonably consistent and constant. The network must provide all users with small variances in delay and throughput characteristics if equipment manufacturers are to trust the network service enough to base product development on it.

The Datakit design goals led to a byte-stream architecture. In order to achieve maximum flexibility in handling user data within the circuit-switched environment that Datakit supports, the designers took as the fundamental unit of data a 9-bit byte where the extra bit distinguishes between data and network control information. A byte-stream architecture allows for fine-grained multiplexing of control and data information, and it enables the Datakit architecture to carry transparently whatever size data envelopes higher-layer protocols wish to use. The Datakit byte-stream architecture contains many elements of the Asynchronous Transfer Mode (ATM) proposal for broadband ISDN and high-speed MANs. For example, ATM propagates data in small fixed-sized cells that are independent of higher-layer data framing.

Unfortunately, the byte-stream architecture brings with it the considerable overhead of data stream processing on a per-byte basis at the receiving end-system. The 9-bit byte structure poses an alignment problem for conventional memory structures that further slows receiver processing. Network-attached computer systems show dramatically better throughput when they can process large blocks of data. To address these efficiency problems, the designers of Datakit developed a set of ideas that became the Universal Receiver Protocol. URP uses a particular style of pipelined receiver implementation that performs block assembly in hardware and delivers completed blocks to a higher-layer processing element.

Since the receiver is burdened with a per-byte examination of the data stream from the network, URP simplifies the receiver as much as possible by reducing the receiver's responsibility and shifting complexity to the transmitter when necessary. The receiver becomes a "clean pipelined path" with incoming data and control information moving through the receiver with little delay. Hardware assistance was anticipated for such a pipelined path, although no silicon has yet been made.[1]

URP's end-to-end control functions allow it to operate as a transport protocol in its own right as well as to serve as the underpinning for a Datakit architecture. The end-to-end functions of URP handle flow and error control as well as data marking for defining the block of data to be presented to the receiving host. Both a block and a character mode are supported, the latter causing each data byte to be delivered to the host immediately upon reception. The receiver is designed to process control information while the data is being placed into buffers in a staging area, and the URP receiver responds with its data delivery status when the transmitter sends status request commands.

While the Datakit project was shaped by wide-area virtual circuit communication and the XTP effort was driven by high-speed LAN technology, XTP was influenced in its design philosophy by the Universal Receiver Protocol. An explicit design goal for the XTP project was the construction of a Protocol Engine, a hardware implementation of XTP and its associated buffering logic, such that a received packet is processed

---

[1.] **This is as of the publication of [FRAS89a].**

within the arrival time of the packet. On a 100 Mbit/sec FDDI network, for example, such "flow through" processing allows only 4.8 microseconds for a typical small (60-byte) packet.

Because the demands on the receiver are so stringent, XTP follows the same path as the Datakit project did in developing a simplified receiver design. The XTP transmitter takes on the complexity of administering the flow and error control policies of the data transfer. With few exceptions, the XTP receiver generates control packets reporting its status to the transmitter only when the transmitter has sent a status request command in a packet's header.

A few elements of the Universal Receiver Protocol's control schemes themselves are echoed in XTP. In particular, to report its status, the URP receiver sends back two sequence number values, one being the highest sequence number correctly received in-order and the other being the highest sequence number delivered in-order to the user. XTP similarly places importance on these two delivery status values in its control algorithms. URP also provides a mechanism very much like XTP's synchronizing handshake for synchronizing the endpoints of a connection. This mechanism allows the transmitter to determine at what point in the data transfer control information was issued.

An overview of the Datakit architecture is presented in [CHES79] and [FRAS83]. The Universal Receiver Protocol and its design principles are discussed at length in both [FRAS89a] and [FRAS89b].

## 3.7   Summary

This final section summarizes the important aspects of the end-to-end protocols examined in this chapter, along with those in XTP. Summarizing and comparing protocol mechanisms is tricky. Some important issues such as the service interface provided to the protocol, the interaction between protocol features, and—perhaps most importantly—implementation-related factors (ease of implementation, variation between implementations, nature of the important decisions left to the implementor) are difficult to quantify. Nonetheless, bearing in mind these caveats, we feel that it is valuable to present a concise representation of the way in which XTP has absorbed innovative ideas as well as selecting conventional techniques.

Table 3.1 was constructed using the sources listed in the bibliography, especially the excellent work found in [DOER90]. In the table, the protocols in this chapter[2] are listed in the chronological order of their first publication dates. Under each item and for each protocol a key phrase or number is placed in the table. A blank entry means that the feature is absent, "N/A" means the feature does not apply, and a checkmark is used if no further description is merited.

[2.] **The GAM-T-103 specification is for an architectural framework, not a particular end-to-end protocol, and is therefore not included in this table.**

| | Communication Model | | | Connection Management | | |
|---|---|---|---|---|---|---|
| | paradigm | primary target environment | supports multicast | number of packets required for reliable transfer | connection establishment | connection release |
| Datakit/ URP (1976) | byte stream | WAN[a] | | 6[b] | hand-shake (2) | hand-shake (2) |
| TCP (1977) | connection | general | | 3 | hand-shake (3) | hand-shake (3) |
| Delta-t (1978) | timer-based connection | LAN | | 2 | implicit (1) | implicit (0)[c] |
| ISO TP4 (1982) | connection | general | | 6 | hand-shake (3) | hand-shake (2) |
| NETBLT (1986) | connection | WAN | | 6 | hand-shake (2) | hand-shake (2) |
| VMTP (1986) | trans-action | LAN | first response[d] | 2 | implicit (1) | implicit (0)[c] |
| XTP (1987) | multiple | general | reliable[d] | 2 | implicit (1) | hand-shake (2) |

[a]·Other than Datakit/URP, the surveyed protocols are designed to operate over an underlying data delivery service that may reorder, duplicate, corrupt, or loose data. Datakit/URP assumes only data loss can occur in its underlying (circuit-switched) network.

[b]·Datakit/URP uses out-of-band signaling messages to establish the connection. The assumption here is that a two-packet handshake is used.

[c]·Delta-t and VMTP can release connections using timer expiration.

[d]·See Chapter 8.

**Table 3.1 — Comparison of Protocol Mechanisms and Services**

It is evident from this table that XTP built much of its functionality on mechanisms and concepts introduced and proven elsewhere. What makes XTP unique is that it combines these good ideas into a protocol whose mechanisms are as much as possible orthogonal to each other.

| | Error Control | | | | Flow Control | | | Rate Control |
|---|---|---|---|---|---|---|---|---|
| | acknowledgement generation | retransmission policy | error reporting | can disable error control | mechanism | can disable flow control | permits buffer reservation | mechanism |
| Datakit/ URP (1976) | sender driven | ARQ go-back-$n$ | NACK | $\sqrt{}$ | window | $\sqrt{}$ | | |
| TCP (1977) | data reception | PAR[e] | implicit[f] | | credit-based window | | | |
| Delta-t (1978) | data reception | ARQ go-back-$n$ | NACK | | credit-based window | | | |
| ISO TP4 (1982) | data reception[g] | PAR[e] | implicit[f] | | credit-based window | | | |
| NETBLT (1986) | data reception | ARQ selective | selective reject | | window, rate-based | | always required | rate, burst para-meters |
| VMTP (1986) | data reception | ARQ selective | selective reject | $\sqrt{}$ | rate-based | | | inter-packet gap |
| XTP (1987) | sender driven | ARQ go-back-$n$, selective | selective reject, NACK | "no-error" mode | credit-based window | "no-flow" mode | "reserv-ation" mode | rate, burst para-meters |

[e.] More flexible schemes are being evaluated.

[f.] The error report is in the form of an expired timer.

[g.] Timer-based acknowledgements that are independent of data reception are optionally provided.

**Table 3.1 — *Continued***

## References

[CHES79]        Chesson, G., "Datakit Software Architecture," *Proceedings of the ICC*, pp. 20.2.1–20.2.5 (1979).

[CHER86]        Cheriton, D. R., "VMTP: A Transport Protocol for the Next Generation of Communication Systems," *Computer Communication Review*, Vol. 16, No. 3, pp. 406–415 (August 1986).

[CHER87]        Cheriton, D. R., and Williamson, C. L., "Network Measurement of the VMTP Request-Response Protocol in the V Distributed System," *Performance Evaluation Review*, Vol. 15, No. 1, pp. 216–225 (May 1987).

[CHER88a]       Cheriton, D. R., "VMTP: Versatile Message Transaction Protocol, Protocol Specification," RFC 1045, Network Information Center, SRI International, February 1988.

[CHER88b]       Cheriton, D. R., "The V Distributed System," *Communications of the ACM*, Vol. 31, No. 3, pp. 314–333 (March 1988).

[CHER89]        Cheriton, D. R., and Williamson, C. L., "VMTP as the Transport Layer for High-Performance Distributed Systems," *IEEE Communications Magazine*, Vol. 27, No. 6, pp. 37–44 (June 1989).

[CLAR87a]       Clark, D. D., Lambert, M. L., and Zhang, L., "NETBLT: A Bulk Data Transfer Protocol," Network Information Center RFC 998, SRI International, March 1987.

[CLAR87b]       Clark, D. D., Lambert, M. L., and Zhang, L., "NETBLT: A High Throughput Transport Protocol," *Proceedings of ACM SIGCOMM 87 Workshop: Frontiers in Computer Communications Technology*, Stowe, Vermont, pp. 353–359 (August 1987).

[COCQ89]        Cocquet, P., "GAM-T-103 Reference Model for Military Real-Time Local-Area Networks (MRT-LAN)," *Proceedings of the IFIP Workshop on Protocols for High-Speed Networks*, Zurich (May 9–11, 1989).

[DARPA81c]      Postel, J., ed., "Transmission Control Protocol—DARPA Internet Program Protocol Specification," RFC 793, USC/Information Sciences Institute, September 1981.

[DOER90]        Doeringer, W., Dykeman, D., Kaiserswerth, M., Meister, B., Rudin, H., and Williamson, R., "A Survey of Light-Weight Transport Protocols for High Speed Networks," *IEEE Transactions on Communications*, Vol. 38, No. 11, pp. 2025–2039 (November 1990).

[FRAS83]        Fraser, A. G., "Toward a Universal Data Transport System," *IEEE Journal on Selected Areas in Communications*, Vol. SAC-1, No. 5, pp. 803–816 (November 1983).

[FRAS89a]       Fraser, A. G., "The Universal Receiver Protocol," *Proceedings of the IFIP Workshop on Protocols for High-Speed Networks*, Zurich (May 9–11, 1989).

[FRAS89b]       Fraser, A. G., and Marshall, W. T., "Data Transport in a Byte-Stream Network," *IEEE Journal of Selected Areas in Communications*, Vol. SAC-7, No. 7, pp. 1020–1033 (September 1989).

[FREN87]        French Ministry of Defense, "GAM-T-103 Military Real-Time Local Area Network Reference Model (Transfer Layer)" February 7, 1987.

[ISO8073]       International Organization for Standardization, "Information Processing Systems—Open Systems Interconnection—Transport Protocol Specification," *Draft International Standard 8073*, July 1986.

[JACO88]        Jacobson, V., "Congestion Avoidance and Control," *Proceedings of the ACM SIGCOMM '88 Symposium*, Stanford, California, pp. 314–329 (August 16–19, 1988).

[MINE89]        Minet, P., "Performance Evaluation of GAM-T-103 Real-Time Transfer Protocols," *Proceedings of the INFOCOM Conference* (April 1989).

[NORD89]    Nordmark, E., and Cheriton, D. R., "Experiences from VMTP: How to achieve low response time," *Proceedings of the IFIP Workshop on Protocols for High-Speed Networks*, Zurich (May 9–11, 1989).

[WATS81]    Watson, R. W., "Timer-Based Mechanisms in Reliable Transport Protocol Connection Management," in **Computer Networks 5**, North-Holland, Amsterdam, The Netherlands, 1981.

[WATS83]    Watson, R. W., "Delta-t Protocols Specification," Lawrence Livermore Laboratory, April 15, 1983.

[WATS89a]   Watson, R. W., "The Delta-t Transport Protocol: Features and Experience Useful for High Performance Networks," *Proceedings of the IFIP Workshop on Protocols for High-Speed Networks*, Zurich (May 9–11, 1989).

[WATS89b]   Watson, R. W., "The Delta-t Transport Protocol," *Proceedings of the 14th Conference on Local Computer Networks*, Minneapolis, Minnesota, pp. 399–407 (October 10–12, 1989).

[WILL89a]   Williamson, C. L., and Cheriton, D. R., "An Overview of the VMTP Transport Protocol," *Proceedings of the 14th Conference on Local Computer Networks*, Minneapolis, Minnesota, pp. 415–420 (October 10–12, 1989).

[WILL89b]   Williamson, C. L., "Dynamic Transport-Level Connection Management in a Distributed System," *Proceedings of the 14th Conference on Local Computer Networks*, Minneapolis, Minnesota, pp. 315–322 (October 10–12, 1989).

[ZHAN86]    Zhang, L., "Why TCP-Timers Don't Work Well," *Proceedings of the ACM SIGCOMM '86 Symposium*, Stowe, Vermont, pp. 397–405 (August 5–7, 1986).

# 4
# Protocol Procedures

Communication, in its most general form, requires a communications channel, a set of mechanisms for exchanging information over the channel, formats for encoding information, and procedure rules for interpreting information exchanges. The collection of these rules and formats constitutes a *communication protocol*. In a packet-switching network, communication protocols are based on the exchange of bounded length data units called *packets*. Procedure rules specify how to use the information within packets to transfer user data. Over the next three chapters we discuss XTP's protocol procedure rules, the various packet formats within XTP, and the underlying structures for these packets. In this chapter we examine the first of these three topics.

## 4.1 Introduction

In order to discuss the procedures of this protocol we first give an overview of the packet structures and packet formats used within XTP. On one hand, a reader should be familiar with the packet structures and the various packet formats before trying to understand the protocol procedure rules that use them. On the other hand, a presentation of many fields and formats without proper motivation has little appeal. Below we provide enough overview to allow a reader to understand the material presented in this chapter; we will cover the formats and packet structures in detail in the next two chapters.

### 4.1.1 XTP Packet Structure Overview

Figure 4.1 shows, as an overview, the general structure of an XTP packet. The Header contains information that specifies how to process this packet, including steering information (the *route* and *key* fields), format and service options information (the *cmd* field), length and sequencing information (the *dlen*, *seq*, and *dseq* fields), priority information (the *sort* field), and validity checks (the *ttl*, *sync*, and *hcheck* fields). The Middle Segment carries protocol information when it is a Control Segment and user data when it is an Information Segment. The Control Segment contains protocol state information used by the rate control (the *rate* and *burst* fields), error control (the *echo*, *time*,

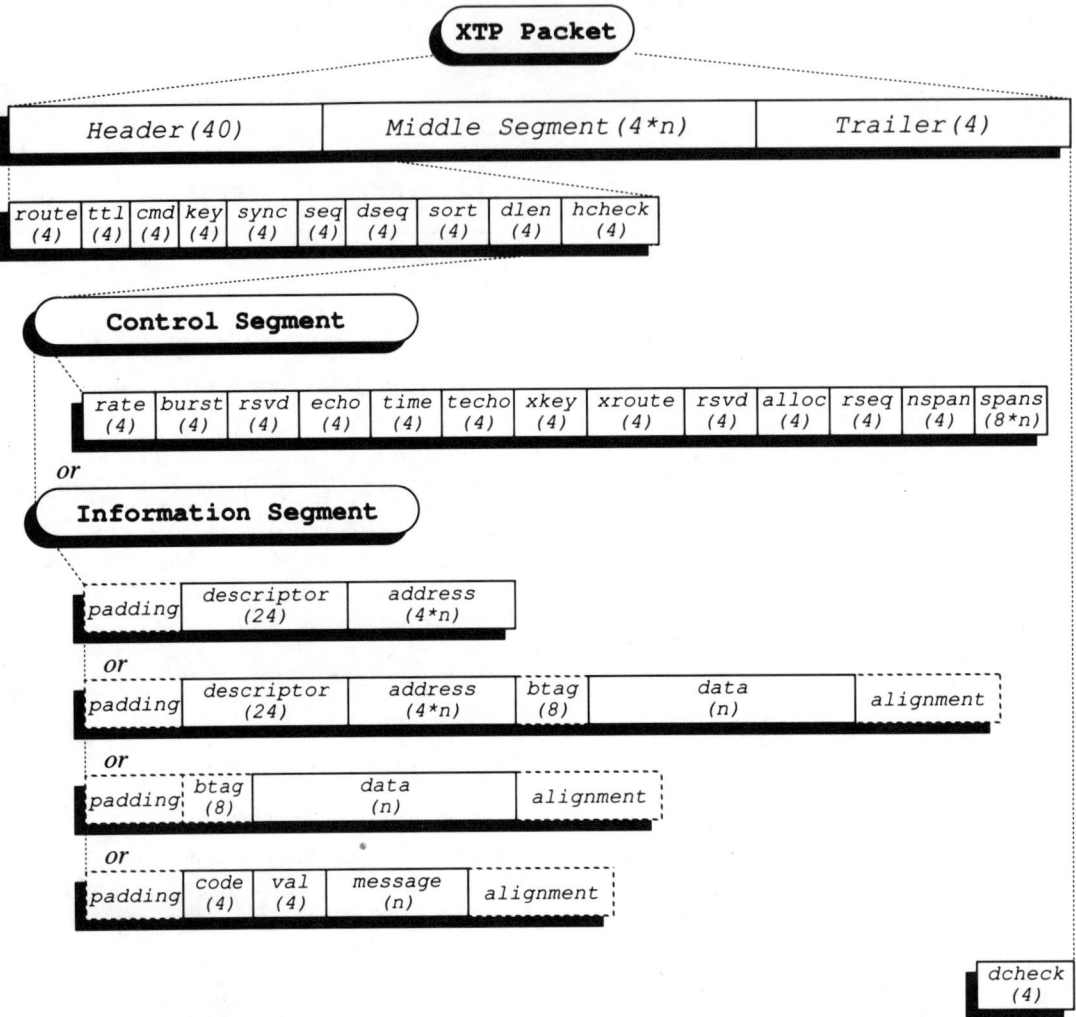

**Figure 4.1 — Packet Structure Overview**

*techo*, *nspan*, and *spans* fields), and flow control procedures (the *alloc* and *rseq* fields), as well as other state information exchange (the *xkey* and *xroute* fields). The Informa- tion Segment contains addressing information (the *descriptor* and *address* fields), user data (the *btag* and *data* fields), both, or managerial messages (the *code*, *val*, and *mes- sage* fields). The Trailer consists solely of the validity check over the Middle Segment (the *dcheck* field).

The *cmd* field, described in detail in Section 5.2.3, contains a couple of subfields of interest, including an *options* subfield and a *pformat* subfield. The *options* subfield is a bit field of options for controlling the various protocol procedures. These options are summarized in Table 4.1. The *pformat* subfield specifies what format is being used for this packet. The next section discusses these formats.

| Protocol Option | Description of Protocol Option |
|---|---|
| NOCHECK | Turns off the checksum over the Middle Segment |
| NOERR | Turns off error control—*no-error mode* |
| MULTI | Indicates that this is a multicast association |
| RES | Indicates that receiver is in *reservation mode* |
| SORT | Indicates that this packet is to be ordered by *sort* value |
| NOFLOW | Turns off flow control—*no-flow mode* |
| FASTNAK | Indicates fast negative acknowledgement policy |
| SREQ | Indicates status requested immediately |
| DREQ | Indicates status requested after previous data delivered |
| RCLOSE | Signals the close of the READER process |
| WCLOSE | Signals the close of the WRITER process |
| EOM | Indicates end of message |
| END | Indicates end of association |
| BTAG | Indicates the presence of a *btag* field in the *data* field |

**Table 4.1 — Protocol Options**

## 4.1.2 XTP Packet Formats

There are nine formats for XTP packets, as shown in Table 4.2. The FIRST and DATA formats are the only packet formats that can contain user data; hence they require that the Middle Segment be an Information Segment. The FIRST packet is used to establish an association. Subsequent user data is exchanged using the DATA packet. The FIRST packet, sent by the initiator of an association, has several effects. As the FIRST packet threads its way through the network switches, it establishes a bidirectional path for all subsequent packets in the association. Upon receipt of the FIRST packet, the receiver activates a context which, together with the context at the transmitting endpoint, defines an association. This FIRST packet may also contain user data. Once an association is established with a FIRST packet, DATA packets can be exchanged in both directions.

The CNTL packet format indicates that the packet is an XTP control packet and hence contains a Control Segment. State information is exchanged using CNTL packets. This state information includes data reception status, rate control parameters, and flow control parameters. By facilitating the sharing of state information, the CNTL packets are also used to synchronize the two (or more) endpoints. CNTL packets may

| Packet Format | Description of Middle Segment Contents |
|---|---|
| DATA | User data only |
| CNTL | Control information and status |
| FIRST | Address information for threading a path and initiating an association; may contain user data |
| PATH | Address information for rethreading a path or joining an in-progress multicast association |
| DIAG | Diagnostic information for fault notification |
| MAINT | Network maintenance information (format undefined) |
| MGMT | Network management information (format undefined) |
| ROUTE | Path release information |
| RCNTL | Control information exchanged between switches |

**Table 4.2 — Packet Formats**

be issued from an association endpoint at any time, but their generation is only required when an incoming packet specifically requests it.

The PATH packet is used to rethread a path through a series of switches if, during the lifetime of an association, the original path becomes unusable or undesirable. It is also used in a multicast association for allowing a receiver to join an in-progress data transfer. The PATH packet consists of an Information Segment with an Address Segment only; no user data is allowed.

The DIAG packet is used for diagnostic messages. It contains an Information Segment that reports error conditions encountered by the protocol machine while trying to process a packet. The DIAG packet attempts to inform the transmitter about the circumstances surrounding a packet's refusal. Its reception helps the protocol decide what course of action to take in order to recover from the error reported.

The MAINT and MGMT packet formats have not yet been fully defined. They will ultimately facilitate end-to-end maintenance and management information exchange.

The ROUTE packet is used for path release. Since paths may remain in place while the associations using them have been destroyed, switches within the network may target a path for dismantling. The ROUTE packet uses a Management Segment to signal to all switches along the path that the path is being released.

Just as the CNTL packet format enables the communication of state information between the endpoints of an association, the RCNTL, or Router Control packet format, allows the communication of state information between XTP switches. An RCNTL packet uses the Control Segment, but only the rate control and route exchange mechanisms are meaningful.

## 4.1.3 XTP Protocol Procedures

The goal of a transfer layer protocol such as XTP is to provide the procedures necessary for the transparent, efficient, and reliable delivery of arbitrarily long messages for an arbitrarily long duration between two or more entities not necessarily sharing the same local network segment. In XTP there are six procedures that aid in meeting this goal: association management, path management, data transfer, flow control, rate control, and error control.

The *association management procedures* enable two or more XTP users to establish an association. Once established, the association uses these procedures to maintain the association as long as the communicants desire the association to remain open. These procedures monitor the association for inactivity and provide the mechanisms for gracefully terminating the association.

The *path management procedures* build, maintain, and eventually destroy the path between the communicants. When this path does not span multiple network segments, the procedures are trivial. However, when packets traverse one or more network segments, the path management procedures dictate how the switches between the segments should ensure proper delivery of packets to their destination hosts.

The transfer of data is the primary goal of a communication protocol. In XTP, data is given to the protocol implementation as a parameter to the **output** command, and is given to the XTP user by the implementation as a result of the **input** command. The *data transfer procedures* are responsible for the movement of data between these XTP users. The *flow* and *rate control procedures* permit efficient use of endpoint and intermediate node resources. The *error control procedures* provide mechanisms for detecting and correcting various failures during communication. They can ensure that data is reliably delivered, in order, in a manner transparent to XTP users.

## 4.1.4 Notational Conventions

To illustrate how a packet format and its contents are used within a procedure, we need a notational convention to describe the type and contents of packets. When describing *key* and *route* field values, $K_A$ and $R_A$ refer to the *key* and *route* values generated by a particular context in Host A. When multiple contexts in Host A are being discussed at the same time, $K_{A_i}$ means the *key* value of the $i$ th context in Host A. Values generated at Host A for use on the return path, the *return key* and *return route* values, are denoted with a prime, as in $K'_A$ and $R'_A$.

When describing an entire XTP packet, the packet's contents are enclosed within square braces ("[" and "]"). The Middle Segment information is enclosed in parentheses ("(" and ")"). When it is completely clear which field contains a certain value, that value is given alone; otherwise, the field/value pair is given by *field = value*. If the encapsulating MAC frame must be shown, it is bracketed by curly braces ("{" and "}"). Consider, for example:

$$\{MAC_R, MAC_A, [K_A, R_A, \text{FIRST}, (address = B), \text{SREQ}]\}$$

This means that the FIRST packet carrying key value $K_A$ and the *route* $R_A$ is being sent to a host and service whose full address is given by $B$. This packet is encapsulated in a MAC frame whose source address is $MAC_A$ and whose destination address is $MAC_R$ for a local switch R. The SREQ bit is set, indicating the request for status.

Packet exchanges are commonly depicted by packet exchange diagrams. These diagrams are used to illustrate points about procedure rules; they are not presented to define these rules. The rightmost and leftmost vertical lines are used to indicate the two endpoints of association. Any vertical lines between these two indicate switches along the path. All vertical lines are labeled above with the node's name. Time progresses from the top of the diagram to the bottom. Actions and packet contents are listed along these vertical lines. Arrow-tipped lines show the "movement" of the packet from one host, possibly through switches, to its destination. Figure 4.2 illustrates these conventions by showing a FIRST packet sent from one host, through a switch, to another host, and the acknowledging CNTL packet sent back in response to the status request (the SREQ flag).

Since packets may be sent in either direction between the two endpoints of an association, we define the *forward* path as being the direction from the endpoint initiating the association to the responding endpoint, and the *return* path as being the direction from the responding endpoint to the initiating endpoint. Thus packets in the forward direction are called *forward* packets, and packets in the return direction are called *return* packets.

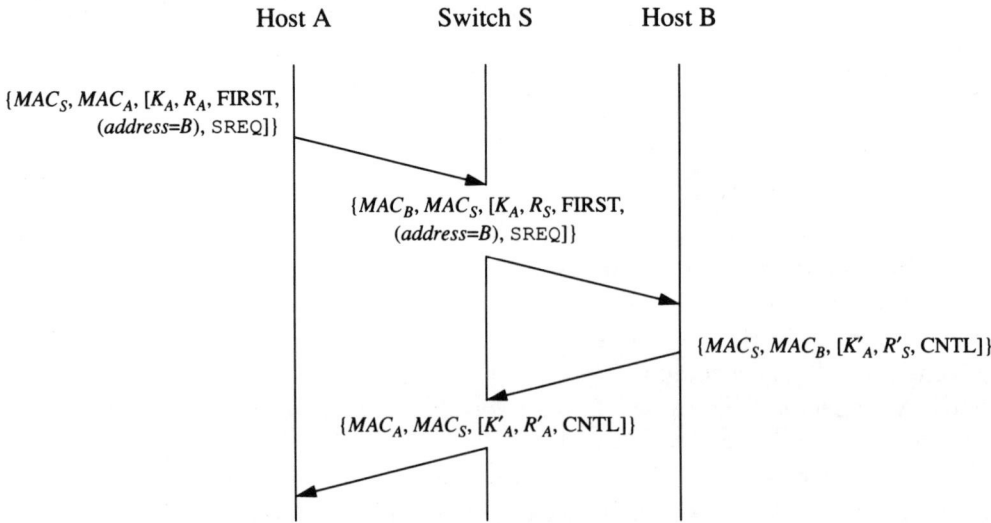

**Figure 4.2 — Illustration of a Packet Exchange Diagram**

## 4.2   Association Management Procedures

The state of an association is reflected first and foremost in the state of the contexts which comprise the endpoints of the association. (Let us for the present limit the association management discussion to the simple two-endpoint case; multicast association management will be addressed separately.) At the highest level of abstraction, a context can occupy one of four states: *Quiescent*, *Listening*, *Active*, and *Inactive*. The states of the Context State Machine are shown in Figure 4.3. The state of a context progresses from Quiescent to Active as that context becomes an endpoint of an association, and from Active to Inactive to Quiescent as the association is terminated. We can thus discuss the establishment, maintenance, and termination of an association by describing the actions which cause a context's state to change.

A context in the Quiescent state may or may not physically exist within an XTP implementation-whether it does or not is implementation-dependent. Abstractly, we

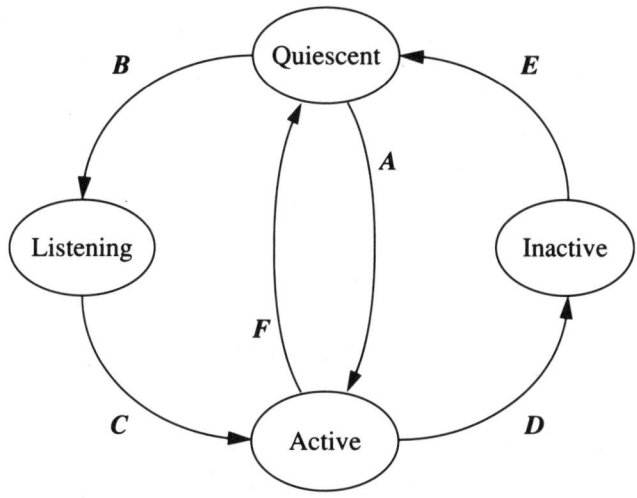

*A*:  Context activated—caused by
    an **output** command

*B*:  Context "listens" for FIRST packet—
    caused by an **input** command

*C*:  Context activated—caused by
    receipt of FIRST packet

*D*:  Close of READER and WRITER

*E*:  Association terminated

*F*:  Association aborted

**Figure 4.3 — Context State Machine**

consider a context to be a shell to hold the state information for a particular association. When it is Quiescent, that shell is empty and resides in a pool of other such quiescent contexts. When a context moves to either the Active or Listening state, it is instantiated with some default and some user-provided information. When the context is in an Active state, it is mapped to some association via the use of a *key* value. In the Inactive state the context is not allowed to receive or deliver user data although the association still exists; it may only exchange protocol information packets. Once an association is terminated, the context becomes Quiescent again and rejoins the pool of empty contexts.

When two or more XTP users decide to communicate, they each issue commands through the user interface to the XTP implementation that starts the association management procedures. At least one XTP user must have issued an **input** command prior to some XTP user issuing a corresponding **output** command. Association establishment procedures begin once both commands have been issued.

During association establishment, an endpoint places the *key* value that identifies its context in the *key* field of the FIRST packet. As part of the association maintenance procedures, the association endpoints may exchange *key* values to simplify the context identification process. The association maintenance procedures also monitor the association for inactivity. As long as the endpoints of the association exchange packets periodically, the association will remain active.

When the XTP users have completed their need for the association, the association is terminated. The association termination procedures allow the association to be dismantled in a graceful manner and resources (like the memory used for the context) to be relinquished. Other termination semantics exist and are discussed in Section 4.2.3.

## 4.2.1 Establishing an Association

Establishing an association between two XTP users involves one user initiating the association while the other user listens for the indication of the start of the association. The user issuing the **input** command will cause XTP to *listen* for any incoming FIRST packet that is addressed to this service address. The **input** command may be issued an arbitrary amount of time prior to the actual association establishment. Although the **input** command on one side must precede the **output** command on the other side, the association is said to be *initiated* by the side that issues the **output** command. Therefore, the context for this side of the association is referred to as the *initiating* context or *initiating* endpoint.

The contexts that will eventually be the endpoints of the association are both initially in the Quiescent state. Upon the issuing of an **input** command, a quiescent context is placed in the Listening state since it is listening for an appropriate incoming FIRST packet. The **output** command causes a quiescent context at the issuing host to move into the Active state, and the FIRST packet is assembled and sent. When the listening context receives this FIRST packet, it then moves into the Active state, and the association is established.

The initiating context builds a FIRST packet that includes several values that are instrumental in the association management procedures and in other procedures as well. This context is assigned a *key* value that is unique within its host; that is, the *key* value is chosen such that there is not, nor will there ever be, two contexts on the same host with the same *key* value. This *key* value will be used to identify outgoing packets (until and unless a key exchange occurs, as described in Section 4.2.2), and to associate any incoming packets with this context. This *key* value is placed in the *key* field of the FIRST packet.

A *route* value is similarly assigned such that the value uniquely identifies an exit port within the host. Once the association is established, this *route* value will be used to help identify the path between the endpoints of the association. It, too, is placed into the FIRST packet.

The FIRST packet contains an Address Segment, which will allow the packet to thread its way through the internetwork of switches, establishing a path along the way. The Address Segment is used to identify the destination host and the destination service within that host. This address can be one of several formats, as discussed in Chapter 7. As the FIRST packet traverses the network, it establishes a path by leaving a *route* value at each switch visited. These *route* values are used instead of the complete addressing format to route subsequent packets traveling in either the forward or return path directions. In the initial path-laying process, the association establishment procedures and the path establishment procedures occur simultaneously; while the association is being built, the path between the endpoints of the association must necessarily be constructed as well.

Also included within the Address Segment are the initiating host's MAC address (*id* field) and suggested rate control parameters (the *rate_req* and *burst_req* fields). The *id* value is included in the Address Segment to identify the original sender of the packet. This field is used to recognize duplicate FIRST packets from the same host. The rate control procedures, discussed later in this chapter, will describe how the *rate_req* and *burst_req* values are used.

Once constructed, the FIRST packet threads its way across the network and is delivered to the destination host and service. When the FIRST packet arrives at its destination host, the protocol must first check to see if the destination context matches any of the currently active contexts; if so, the packet is discarded as a duplicate sent as a result of some error control procedures. If the FIRST packet does not match an existing context, its Address Segment is compared with a set of *filters* which represent the listening contexts. These filters are compared with the destination address within the Address Segment of the FIRST packet. If a filter matches the address, the context associated with that filter is activated, the information within the FIRST packet is recorded at the activated context, and the association is established.

Figure 4.4 shows how this single FIRST packet can establish the association. All of the components are in place for a duplex conversation: the structures which contain the association's state are completely active, each context can be identified uniquely, and the path in both directions is established. However, given the possibility of prob-

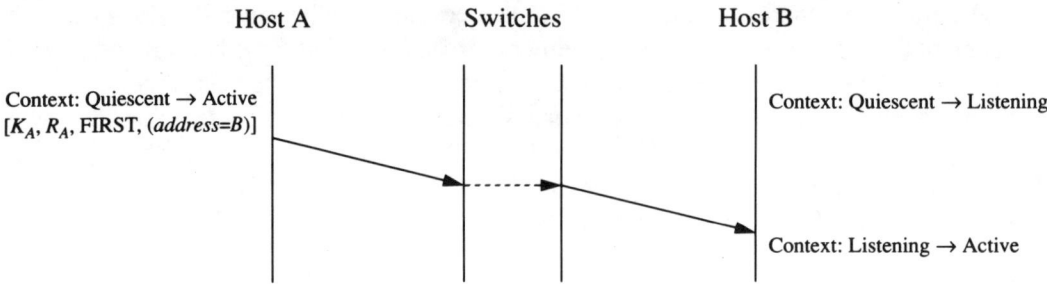

**Figure 4.4 — Association Establishment Packet Exchange**

lems in establishing this association, the association establishment procedures may require acknowledgement of success. In XTP, these acknowledgement mechanisms are orthogonal to the association establishment procedures. Rather than the request-acknowledge-confirm procedures of TCP and ISO TP4, XTP allows the XTP user to control the degree of reliability it requires on association establishment, and indeed in any packet exchange. It is the error control procedures, however, that provide these mechanisms.

When an association is established, the host that received the FIRST packet must create a mapping between certain identifying information in the FIRST packet and the destination context so that any other packets destined for this same context can be properly delivered. In the case of the FIRST packet, the appropriate context is found and activated using filters and the information within the Address Segment. Subsequent packets on an association do not have this Address Segment information. Therefore, as part of establishing the association, the host receiving the FIRST packet must form a mapping from the FIRST packet's *key*, *route* and MAC address (from the MAC frame which contained the XTP packet[1]) values to the destination context. Performing the mapping from a triple <MAC address, *key* value, *route* value> to a context is called the *full context lookup*. The necessity of a full context lookup is explained in Section 4.2.2 on association maintenance procedures since that section deals with the subsequent packet exchanges after association establishment.

Recall that a FIRST packet can carry data. Thus, although the main purpose of the FIRST packet is to establish the association, it can also be a data-bearing packet. Since the presence of data is a possibility, the listening context may have acquired some XTP buffer space to hold this data. The amount of data present in the FIRST packet is bounded by the size of the MAC frame. If no buffer space is available, the FIRST

---

[1] This MAC address is distinguished from the value in the *id* field of the Address Segment in that the *id* value is the MAC address of the initiating host, while the MAC address used here is directly from the source address field of the MAC frame which contained this packet. If the XTP packet had to traverse one or more switches, the MAC address from the MAC frame will not be the same as the MAC address in the *id* field.

packet still establishes the association and relies on the association's error control procedures to recover from the loss of this data.

The following list summarizes the protocol's activities at the local host when an
XTP user issues an **output** command:

1. Context is placed in Active state.
   a. A unique *key* value is created and associated with the context.
   b. Parameters from the **output** command help fill the context data structure.
   c. A unique *route* value is assigned.
2. A FIRST packet is generated with:
   *key* value (*key* field)
   *route* value (*route* field)
   network address (Address Segment)
   requested *rate* and *burst* values (*rate_req* and *burst_req* fields)
   sequence number in forward data stream (*seq* field)
   requested starting sequence number in return data stream (*dseq* field)
3. If an acknowledgement request is included in the FIRST packet (i.e., SREQ is set), a wait timer (WTIMER) is started.

Similarly, these actions are taken when an XTP user issues an **input** command:

1. A context is placed in Listening state, and a filter representing that context is placed in the set of waiting filters.
2. Context moves to Active state upon its filter matching an incoming FIRST packet.
   a. Mapping made from <MAC address, *key*, *route*> triple to context.
   b. Parameters and identifiers from the FIRST packet are recorded, including:
   *key* value (from *key* field)
   *route* value (from *route* field)
   network address (from Address Segment)
   requested *rate* and *burst* values (from *rate_req* and *burst_req* fields)
   sequence number for incoming data stream (from *seq* field)
   requested starting sequence number for outgoing data stream (from *dseq* field)
3. Data, if present, is placed in buffers.
4. If requested, an acknowledgement in the form of a CNTL packet is returned.

These two sets of actions, and the shared event of the exchange of the FIRST packet, establish the association.

## 4.2.2 Maintaining the Association

Maintaining an association, once established, requires providing the procedures for exchanging packets subsequent to the FIRST packet, and delivering those packets to their proper context. Since the full addressing information is carried in only the FIRST packet, the association maintenance procedures describe how packets subsequent to the FIRST packet are to be mapped to their destination contexts. Specifically, association maintenance procedures include the *full context lookup* procedure and the *return key* and *key exchange* procedures.

When a FIRST packet threads the forward path and establishes an association between two endpoints, the packets that follow the FIRST packet in this forward direction use the same *key* and *route* values as the FIRST packet. Recall that when a FIRST packet is received by the destination host, a listening context is activated and a mapping is created from the information in the FIRST packet to this destination context. Subsequent received packets which contain this same information will be mapped to this context, eliminating the need for a full address.

The *translation map* is the database that is used with certain information within a packet to "look up" the context to which this packet must be delivered. Each XTP implementation maintains a translation map. XTP uses the information within the packet as the index to the translation map; the translation map returns the context matching that information. In the most general case, the information required from an incoming packet to determine its destination context is the *key* value, the *route* value, and the MAC address value; these three values are used in a full context lookup.

Initially, packets sent from the initiating host in the forward direction require a full context lookup to match them with their destination contexts since the *key* value was not generated at the destination host. The *key* value alone therefore can not uniquely identify the destination context. The MAC address value identifies the last node to have forwarded the packet, but if this node were a switch, it is possible that packets from two different sending contexts coincidentally used the same *key* value *and* used the same final switch on the way to the same host (although to different destination contexts). Since the *route* values generated by a node are guaranteed to be unique, packets with the same *key* and MAC address values can be distinguished by examining the *route* value. Thus the triple <MAC address, *key* value, *route* value> fully and uniquely identifies any incoming packet's destination context, and is therefore used as the index into the translation map in a full context lookup.

Packets sent from the destination context back to the initiating context use *return key* and *return route* values. The *return key* value is derived from the *key* value within the FIRST packet by setting the most significant bit (MSB) of that *key* value. (It is a rule in the XTP Definition that *key* and *route* values in a FIRST packet are always generated such that the MSB is not set.) Likewise, the *return route* value for the return packet is formed by setting the MSB of the *route* value from the FIRST packet. For example, if Host A generates the key value $K_A$ for a context within Host A, any packets arriving at Host A with the *key* value $K'_A$ (the value $K_A$ with the MSB set) will be delivered to that context. The use of the *return key* in return packets allows Host A to match the packet with the proper context using only the value in the *key* field instead of a full context lookup.

A host recognizes that an incoming packet contains a *return key* value by checking the MSB of the *key* field. Since the original *key* value was generated by this host, and the original *key* value is guaranteed unique within this host, the *return key* unambiguously identifies the context within this host that is the proper recipient of the return packets. Using a *return key* alone to map an incoming packet to its context is called an *abbreviated lookup*.

### Example 4.1

This example shows why the XTP Definition requires the destination context to use the *return key* value for all return packets.

Consider the situation where Host A initiates an association with Host B using the *key* value $K$. Assume (contrary to XTP) that Host B is not required to use the *return key* value $K'$ for return packets sent to Host A, and instead packets are sent on the return path using $K$ as their *key* field value. Now suppose by chance a Host C initiates an association with Host A using the *key* value $K$ as well. If Host B and Host C must use the same final switch along the path, then the MAC address in the MAC frames containing the XTP packets coming to Host A will be the same. Moreover, if the switch uses the same *route* value (as it would in route sharing, Section 4.3.2), Host A can not distinguish between return packets from Host B and forward packets from Host C.

Since the XTP Definition requires a destination host to use a *return key* value in all return packets, all incoming packets at a host can always be mapped to their proper context.

Unfortunately, the abbreviated lookup using *return key* values only works in the return direction. To allow abbreviated lookups to be used in both directions, the two endpoints must perform a *key exchange procedure*. Under key exchange the destination context informs the initiating context what *key* value to use in packets in the forward direction. This mechanism allows the equivalent of a *return key* to be defined for the forward path. Unlike the use of the *return key*, the key exchange procedure is not necessary for the correct working of the protocol since any return packet can be identified with its proper context by using the full context lookup procedure. Instead, the key exchange procedure is an optimization in that it alleviates the need for a full context lookup, as in the *return key* case, by allowing an incoming packet to be matched with its context using only the value in that packet's *key* field.

The exchange key field (*xkey*) in a CNTL packet provides the mechanism for eliminating the full context lookup at the destination host in favor of an abbreviated lookup. Host B generates a unique *key* value (say $K_B$), sets the MSB to make it a *return key* ($K'_B$), and puts it in the *xkey* field in the Control Segment of the CNTL packet it sends to Host A, as shown in Figure 4.5. Host A then stops using $K_A$ for the *key* value in A-to-B packets, and instead uses $K'_B$ (retrieved from the *xkey* field). Now both directions, A-to-B and B-to-A, use *key* values that were generated at the packet's destination

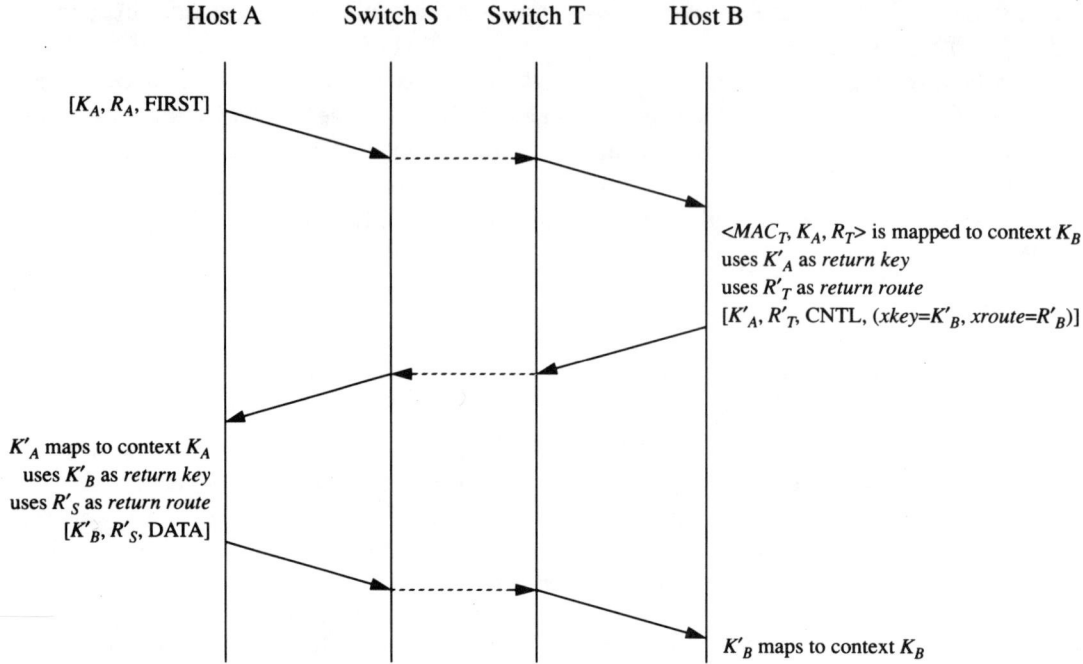

**Figure 4.5 — Packet Exchanges for Using *xkey* and *xroute***

and are thus guaranteed to be unique at that host. Packets in the network which coincidentally have the same *return key* value can never be destined for the same host. Since this is true, an abbreviated lookup is now sufficient to find the proper context in both directions.

If the MSB of the *key* field of an incoming packet is set, the abbreviated lookup is all that is necessary. Any packets other than FIRST packets which arrive with the MSB not set in the *key* field are matched with their contexts by using the full context lookup. Note that the key exchange is not required, and in multicast it is forbidden (see Chapter 8). Also note that the full context lookup remains valid even if the key exchange occurs.

## 4.2.3 Terminating the Association

Associations are designed to handle an arbitrary number of messages over an arbitrary length of time. At some time, however, it will become necessary to end the association and relinquish the structures held for that association. XTP provides the mechanisms for several different termination semantics, from an independent graceful close to an immediate abort. An independent graceful close ensures that all outstanding data in either direction on the association is reliably delivered before the association is terminated. An abort immediately closes the association without regard to data delivery assurance. A forced close is a graceful close on one data stream concurrent with an abort on the other.

After an arbitrary length of time, and after an arbitrary number of messages have been exchanged, one or both of the endpoints starts the association termination procedures. In contrast to the rapidity of association establishment, terminating an association gracefully requires a series of carefully guarded state changes so that the contexts in the association, before returning to the Quiescent state, are assured that all data that was to be delivered has been in fact delivered. Since each association is actually two simplex data streams, each endpoint of the association represents a WRITER to and a READER from that data stream (recall these procedures from Chapter 2). Consequently, each data stream must be independently closed before either endpoint can be released.

There are three bits in the *options* field in the Header of XTP packets which indicate the progression toward association termination: the WCLOSE, the RCLOSE, and the END bits. Since a data stream is unidirectional, one context is the sender and the other is the receiver. When a data stream is being gracefully closed, the sender sets the WCLOSE bit in an outgoing packet. This indicates that the sender's WRITER process is closed, and hence no new data will be sent. Retransmissions, if necessary, are still allowed even after the WRITER closes, but the sequence number associated with this data stream will not advance. Upon receipt of the WCLOSE bit, the receiver sets the RCLOSE bit in an outgoing packet. This indicates that the sender's READER process is closed, and hence no new data will be read from the network. After the RCLOSE bit has been set, the receiver will not accept any packets which advance the sequence number associated with this data stream. Once one of these bits is set, it stays set in the Header of every subsequent packet sent by the context which set the bit. The END bit indicates that the context setting it is being relinquished, and no other communications of any kind are allowed. The END bit from either context will terminate the association at any time; it is the coordinated use of the WCLOSE and RCLOSE bits which enables a graceful close.

Below, we describe the packet exchanges which cause a context to move from the Active state to the Quiescent state. Although the error control procedures are independent of the association management procedures, in the following discussion we will assume that the data is acknowledged and, when a data stream is closed, it is assumed that the appropriate number of acknowledgements and any retransmissions necessary have occurred prior to the closing. In the discussion and examples below, the SREQ bit will be set on the packets carrying any of the association termination bits to ensure rapid response, although it should be noted that setting any response request bit is not required as part of the termination procedures.

A data stream becomes inactive when the WRITER process is closed at one endpoint and the READER process is closed at the other. The graceful closing of a data stream requires a two-way handshake: the WRITER closes first, after which the remote READER closes. Similarly, a context becomes inactive when both its WRITER and READER processes are closed since this implies both the incoming and outgoing data

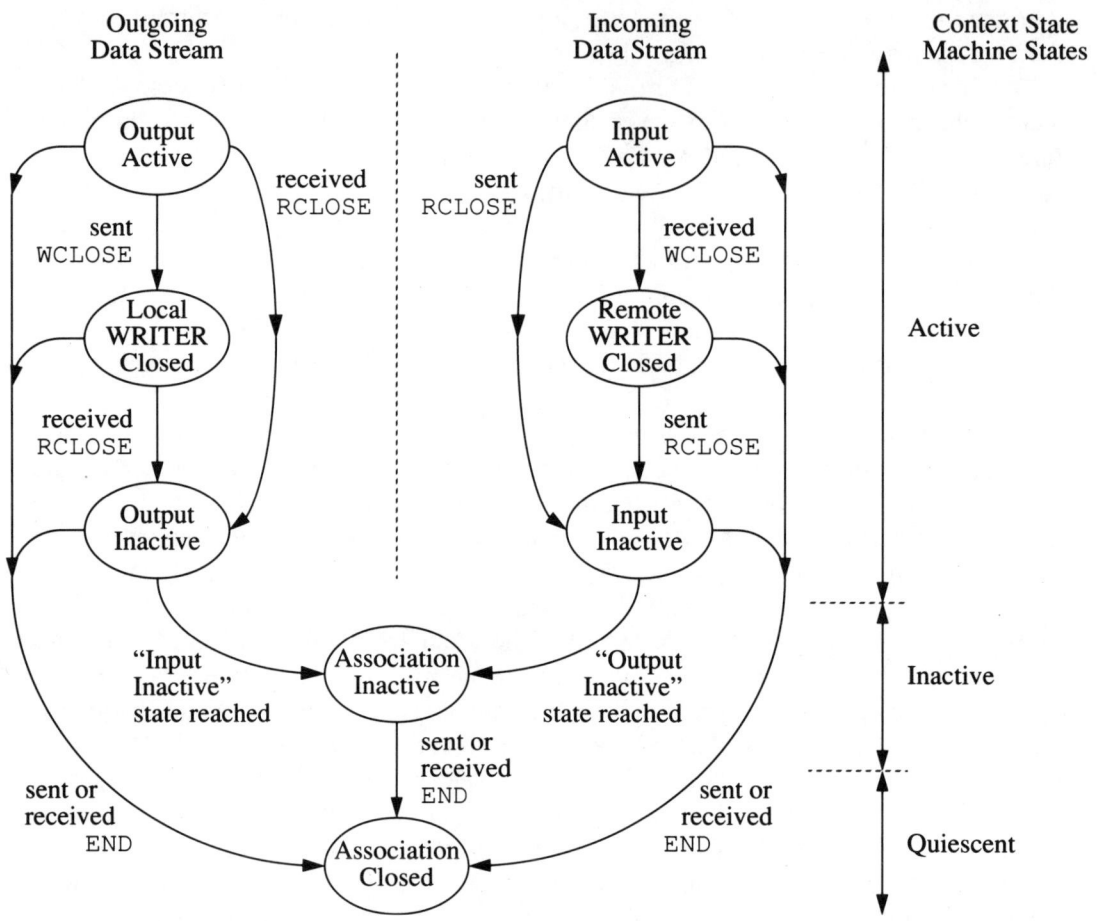

**Figure 4.6 — Association Termination State Machine**

streams are inaccessible. Figure 4.6 shows the Association Termination State Machine diagram for the association termination procedures for both sides of a context. Since each data stream must be independently closed for a graceful termination of the association, the state machine for a context has two symmetric halves. The outgoing data stream starts in the Output Active state and the input data stream starts in the Input Active state since the Context State Machine (shown in Figure 4.3) is in the Active state. As the outgoing or incoming data stream begins termination procedures, the local or remote WRITER process, respectively, is closed. When the outgoing data stream enters the Output Inactive state, and the incoming data stream enters the Input Inactive state, the two partial state machines merge and enter the Association Inactive state. This state corresponds to the Inactive state of the Context State Machine since the context can not be active if the association in which it participates is inactive. Likewise, when the Association Termination State Machine enters the Association Closed state, this corresponds to the Quiescent state of the Context State Machine.

When the context has no more data to send, it issues a packet (possibly the last DATA packet) with the WCLOSE bit set. This moves the outgoing data stream side from the Output Active state to the Local WRITER Closed state. As a consequence no more data may be sent by this context. After the context receiving the WCLOSE has ensured that all of the data which has been sent has also been received, it sends a packet with an RCLOSE bit set. The reception of an RCLOSE causes the outgoing data stream side of the context to transition to the Output Inactive state, since the context can not send (nor can the corresponding READER receive) any more data on this data stream. The outgoing data stream is now closed, and half of the association is terminated.

The context may send or receive a packet with an END bit set while in any state. Since the END bit indicates that the sending context has been relinquished, there can be no further communication in either direction. As a result the receiving context is immediately relinquished and the Association Termination State Machine enters the Association Closed state.

The incoming data stream side of the context (i.e., the right half of Figure 4.6) remains active until the context receives a packet with the WCLOSE bit set. This indicates that there will be no more new data to read from this data stream. The incoming data stream side of the context then moves to the Remote WRITER Closed state. After all data is received, this context sends a packet with an RCLOSE bit set, indicating that it understands that no more data will be sent and that it is therefore closing its READER. The incoming data stream side of the context moves to the Input Inactive state since this data stream is now closed.

When both of the data streams of the context have become inactive, the association becomes inactive, and the Association Termination State Machine moves to the Association Inactive state. Either of the two contexts then sends a packet with an END bit set. The sender immediately moves to the Association Closed state since the END bit indicates that the sending context has been relinquished. The receiver immediately moves to the Association Closed state upon receipt of the END bit since there is no other endpoint with which to communicate. The association, therefore, is terminated.

Since the data streams are independent, and the mechanisms for closing them are orthogonal, many interesting combinations and orderings arise. One such case is the independent graceful close, where each data stream is closed independently of the other. Figure 4.7 shows a context within Host A sending DATA packets to a context in Host B, the last of which contains the WCLOSE bit set. Host B receives the WCLOSE and (assuming all the data is accounted for) returns a CNTL packet with the RCLOSE bit set. Meanwhile, Host B may have been sending an arbitrary number of DATA packets to Host A. Since every outgoing packet carries the closing bits already set by that host, every DATA packet on the B-to-A data stream now carries the RCLOSE as well. When Host B is ready to terminate its outgoing data stream, it sets the WCLOSE bit in the last DATA packet.

When the WCLOSE bit is received, the context within Host A becomes inactive since both its outgoing and incoming data streams are closed. It responds by setting the RCLOSE bit in an outgoing CNTL packet and asking for an acknowledgement by

Host A          Host B

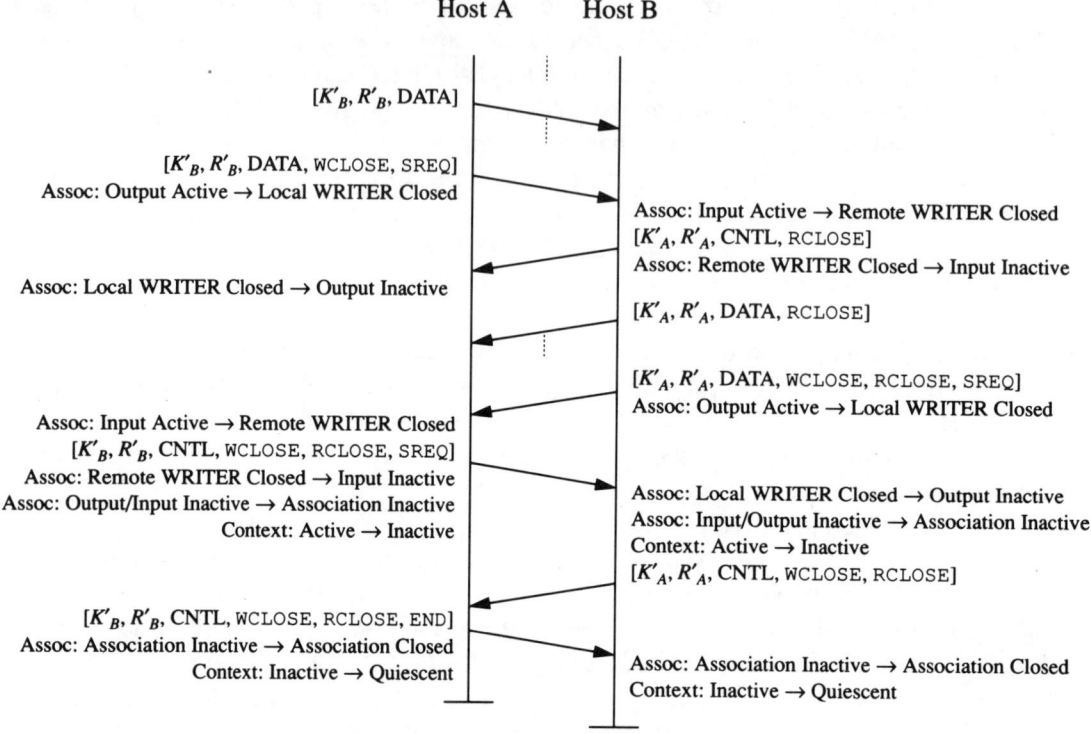

**Figure 4.7 — Independent Graceful Close**

setting the SREQ bit. The context within Host B sends a CNTL packet with both the WCLOSE and RCLOSE bits set since these bits are set in all subsequent outgoing packets. At this point Host A issues a CNTL packet with the END bit set as well as WCLOSE and RCLOSE. The context $K_A$ in Host A is now quiescent. Host B also becomes quiescent after processing the END bit. The association between the contexts at Hosts A and B is terminated.

When an association is being used mostly for one-way traffic, it is typical that the closing of one data stream is the signal that the entire association is ready for termination. If this is the case, the termination procedures may be abbreviated by combining packet exchanges. In general, both data streams may be closed independently, but since XTP allows combinations of bit indicators to be set in one packet, some packet exchanges may be foregone.

Figure 4.8 illustrates the abbreviated graceful close. Host A sets the WCLOSE bit in its final DATA packet to Host B. Host B responds to this WCLOSE by setting the RCLOSE bit in the next outgoing CNTL packet. At this point Host B has closed its incoming data stream. However, Host B may also set the WCLOSE bit in this packet to indicate that it wants to shut down its outgoing data stream at this time as well. Host A processes the RCLOSE bit to close its outgoing data stream, and responds to the

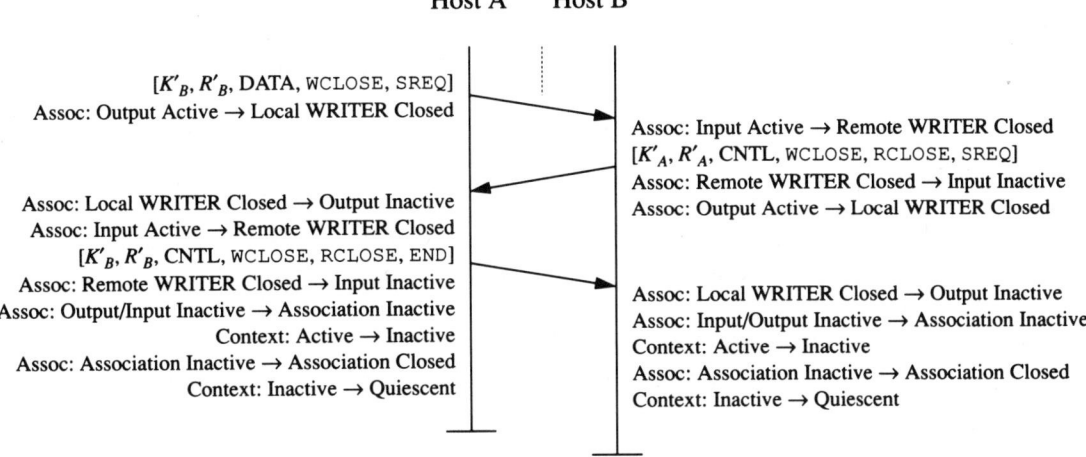

**Figure 4.8 — Abbreviated Graceful Close**

WCLOSE bit by sending a packet which acknowledges the closing of the incoming data stream with an RCLOSE, and ends the association with the END bit. This example shows the packet exchanges necessary to gracefully close both data streams and terminate the association.

Figure 4.9 shows the case where one endpoint of the association "forces" the other endpoint to close its outgoing data stream. Host A sends a packet with the WCLOSE bit set, indicating the start of the graceful close of its outgoing data stream. It also sets the RCLOSE bit. If this bit is set by an endpoint prior to that endpoint receiving the appropriate WCLOSE indication, the setting endpoint forces its incoming data stream to close abruptly. Host B responds to the WCLOSE with an RCLOSE to indicate the graceful

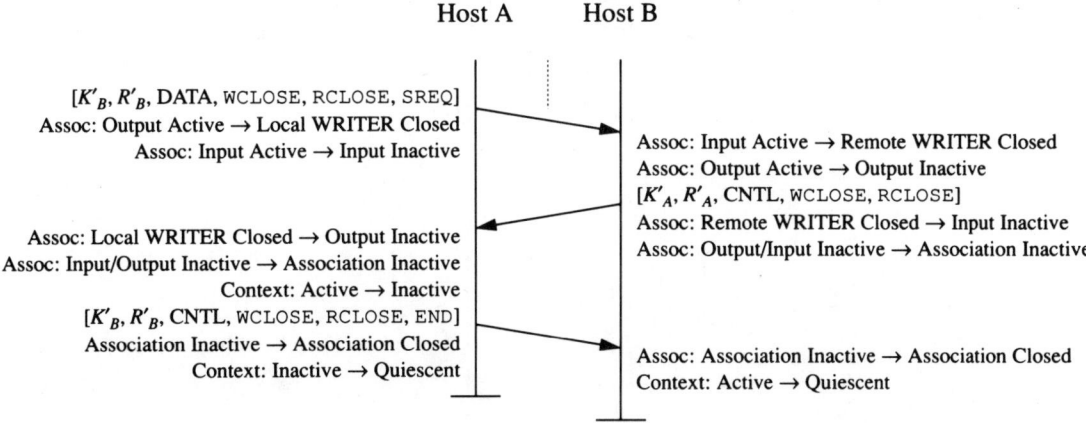

**Figure 4.9 — Forced Close**

close of its incoming data stream, but it can only respond to the RCLOSE by setting the WCLOSE bit. Since this exchange can not represent a graceful close of the outgoing data stream, the Association Termination State Machine moves from Output Active to Output Inactive immediately. Host B also has the option of setting the END bit, but in this example Host B defers to Host A since Host A is the endpoint that initiated the termination procedures.

Either endpoint may decide to end the association abruptly by simply setting the END bit in any outgoing packet, as shown in Figure 4.10. Immediately upon setting this bit the Association Termination State Machine moves to the Association Closed state, and the Context State Machine moves to the Context Quiescent state. Likewise, upon receipt of any packet with the END bit set, the Association Termination and Context State Machines for that endpoint move to the Association Closed and Context Quiescent states, respectively. This aborts the association with no regard for data that has not yet been received or acknowledged.

## 4.2.4 Interesting Paradigms

XTP resembles a connection-oriented protocol in the sense that connection state information is maintained at both ends of the association. However, XTP differs from the conventional connection-oriented transport protocols in its flexibility for providing user-imposed service policies, rather than imposing the policy on the user. Below we offer examples of widely known communication paradigms whose behavior can be mimicked by XTP.

### ISO Connection

The ISO Transport Protocol class 4 (TP4) connection paradigm is built upon three service primitives: T_Connect, T_Data, and T_Disconnect. A connection is established by issuing a T_Connect.request to the transport service provider. The destination service is notified by a T_Connect.indication, and responds with a T_Connect.response.

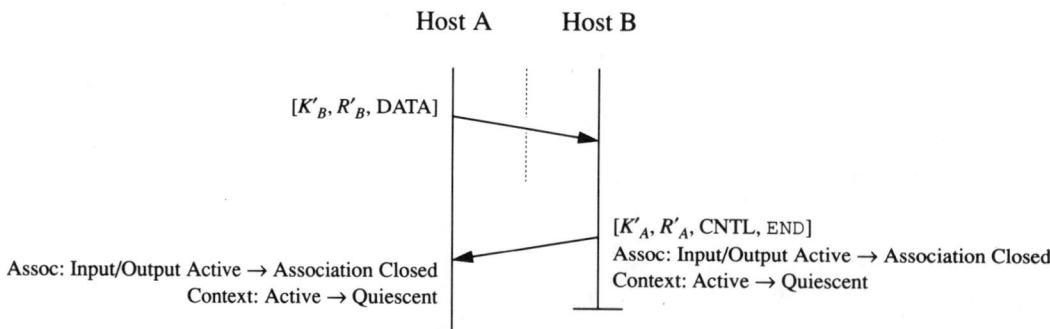

**Figure 4.10 — Abort**

The initiating user is notified of connection establishment by a T_Connect.confirm. This two-way handshake allows the two endpoints to exchange any connection-related information prior to the actual data transfer. Data is transferred using a T_Data.request and T_Data.indication pair. The connection is terminated when one side issues a T_Disconnect.request and the other side is notified by a T_Disconnect.indication. Since TP4 provides a reliable service, all primitives are explicitly acknowledged within the protocol by special Acknowledgement packets, though these acknowledgements are transparent to the user.

Figure 4.11 shows an XTP packet exchange and the equivalent TP4 primitives. Note that, although the FIRST packet may carry data, when emulating the TP4 connection paradigm no data is exchanged until the connection is established. The connection-related information of *xkey* and *xroute* is exchanged at this time, along with flow and rate control information useful during the data transfer phase of the connection. Also note that the connection termination prescribed by TP4 is the same as the forced close shown in Figure 4.9.

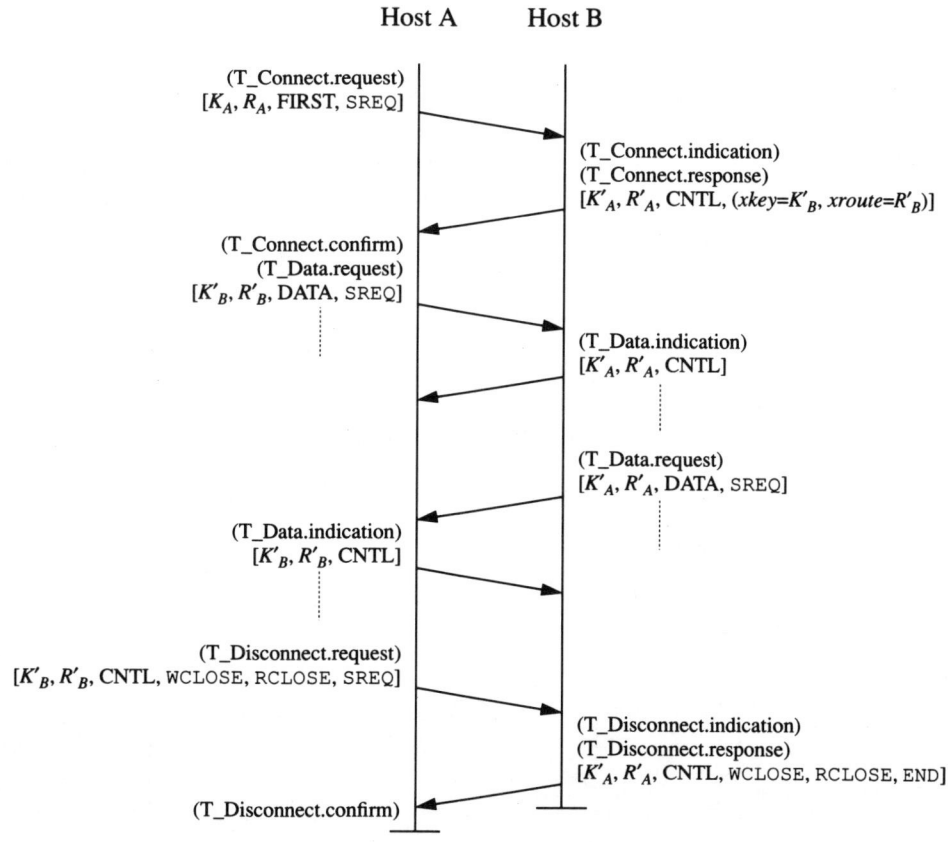

**Figure 4.11 — Packet Exchange for ISO Connection Paradigm**

## Transaction

In transaction-oriented protocols like VMTP, the client sends a request to a server, where the request is processed, and the server responds. The transaction is initiated by a request and terminated by the response; there are no other operations specifically designed for establishing the connection prior to the information exchange, or for terminating the connection once the exchange is completed.

Figure 4.12 shows how XTP can provide a transaction paradigm. The FIRST packet carries in its data field all of the information necessary for the client to make its request of the server. The FIRST packet's powerful association establishment mechanisms resemble the on-demand transaction setup inherent to transaction-based protocols. In this environment the server's response, a DATA packet containing the information requested, often serves as a higher-layer acknowledgement, although the SREQ and DREQ bits would allow for an explicit XTP acknowledgement if desired by the XTP user (client). As per the transaction paradigm, the DATA packet sent from the server has all the bit indicators set to shut down the exchange.

## Datagram

Connectionless transport protocols, such as ISO Transport Protocol 8602 and User Datagram Protocol (UDP), provide a *connectionless* mode service, typically called a *datagram* service. A datagram is constructed and sent with the understanding that the service provider does not guarantee delivery of the message. Since datagram service does not usually provide segmentation and reassembly, the user's message is generally limited to what can fit in a single packet. Figure 4.13 shows a single XTP packet which is a FIRST packet containing the datagram information. The EOM bit is set to indicate that this packet also concludes the message. The association termination indicator bits WCLOSE and RCLOSE may also be set here, but since the datagram does not require graceful closing, the END bit is all that is necessary. Because there is no overhead associated with ensuring reliability, the datagram is an inexpensive communication alternative.

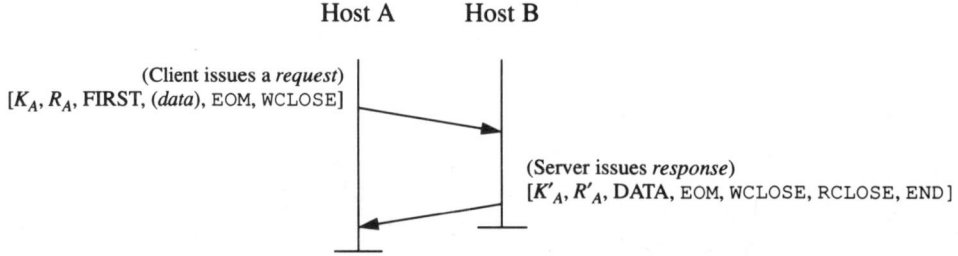

**Figure 4.12 — Packet Exchange for Transaction Paradigm**

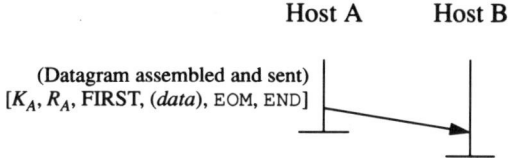

Host A        Host B

(Datagram assembled and sent)
[$K_A$, $R_A$, FIRST, (*data*), EOM, END]

**Figure 4.13 — Packet Exchange for Datagram Paradigm**

## Reliable Datagram

The reliability of the connection and the cost-effectiveness of the datagram can be combined; Figure 4.14 shows a *reliable* datagram service. The XTP transmitter requests acknowledgement of the single-packet message by setting the acknowledgement request bit DREQ (or SREQ). The DREQ bit instructs the receiver to issue a CNTL packet only after the user has been given the data.

# 4.2.5 Multicast Association

The term *multicast* refers to a data transfer service that supports a one-to-many data flow. An XTP multicast association consists of a context serving as a transmitter and an arbitrarily large set of contexts serving as the *receiver set*. A multicast association is restricted to a single flow of data, from the transmitter to the receiver set, since it is not clear how to apply the abstraction of a data stream to a many-to-one transmission.[2] The transmitter issues data-bearing and control packets, and each receiver in the receiver set accepts the data. The receivers, however, are not allowed to send data-bearing packets in return.

Multicast association establishment begins when an XTP user submits an **output** command for a multicast address. An initiating context is activated, and a FIRST packet carrying the group address in its Address Segment is issued. Since the multicast facility in XTP is designed for media which support a multicast or broadcast capability, the destination physical address for the FIRST packet is ordinarily a physical multicast or broadcast address. At some time prior to the arrival of this FIRST packet a set of XTP users have issued **input** commands, causing contexts to "listen" on the multicast group address. The FIRST packet is delivered to each host belonging to the multicast group address, and listening contexts at those hosts, together with the transmitting context, form the multicast association.

As with the unicast association, the FIRST packet of a multicast association may carry data and set any of the bits in the *options* field in the Header except DREQ. In

---

[2.] **Many-to-one transmissions, or *concentrations*, can be accommodated by using a separate context for each of the many incoming data streams. In this way each data stream can be managed using already existing XTP mechanisms.**

Host A     Host B

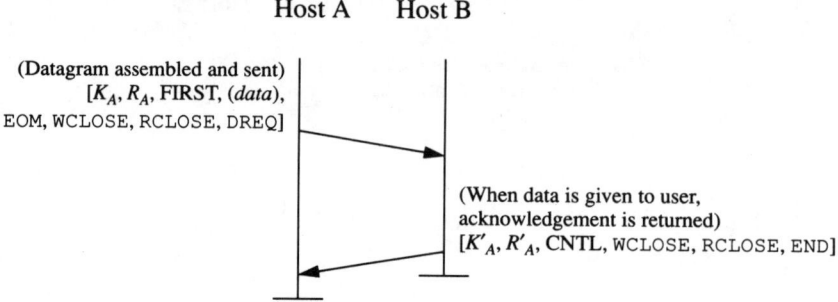

**Figure 4.14 — Packet Exchange for Reliable Datagram Paradigm**

particular, the FIRST packet of the multicast association, and every packet in this association thereafter, must set the MULTI bit in the *options* field. The MULTI bit informs each receiver that it is part of a receiver set for a multicast association.

Once established, the multicast association can transfer an arbitrary amount of data. At some point in time, the transmitter may wish to discover the reception status of the receiver set. Unlike the unicast case, the multicast transmitter is not aware of the size or composition of the receiver set, and must therefore synthesize the reception status information from the responses of the receivers in the receiver set. To ensure that the response is immediate, the transmitter is required to use only the SREQ bit, and never the DREQ bit, in requesting a CNTL packet. As a result of receiving a packet with the SREQ bit set, each receiver in the receiver set immediately issues a CNTL packet with the MULTI bit set and with reception status, flow, and rate control information included. These CNTL packets are multicast on the group address. Each receiver in the receiver set, as well as the transmitter, receives them. Since the transmitter does not know how many receivers there are in the receiver set, it does not know how long to collect CNTL packet responses. Chapter 8 addresses the issue of how long a transmitter should wait for responses. The transmitter infers the reception status of the entire receiver group based on the CNTL packet responses.

Since there is a danger that old CNTL packets may be included in the transmitter's synthesis of the reception status, only the SREQ bit can be used in packets issued by the transmitter. When the transmitter issues a packet with the SREQ bit set, the transmitter performs a "synchronizing handshake" (as described in Section 4.7.4) with each receiver in the receiver set.

Recall from the association maintenance procedures that the key exchange is an optimization which allows the packets on the forward path to be matched with their proper contexts via an abbreviated lookup. Because there are multiple receivers there can be no agreement on the *return key* for the forward path. Therefore multicast receivers must perform a full context lookup for each incoming packet. Note, however, that the CNTL packets sent back to the transmitter do indeed carry the *return key* value in the *key* field. Thus a packet with a *return key* value in the *key* field is a packet from a receiver in the receiver set, and a packet with a regular *key* value in the *key* field is from the transmitter.

In a unicast association both endpoints, as members of the association, are essential. In the multicast association, the transmitter is essential, but the receiver set membership may vary. Certainly, this set must have at least one active member but, over the lifetime of the multicast association, the receiver set membership may expand and contract. When a receiver must leave the receiver set, it simply ceases to participate in receiving packets and responding to requests for status. This does not affect the transmitter unless the receiver set becomes empty. If, however, an XTP peer wishes to join an in-progress multicast association, it may do so with the *join* procedure.

The XTP peer must have a context activated in order to join the receiver set. This context issues a PATH packet containing the multicast group address and a value of zero in the *key* field. This PATH packet is multicast on the group address; the XTP Definition requires other receivers to ignore this packet. When the transmitter receives such a PATH packet it responds by issuing a PATH packet containing the multicast group address, but also containing the *key* value for this transmitter context. The new receiver receives this PATH packet and begins to accept packets with this *key* value.

Graceful termination semantics for multicast fall under the graceful close with forced termination (see Section 4.2.3) since there is no reverse direction (i.e., many-to-one) data flow. Accordingly, for a graceful close, the transmitter issues a packet with the WCLOSE, RCLOSE, and SREQ bits set. Upon reception of this packet, a receiver responds with a CNTL packet having the WCLOSE and RCLOSE bits set. After satisfying any retransmission requests, the transmitter then issues a final CNTL packet with the WCLOSE, RCLOSE, and END bits set. Only the transmitter can issue a packet with the END bit set. The multicast association is now terminated.

Group communication in general, and XTP multicast in particular, are discussed in more depth in Chapter 8.

## 4.3  Path Management Procedures

XTP is a *transfer* layer protocol, and hence by design it subsumes not only the reliable data transfer functionality of the transport layer but also the routing functionality of the network layer of the OSI Reference Model. The path management procedures directly address the question of end-to-end packet delivery across an internetworking system. In establishing a path, these procedures put into place the facility by which packets may be delivered to the destination host; association management procedures ensure delivery once the packets are within the host.

XTP uses a technique called *cut-through switching*, where the initial packet of an association (the FIRST packet) "cuts" the path from the initiating endpoint to the destination by leaving a trail of references in the intermediate nodes. The ordered sequence of these references constitutes a path from one endpoint to the other, which can be used by packets traveling in either direction.

The path management procedures are responsible for establishing, maintaining, and releasing the structures within the endpoints and the intermediate nodes which represent the path. This section describes these procedures, as well as the conditions and actions necessary for such auxiliary procedures as *route exchange* and *route sharing*.

## 4.3.1 Path Establishment

The path establishment procedures occur concurrently with the establishment of the association; indeed, the association could not be established if the path between the two endpoints were not established as well. The context at the host initiating the association creates a value with which to identify the local exit port for the outgoing data stream. This identifier is called the *route* value for this host's outgoing data stream. It is generated in a manner similar to the way in which *key* values are generated: the *route* value must be unique within the host's XTP implementation that generates it, and the most significant bit must be cleared. The *route* value identifies the exit port for packets that will be sent on the outgoing data stream, and subsequent packets sent on this data stream need only use this *route* value to ensure that they are delivered to their destination hosts.

### Example 4.2a

Suppose Host A were initiating an association with Host B. It selects a *route* value, say $R_A$, which is unique among all other *route* values used within Host A. Since Host A is selecting this value, $R_A$'s MSB is not set. The FIRST packet is constructed thus: $[K_A, R_A, \text{FIRST}, (address = B)]$. Suppose further that two intermediate nodes lay in the path between Host A and Host B; call these nodes Switch S and Switch T. Since Host B is not a local host, the exit port identified by $R_A$ directs the packet to Switch S.

The FIRST packet of the association is sent from switch to switch as it establishes a path between the two endpoints of the association. At each switch the following things happen. If the *route* value has its MSB set, then it is used to look up certain pertinent path information. Otherwise, the <MAC address, *route* value> pair is used to check if the path already exists. If so, the path information contained in the path database within the switch is found using the <MAC address, *route* value> pair. The situation where a path on which the FIRST packet can travel already exists may arise if the path is being shared (route sharing is described in next section). If the path does not currently exist, the pair <MAC address, *route* value> is mapped to an exit port within the switch, and a new *route* value is generated to identify this exit port within the switch. This newly generated *route* value must be unique within the switch and must have its MSB cleared. The switch replaces the current *route* value in the *route* field of the FIRST packet with the *route* value that it has generated. The FIRST packet is then sent out the exit port to the next switch or the destination host. At the destination host the triple <MAC address, *key* value, *route* value> is mapped to the newly activated context. The path is now established and is represented by the ordered series of *route* values from the initiating host to the destination host.

### Example 4.2b

Continuing with Example 4.2a, Switch S generates a new *route* value, say $R_S$, and replaces $R_A$ in the FIRST packet with it. Thus, $[K_A, R_S, \text{FIRST}, (address = B)]$ is sent to the next node, Switch T. At this node the same procedure occurs, and the packet $[K_A, R_T, \text{FIRST}, (address = B)]$ is sent to Host B. The path between Host A and Host B is fully represented by the ordered sequence $(R_A, R_S, R_T)$.

It should be mentioned that the *route* value of zero has a special meaning. When an association is established between endpoints on the same local network, no switches are required, and hence the path is (an ordered sequence of) one *route* value. The *route* value of zero indicates that the packet is destined for some host within the local network and does not need the services of a switch.

Once established, the state information in switches and endpoints indexed by *route* values remains in place until it is explicitly released or until the path fails.

## 4.3.2 Path Maintenance

The procedures for maintaining the path, once established, are purposefully similar to those used to maintain the association. The *full route lookup* procedure handles forwarding packets along the path in the forward direction. The *return route* is used to guide packets in the return direction. The route exchange procedure optimizes lookups at the switches in a manner similar to key exchange. Since paths are independent of associations, the route sharing procedure enables associations to share a path.

After the FIRST packet has established a path, subsequent packets in the forward direction in the association need only carry the *route* value in order to use this path. At each switch, the *route* value within the packet is replaced with the *route* value that was generated by this switch for this path. Each switch along the path uses the <MAC address, *route* value> pair from the incoming packet to perform a full route lookup. That is, the pair identifies the appropriate *route* value used to forward the packet. The full route lookup procedure is necessary for packets in the forward direction.

The *return route* value is derived from the *route* value by setting the MSB in that value. A packet sent from the destination host back to the initiating host includes the *return route* value in the route field of the packet. Since the destination host has noted from which node the incoming FIRST packet was sent, the exit port identified by the *return route* value directs the return packet to that node. When the packet arrives at the first switch along the return path, its *return route* value is used to look up the next *return route* value to be used in this packet's route field. The switch now overwrites the value in the *route* field with this new *return route* value, which enables the packet to be forwarded to the next switch on the return path. The process is repeated at each switch along the path until the packet arrives at the initiating host.

Note that the *return route* value enables a switch to use a single-valued lookup procedure to find the next value to place into the *route* field. This action is analogous to an end-node using a *return key* value in an abbreviated lookup to map an incoming packet to its context. In both cases the value used for the lookup has been locally generated and is thus unique within the XTP implementation in this node. Example 4.2c illustrates the *return route* procedure in the continuing example.

### Example 4.2c

When Host B sends a packet along the return path, it includes within the *route* field of that packet the *return route* value derived from the *route* value of the FIRST packet. Since Switch T was the last switch along the path before the FIRST packet arrived at Host B, the *route* field of the FIRST packet contained the value $R_T$ when it arrived at Host B. Host B places $R'_T$ in the *route* field of the return packet and sends $[K'_A, R'_T,$ CNTL] since a CNTL packet was requested. Host B sends this packet to Switch T, whose MAC address was recorded when the FIRST packet arrived at Host B. Switch T uses the value $R'_T$ to look up $R'_S$, the *return route* value to be used. Switch T learned during path establishment the MAC address of Switch S, the next switch on the return path. Switch T replaces $R'_T$ with $R'_S$, and sends $[K'_A, R'_S,$ CNTL]. Switch S likewise finds $R'_A$ and the MAC address for Host A by using $R'_S$ as the lookup value. The packet sent from Switch S to Host A is $[K'_A, R'_A,$ CNTL].

In this way we see that the return path, like the forward path, is an ordered sequence of *route* values. In this example it is $(R'_T, R'_S, R'_A)$.

As with a *return* key, the presence of a *return route* value signals to the XTP implementation that a full route lookup is not necessary. Since the *route* value used on the forward path was generated locally with uniqueness guaranteed within this implementation, the corresponding *return route* value (e.g., the *route* value with the MSB set) is guaranteed to remain unique. Thus the pertinent return path information, namely the next *return route* value and the MAC address of the next node along the path, is found using only the incoming *return route* value as the index into the database.

The route exchange procedure is used to allow switches handling packets in the forward direction to benefit from an abbreviated lookup just as they are afforded when they handle packets in the return direction. The route exchange procedure begins when a CNTL packet traverses the path in the return direction with a valid value in its *xroute* field. This value, generated by a node, is the *route* value requested by that node for placement in forward packets. In the same way that the *return route* value is the value sent back to the node that generated it, the *xroute* field indicates to the next node along the path what *route* value the downstream node would like to receive in the future. Since the *xroute* value is generated by the node that will be receiving it, it must have its MSB set. Once the route exchange procedure is complete (or equivalently, a route exchange has occurred), nodes sending packets in both directions will be using *route* values with the MSB set, which indicates that the value in the *route* field is sufficient for use in the abbreviated lookup.

### Example 4.2d

When Host B sends a CNTL packet on the return path to Host A, it may communicate to Switch T that it would rather see a different *route* value in the *route* fields of any subsequent incoming packets. Host B does this by placing a locally generated *return route* value into the *xroute* field of the CNTL packet. Let Host B choose $R'_{B_I}$. The CNTL packet sent, then, is $[K'_A, R'_T, CNTL, (xroute = R'_{B_I})]$. This information is for use by Switch T only. If Switch T sends a new *route* value in the *xroute* field of the CNTL packet that travels from Switch T to Switch S, then Switch T similarly establishes a new *route* value for use in its link with Switch S. Switch S may do the same thing with Host A. If a route exchange occurs between each pair of nodes on this path, the new forward path is given by the ordered sequence $(R'_{S_I}, R'_{T_I}, R'_{B_I})$.

As with the key exchange, route exchange is not required for the proper maintenance and operation of the path; it only constitutes an optimization for path information lookups within the switches. However, the *xroute* field is interpreted in every CNTL packet. If route exchange is not desired, the *xroute* field in the CNTL packet must contain the value zero. Also, after a route exchange is completed, the *xroute* field must contain a zero until and unless a new route exchange is to occur.

The route sharing procedure is another optimization for delivering packets. If the situation arises that there exists a path between two hosts, and those two hosts wish to establish another association, then the existing path may be used to deliver the packets for both associations to their common destination host. Recall that the lifetime of a path is independent of the lifetimes of the associations that it supports. Hence, it may not be uncommon that a path already exists when a new association is being established.

If an initiating host is aware of an existing path between it and the destination host, that initiating host may simply use the *route* value that identifies the exit port to the existing path for the FIRST packet of the new association. Since the *route* value is all that is required for a packet to be delivered to the host at the other end of the path, the packets for this new association will use the trail of references already in existence as they traverse the network to the destination host. The FIRST packet will, of course, have to carry the Address Segment, but the use of the shared route means that this Address Segment will not be needed within the switches to ensure delivery to the proper destination host.

Within this scenario there are two cases to be considered. The first case is where a route exchange has occurred. Since the value in the *route* field in each packet has the MSB set, the switches along the path simply use this *return route* value for the path information lookup. When such a path is shared, the packets from the new association are indistinguishable at the switches from packets from the old association, and the sharing is trivial. The second case is where the route exchange has not occurred. That is, packets in the return direction have the *return route* values so that the lookup is abbreviated, but packets in the forward direction do not have the MSB set. The full route lookup is required here. However, recall that a full route lookup requires only the pair <MAC address, *route* value>, and since the key value is the only way to distinguish between the packets in different associations, the path can be shared without additional effort. Example 4.2e illustrates an instance of route sharing in our continuing set of examples.

### Example 4.2e

Consider a newly activated context, identified by $J_A$, within Host A. This context is to be the endpoint of a new association of which the destination host is Host B. If Host A recognizes that it already has a path between Hosts A and B, then packets from context $J_A$ can use the same *route* value as those used by context $K_A$. Since a path already exists, there is no need to create a new path. Assuming that a route exchange has occurred, the FIRST packet for context $J_A$ is issued as $[J_A, R'_{S_1}, \text{FIRST}]$, and it passes through each intermediate node along the established path.

Recovering from a damaged or inadequate path is also part of the path maintenance procedures. The PATH packet is used to rethread a path for an existing association. The PATH packet has only an Address Segment within its Middle Segment. An endpoint of an association, under the proper error control conditions or when rate control parameters become unacceptable, issues a PATH packet addressed for the other endpoint of the association, which contains a new, unique *route* value. The PATH packet creates a path in the switches in exactly the same manner as the FIRST packet. Upon receiving a PATH packet, the other endpoint uses the new *route* value to derive the *return route* value for all of its return packets on that association. Upon receiving a return packet with this new *return route* value, the endpoint which issued the PATH packet ceases to use the old *route* value and begins to use this new one. A route exchange (as described above) may now occur on this new path. As a consequence, therefore, of the PATH packet, the association begins to use a new path without having to terminate and rebuild the entire association. The old path is simply not used for this association after the change, but since it may have some other associations using it, it can not be discarded. Eventually, it will be released by the path release procedure when the proper conditions are met.

The RCNTL packet serves as the control packet for use between nodes along the path. While CNTL packets carry mostly end-to-end association related information, RCNTL packets are strictly for exchanging path related information on a hop-by-hop basis. Consequently, only the value from the *route* field is needed to determine what agent should process the packet's information. Since only path-related values are relevant, the *rate*, *burst*, and *xroute* fields are the only fields from the Control Segment that are used. Thus, RCNTL packets allow switches to communicate path maintenance information between each other without involving any of the associations using the path.

## 4.3.3 Path Release

Since more than one association may share a path, there is no practical way to know exactly when a path is no longer useful. After some implementation-dependent amount of time some node along the path may initiate the path release procedure if the conditions suggesting that a release is warranted are met. This release procedure requires a request/acknowledge handshake to ensure that any association still relying on the path can make its presence known.

Each node along the path keeps a packet count for each path through or originating at that node. As a packet traverses the path, it is counted at each node along that path. An activity timer is used to periodically check these packet counts to detect any paths that have had no activity for some time interval. If such a path exists, then the path release procedure begins on that path. It is important, therefore, that the activity timer for paths be at least as long as the timers used to detect inactivity on an association.

Table 4.3 shows the codes used within ROUTE packets. When some node on the path decides to initiate the path release, it issues a ROUTE packet with the *route* value in the *route* field set for this path and the *code* value set to 1, the "release route" *code* value. The ROUTE packet traverses the path. If the release initiator is an intermediate node of the path, it sends a ROUTE packet in both directions. Upon sending the ROUTE packet, the release initiator sets a timer (the WTIMER, discussed in the error control procedures of Section 4.7). Once the ROUTE (*code* = 1) packet arrives at an endpoint of the path, a check for activity on this endpoint is conducted. If no activity has been detected for this path for some time interval, the endpoint issues a ROUTE packet with *code* value set to 2, for "release acknowledge." As each node along the path receives and forwards this packet, it releases all internal structures associated with the path. Note that the intermediate node initiating path release should receive two such ROUTE packets as acknowledgements since two route release ROUTE packets were sent.

If any node along the path wishes to reject the release procedure, it does so by simply failing to forward the ROUTE (*code* = 1) packet. The node would choose to do this if it had some knowledge that the path should not be released. Failing to forward the ROUTE packet does not terminate the release procedure; rather, it merely stalls the release. The initiator will eventually time out waiting for the ROUTE (*code* = 2) packet, and retry. The only way for a path to be saved from release, once release is initiated, is for some packet (other than a ROUTE packet) to be sent across the path.

| Value of *code* field | Message Category |
|:---:|:---|
| 1 | Release Route |
| 2 | Release Acknowledged |

**Table 4.3 — ROUTE Packet *code* Values**

If this occurs at any time during the release procedure the release is immediately termi-nated.

The release initiator will do one of three things: (1) receive a ROUTE (*code* = 2) acknowledgement, (2) receive some other packet on this path, or (3) time out waiting for one of these two events. If the initiator receives the acknowledgement, at least that portion of the path is released. If the initiator is awaiting two acknowledgements and both arrive, it releases its path management structures and the path is released. If some other packet is received, the path release procedure is terminated and (at least a portion of) the path remains intact. If, after an implementation-dependent number of retries on the ROUTE (*code* = 1) packet have occurred, the release initiator must assume that the path has been severed by failure or partial release, and it removes its path management structures.

Note that if an intermediate node initiates a path release there is the danger that only one half of the path will be released while the other half is still functioning. Since only a new packet using the path can prevent its release, such a packet will eventually encounter a portion of the path that has been released. Error control procedures will eventually recover from this by causing a PATH packet to rethread a new path for the associations affected.

# 4.4   Data Transfer Procedures

The data transfer procedures begin when data is passed to the XTP implementation from an XTP user as a parameter to an **output** command. They continue until the data stream carrying this data is closed. While data buffer management is implementation-specific, the data transfer procedures implement the movement of data from a transmit-ting XTP user data buffer space to a remote receiving XTP user data buffer space. This data transfer includes the following phases: moving the data from XTP user data buffer space into XTP data buffer space, placing it into *data* fields of either the FIRST packet or subsequent DATA packets, traversing the network, placing the data into receiving XTP data buffer space, and finally delivering the data into the receiving XTP user data buffer space.

Data transfer procedures use the various mechanisms present in the packet struc-tures. These procedures are conceptually separate from the association and path man-agement procedures (which provide the infrastructure for the data transfer), the rate and flow control procedures (which regulate the data flow), and the error control proce-dures (which provide the safeguards to ensure correct data flow).

Data is given to an XTP implementation for transfer to some remote XTP user. When the local XTP user issues an **output** command, the data is placed in XTP buffers, and when appropriate, is copied into the *data* fields of outgoing data-bearing packets. The data is identified by assigning a sequence number to each byte such that a range of sequence numbers implies a contiguous group of data. The *seq* field of a data-bearing packet specifies the sequence number of the first byte of data (or addressing information, if this is a FIRST packet) contained within that packet. The amount of data in the packet is conveyed in the *dlen* field.

When a data-bearing packet is received by the destination XTP implementation, its contents are placed into XTP data buffers according to the sequence number in the *seq* field. As each byte is identified by a sequence number, simple offset calculations can produce the position of the data in the receive buffers. The receiving context keeps track of outstanding data and, when asked via an **input** command, delivers contiguous data to the XTP user. When data is delivered to the XTP user, it leaves the XTP domain and the transfer is complete.

There is a facility within the data transfer procedures that allows the sending XTP user to place markers in its data. This is called "tagging." The receiving XTP user is given an indication when the data is tagged. The mechanism for tagging data is the *btag* field. This field only appears in the Data Segment when the BTAG bit is set in the *options* field of the Header. The BTAG bit indicates that the first eight bytes of user data in the packet are tagged. Tagged data may be "out-of-band" data, user-understood event marks, higher-layer encapsulating mechanisms, or other application-dependent schemes.

While XTP has no control over the data placed in the tagged-data channel, the XTP Definition requires every XTP implementation to reserve a special value for the *btag* field for the sending of an error-controlled DATA packet with a zero-length *data* field. Since sequence number space is the only means for identifying data, and hence is instrumental in the error detection and recovery procedures, a zero-length *data* field in a DATA packet can not be protected. If such a packet were to be lost, its absence would not be known since it did not consume any sequence number space. Therefore, in order to cause some sequence number space to be consumed without sending any XTP user data, the XTP Definition specifies the use of the *btag* field with a special value (all bits set) in the 8-byte tag. Thus, a DATA packet carrying no user data can be sent such that it consumes sequence space, and is therefore protected from loss.

The data priority mechanism in XTP is provided by the *sort* field. When data is given to the XTP implementation via an **output** command, the command may contain a *sort* value for use in ordering the protocol processing of this data. The context "inherits" the *sort* value from the **output** command as the context processes the data from that command. Thus the servicing of contexts is ordered according to the *sort* values of the data they contain. Active contexts, i.e., those not blocked by flow or rate control restrictions, are serviced in order from lowest *sort* value to highest. Contexts with "unsorted" data are serviced only after all other contexts are serviced. A packet issued as a result of servicing a context with a *sort* value carries that *sort* value in the packet's *sort* field and sets the SORT bit in the *options* field. Unsorted packets are issued with the SORT bit cleared. Each switch on the path processes packets in *sort* value order. The destination endpoint uses the *sort* values to order the servicing of the **input** commands, which deliver the data and the data's *sort* value to the XTP user.

XTP uses a special mechanism to mark the end of a message. XTP user data is conceptually one or more *messages*, where a message is a user-defined grouping of the data. The association is equipped to handle an arbitrary number of messages over its lifetime. When a data-bearing packet is carrying the end of the message, the EOM bit is set in the *options* field. This indicates that the last byte of data in the *data* field is the last byte of data for the message.

Data transfer may not be limited to only two users; in fact, XTP supports one-to-many and many-to-one data flows. In the former case this transfer is referred to as a *multicast*; in the latter it is referred to as a *concentration*. Multicast associations are restricted to transferring data only from the transmitter (initiating context) to the set of receivers. This is because there is no general solution for how a single context can map the data from multiple data streams onto its buffer space. If a reverse data transfer, or concentration, is desired, the single receiver must activate a separate context for each of the data streams coming into it. Chapter 8 continues and expands upon this discussion.

# 4.5   Flow Control Procedures

*Flow control* regulates the volume of data flowing between the endpoints of an association according to policies enforced by the receiver (or receiver set, in the case of multicast). XTP provides the mechanisms and the procedures for an end-to-end credit-based sliding window flow control algorithm. As the receiver is able to accept more data, more sequence numbers in the data stream are allocated to the transmitter, thus moving the upper edge of the transmitter's window forward. As a receiver acknowledges data received, the lower edge of the transmitter's window is moved forward. Thus the transmitter's window slides across the sequence number space of the data stream at a rate dictated by the receivers' ability to accept and acknowledge new data. This section describes those procedures and mechanisms within XTP that implement this sliding window flow control.

The sequence number space for a data stream is a mapping of every byte in the data stream to an integer, which imposes an ordering on the data—hence the term *sequence* number. It also places an identification tag on each piece of data so that that piece of data can be accounted for during data transfer. The ability to account for and recover from missing data is part of the error control procedures described in a later section, including the ways in which policies for acknowledging data can be effected, but the fact that data is acknowledged is an essential aspect of the sliding window flow control procedure.

The packets exchanged between two endpoints carry the information necessary to allow progress in the data transfer, and hence allow the flow control window to slide across new sequence numbers. The fields involved are the *seq* and *dseq* fields from the Header of every packet, and the *alloc* field from the Control Segment of a CNTL packet.

The value of the *seq* field in data-bearing packets represents the first byte of the Information Segment, excluding any padding. In CNTL packets, however, the value of the *seq* field represents the next byte expected on the forward data stream. For example, if 1000 bytes of data, starting with the sequence number 200, are sent in a DATA packet, then the *seq* field for that packet would contain the value 200. If the SREQ bit were set in that DATA packet, the CNTL packet sent in return would carry the value 1201 in its *seq* field.

The *dseq* field is present in all packets. The value in the *dseq* field in an incoming packet applies to the data stream outgoing from the host receiving the packet. The *dseq* value communicates the first unacknowledged byte on this data stream. Hence, if all data up to sequence number 3000 were delivered to the XTP user, the *dseq* field of any packet traveling back to the sender would carry the value 3001.

The *alloc* field from a CNTL packet indicates the highest sequence number that the receiver on this data stream will accept. Its value is the sequence number one greater than the highest sequence number acceptable, and hence represents the beginning of unallocated sequence space.

Let us first examine the flow control procedures from the transmitter's point of view. The window in the transmitter represents the sequence number space of data that the receiver is willing to accept. Consequently, the receiver must communicate to the transmitter the bounds for the window. Since the *dseq* field contains the first byte of unacknowledged (and hence outstanding) data, the value in this field in any incoming packets represents the lower edge of the transmitter's window. The upper edge is set using the value of the *alloc* field of incoming CNTL packets. Hence, the window of sequence numbers acceptable to the receiver is (*dseq..alloc*−1). As the receiver can accept more data, the *alloc* value is advanced.

Since the value of the *alloc* field may be changed with each CNTL packet from the receiver, the flow control window may be expanded, contracted, or even closed completely. It is therefore important that the transmitter be able to recognize old or stale CNTL packets in order to ensure that the *alloc* value being processed represents the current state of the receiver. The synchronizing handshake described in the error control section enables a transmitter to recognize old or stale CNTL packets.

Now we look at the flow control procedures from the receiver's point of view. The receiver keeps two variables, **r_dseq** and **r_alloc**, whose values represent the values placed in the *dseq* and *alloc* fields of outgoing packets. Clearly, the sequence numbers of incoming data should fall within the range of the **r_dseq** and **r_alloc** values maintained by the receiver. As data is delivered to the XTP user, the value of **r_dseq** is advanced. As buffer space becomes available for this association, the value of **r_alloc** is advanced. When a data-bearing packet is received, the data that falls within the range (**r_dseq..r_alloc**−1) is placed into receive buffers.

### Example 4.3

Figure 4.15 shows how the transmitting window at Host A is maintained by the information obtained from the CNTL packets sent from Host B. Host A begins with an initial allocation (window size) of data stream space of 50 bytes. It sends a FIRST packet with 50 bytes of data (some of these bytes are from the Address Segment). Since the

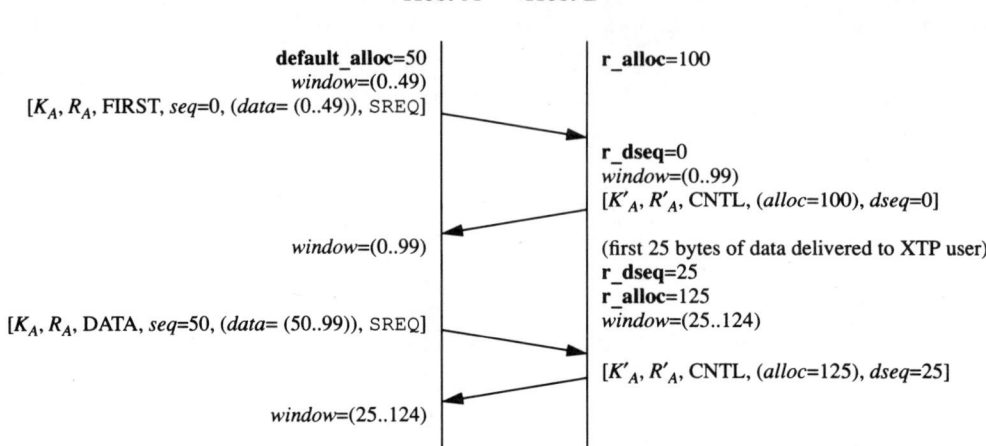

**Figure 4.15 — Packet Exchange Showing Flow Control Window**

FIRST packet has the SREQ bit set, a CNTL packet is immediately generated. It carries the values of **r_alloc** and **r_dseq** in its *alloc* and *dseq* fields. For the receiver, these two variables constitute the receiving window, shown to be (0..99). The transmitter receives the CNTL packet and updates its window to reflect the new information. Since it may send 50 more bytes of data, it does so, thus filling the transmit window with outstanding data. Meanwhile, 25 bytes of data are delivered to the XTP user. This is reflected by the update of the **r_dseq** variable. The receiver updates **r_alloc**. These values are transmitted in the next CNTL packet, and the lower and upper edges of the transmitter's window are moved to reflect the new range of sequence numbers which may be transmitted; in this case it is (25..124).

It should be pointed out that the flow control procedures work independently for each data stream, although DATA packets on one data stream may carry flow control information (namely *dseq* values) for the data stream in the other direction. Also, the *seq* field of *any* outgoing packet will always reflect the sequence number of the next byte to be sent on that context's outgoing data stream. For instance, assume Host A sends a FIRST packet with *seq* = 0 and *dseq* = 1000, indicating that Host A's outgoing data stream will start with sequence number 0 and its incoming data stream will start with sequence number 1000. Host B, upon receiving this packet, will set the *seq* field in its next outgoing CNTL packet to 1000, even though that CNTL packet is not necessarily generated for the data stream for which 1000 is the starting sequence number.

In general, the receiver uses some local policy on buffer space for setting the *alloc* value and thus controls the transmitter's flow rate. However, the transmitter may make the receiver use a conservative policy by setting the RES bit in the *options* field of the Header of the first packet sent on that data stream. When the transmitter sets this bit, the data stream is forced to operate in *reservation mode*, and the receiver is constrained to set the *alloc* value based only on the buffer space dedicated to this association. Although the transmitter sets the RES bit, and thus dictates which allocation policy the receiver should use, no other aspects of the flow control procedures are changed.

Another policy bit may be set by the transmitter in order to turn off the flow control procedures on the outgoing data stream. The NOFLOW bit in the *options* field of the Header indicates "no-flow" mode. Once a packet is received with this bit set, the receiver may accept this policy of no flow control or reject it. By accepting the policy, the receiver understands that the *alloc* values it provides to the transmitter will not be heeded. The transmitter must set the NOFLOW bit in all outgoing packets since this policy can not be toggled. If the receiver declines to accept the suspension of flow control, it rejects the connection by issuing a DIAG packet with the proper *code* and *val* values. If the receiver on either data stream rejects the NOFLOW offer, the whole association is terminated with the DIAG rejection packet.

As in the unicast association, the transmitter in a multicast association observes the default flow control parameters when the multicast association is established. As the transmitter requests CNTL packets from the receiver set, the transmitter updates its flow control parameters based on the flow control values received in the returned CNTL packets.

# 4.6   Rate Control Procedures

While flow control applies to data transfer in an association and reflects the ebb and flow of XTP buffer space at the endpoints of that association, *rate control* is an attribute of a path, and each XTP node along the path participates (even when the path only includes the end-nodes). Since each node in the path receives packets and forwards them, each pair of nodes in the path forms a producer/consumer pair. Rate control regulates the rate at which data is produced at one node so as not to overrun the downstream consumer. That consumer node then becomes the producer for the next XTP node along the path, until the destination end-node is finally reached. Since it is possible that the generation of many packets within a short amount of time could overrun a node along the path, XTP provides mechanisms (*rate* and *burst* fields in the Control Segment of CNTL and RCNTL packets) and the procedures with which consumers may throttle producers.

The initiating context of an association begins with default values for *rate* and *burst* parameters. The *rate* value specifies in bytes per second the (supposed) maximum rate at which data can be consumed by the receiver. The *burst* specifies the (supposed) maximum number of bytes which can be consumed in one burst of packets, that is, packets sent in rapid succession. These values are "supposed" since they are defaults and thus are not based on actual feedback from the receiver. The XTP Definition defines a countdown timer called the RTIMER (for refresh timer) for each association, which will mark regular periods over the lifetime of the association. The value placed in the RTIMER is the quantity *burst* divided by *rate* since this quotient gives us the period of time during which *burst* number of bytes can be transmitted. An association variable, **credit**, is loaded with the value in *burst* each time the RTIMER is reset. As packets are transmitted, **credit** is decremented by the amount of data sent. When the value in **credit** reaches zero, the transmission of data packets is suspended until the RTIMER expires. At this time the RTIMER is refreshed, the **credit** is renewed, and transmission of data packets is once again enabled.

By setting *rate* and *burst* with certain values transmission can be constrained or halted. A value of zero for *burst* means that the transmission is unconstrained. This test is performed first. If the *burst* is not zero but the *rate* value is (hence, a divide-by-zero fault would occur), the transmission is halted immediately and not restarted until either a nonzero value for *rate* or a zero value for *burst* arrives.

The initiating endpoint may suggest to its remote receiver values for use in the rate control procedures for the forward data stream of the association. This is done by using the *rate_req* and the *burst_req* fields in the Address Segment of the FIRST packet. The XTP Definition does not dictate how the receiver must act on these values. When the receiver sends CNTL packets back to the initiating endpoint, it includes up-to-date values in the *rate* and *burst* fields of the Control Segment. These values must be used to update the rate control variables at the initiating endpoint. The receiver may change these values at any time during the lifetime of the association by including updated values in outgoing CNTL packets.

The receiving end-node sets the *rate* and the *burst* values by determining how much data it can process over a period of time. The rate control procedure provides a method of bandwidth allocation, where the receiving end-node allocates packet-processing capacity to those who wish to send packets to it. The policies and heuristics that are used for controlling this bandwidth allocation through the rate control procedures are not within the scope of the XTP Definition; however, the ability to do so is present.

Each one of the intermediate nodes along the path between the endpoints of the association may participate in the rate control procedure. Switches are permitted to reduce the values of the *rate* and *burst* fields of any CNTL packets passing through them. The rate of data generation at the transmitter is thus the minimum acceptable rate of all of the nodes along the path. Also, the switches may adjust rate control values by using RCNTL packets. Chapter 5 discusses how RCNTL packets are used to exchange path-related information, including the rate control parameters. Switches may use these packets at any time during the lifetime of the path to set rate control parameters.

Rate control involves the path between endpoints. Since this path may be shared by two or more associations, the rate control information applies to all associations using this path.

# 4.7   Error Control Procedures

In order to provide a data transfer service that claims to be *reliable*, there must be procedures present in the service provider that can monitor the data transfer and supporting procedures to detect, notify, and, if possible, recover from any error conditions that may arise. The error control procedures within XTP are designed to facilitate reliable data transfer. The procedures provide error detection and recovery in five ways: (1) by protecting against corrupted data, (2) by monitoring the data transfer for data loss, (3) by supporting resynchronization when endpoints of an association lose synchrony, (4) by removing packets that are known to be too old, and (5) by providing notification to proper agents when error conditions are unrecoverable.

Error detecting codes, in the form of *checksums*, are used to protect the data within a packet from bit errors occurring during transmission or during processing at an intermediate node or endpoint. Corrupted control information, namely that within the Header of a packet, is considered harmful enough to warrant the abandonment of any further processing on that packet. A checksum over the Header fields protects the packet from such errors. An optional second checksum protects the Middle Segment information as well; if this protection is required, then errors in the Middle Segment can also cause a packet to be abandoned.

Certain conditions that cause packets to become lost may arise in the network, such as improperly addressed packets, erroneous routing tables, or a failure of a node along the path. Data-bearing packets in a reliable service are protected by a sequence number space, which associates each data byte with an integer in a continuous range. The data may be acknowledged and retransmissions requested by referring to the data by its sequence numbers.

The contexts which constitute the endpoints of the association must share protocol state information in order to provide data transfer effectively and efficiently. Hence the protocol must provide procedures for recovery from the failure to maintain synchrony in state between the state machines of the endpoints. This procedure, called the *synchronizing handshake*, provides the means by which protocol state information contained within the CNTL packets can be considered up-to-date.

Certain aspects of the error control procedures rely on timers to signal when an expected event has failed to occur. Without the use of timers the protocol risks deadlock. When a timer expires, the error control procedures are notified that some action is necessary. In particular, there are three timers used in the error control procedures: one providing the length of time a context will wait on a requested status update in the form of a CNTL packet (WTIMER), another for setting a limit on the duration of an inactive association (CTIMER), and the third for bounding the time spent trying to revive an inactive association (CTIMEOUT).

It is possible within a network that a packet is held for a long time before being allowed to continue. Circumstances like corrupted routing tables may cause a packet to circulate through a network for some time before eventually finding its destination host. Such packets may "live" longer than the information contained within them is valid. A *time-to-live* field within each packet ensures that after a certain amount of time without delivery the packet will be removed from the network.

Finally, errors discovered in an attempt to process an incoming packet may cause a diagnostic (DIAG) packet to be generated, thus notifying the packet's sender of the reason for failure. DIAG packets provide an informative and timely notification of certain packet processing errors. This allows smoother, more timely error recovery transitions in the protocol state machine.

This section describes the procedures that implement the error control facility within XTP. XTP provides the mechanisms for a robust data transfer protocol, as well as controlled ways of relaxing error control procedures such that certain errors are tolerated if the user so directs.

## 4.7.1 Checksums

It is important to the XTP protocol state machine that the integrity of certain parts of a packet be ensured. Upon detection of breached integrity, a packet is discarded. If the discarded packet falls under error-controlled transmission, its loss will be detected and recovered at the packet's originator. In particular, the contents of the Header fields must remain uncorrupted since protocol state information is shared via the fields. Inaccurate information in these fields is more dangerous to the operation of the protocol and more difficult to recover from than the loss of information that results from discarding these packets.

The XTP checksum algorithm provides the error-detecting code for the XTP packet information. Briefly, the checksum is a two-part sum of a block of information. The first part is a straight "vertical" exclusive-or of each 16-bit short word in the block. The second part is a rotated "spiral" exclusive-or of each 16-bit short word. By taking the straight vertical exclusive-or, the checksum is equivalent to a parity check of each bit position in each short word. By spiraling through the information with a rotating exclusive-or, the second part of the checksum provides a parity check which is not as strongly position dependent. This checksum misses only a few patterns involving an even number of errors.

Each packet carries two checksum values, one over the Middle Segment of the packet, and one over the fields in the Header of the packet. The segments covered by these two checksums are mutually exclusive, partitioned so that protection can be provided over data delivery and state information without requiring that the same level of protection be required of the information carried in the Middle Segment of the packet. While the checksum over the Header information must always be used, the checksum over the Middle Segment can be disabled on a per-packet basis as befits the application.

The NOCHECK bit in the *options* field of the Header indicates whether a checksum has been calculated over the Middle Segment of this packet. If the NOCHECK bit is set, the checksum is disabled. When the checksum is enabled, the result of the checksum, which covers the entire Middle Segment, including any padding or alignment bytes, is placed in the *dcheck* field in the Trailer.

The result of the checksum over the Header fields is placed in the *hcheck* field in the Header. Whereas the checksum over the Middle Segment can be disabled, the checksum over the Header fields is mandatory. All fields in the Header except for the *route* field, the *ttl* field, and the *hcheck* field itself are included in the checksum result which is placed in the *hcheck* field. Since the *hcheck* field is the last four bytes of the Header, the checksum calculation can simply stop four bytes early (which is the same as clearing the four bytes and proceeding with the calculation over them as well).

The Header is checked for errors at each intermediate node by recalculating the checksum and comparing the result to that carried in the *hcheck* field. In this way the integrity of the information is maintained through each switch on the path. Each switch must be assured that it is handling a valid packet, so the Header fields are tested for integrity each time their contents are used. The integrity of the data within the Middle Segment, however, is an end-to-end issue. Thus, when the NOCHECK bit is clear, the checksum is calculated at the transmitting endpoint and the result compared with the value of the *dcheck* field only at the receiving endpoint.

## 4.7.2 Acknowledgements and Retransmissions

The error control procedures detect and recover from lost data by acknowledging received data and retransmitting data known or suspected of being lost. These acknowledgement and retransmission procedures are related to the flow control procedures in that the window for flow control also represents the amount of outstanding data awaiting acknowledgement. Data from within this window is retransmitted as needed, either from lack of acknowledgement or explicit negative acknowledgement.

The *dseq* and *rseq* fields represent two kinds of acknowledgement in XTP. The acknowledgement that moves the lower edge of the flow control window indicates that the data prior to a particular sequence number, given by the *dseq* value, has been reliably delivered to the XTP user. Any transmit buffers holding this data may now be released. The second kind of acknowledgement, represented by the *rseq* value, indicates that the data has been received at the destination endpoint. The data so acknowledged will not require retransmission but the XTP buffers can not be released until the lower edge of the window slides past the data they hold. The error control procedures that direct the acknowledgement and retransmission of data are concerned primarily with this second level of acknowledgement.

Data is sent from a transmitting endpoint to a receiving endpoint via data-bearing packets. At some point the receiving endpoint may receive a packet with either an SREQ or DREQ bit set, indicating that a CNTL packet is requested by the transmitter. If the SREQ is set, the endpoint receiving this indication issues a CNTL packet immediately. If the DREQ is set, the CNTL packet is issued only after all data currently in XTP receive buffer space is delivered to the XTP user. In either case, the CNTL packet that is generated contains acknowledgement and retransmission information.

Specifically, a CNTL packet contains three fields that facilitate acknowledgement and retransmission: the *rseq*, the *nspan*, and the *spans* fields. The *rseq* field contains the sequence number of the first byte of the first gap in the data. The *nspan* field specifies the number of spans present in the *spans* field, where each span is a pair of sequence numbers representing a group of contiguous data received. The use of the *spans* field, either by the receiver or by the transmitter, is optional since the *rseq* value is the only information required to conduct retransmissions. If present, the spans information, along with the *rseq* value, indicates what data has been received into XTP receive buffer space, and by inference, what data has not.

To illustrate acknowledgement and retransmission we define two variables, **bseq** and **eseq**. These variables are not part of the XTP Definition, but represent one way of implementing the mechanisms that must be present for error detection and correction to work properly. Let **bseq** be the beginning sequence number of sent but unacknowledged data, and let **eseq** be one greater than the ending sequence number of sent but unacknowledged data. The range (**bseq**..**eseq**−1) represents all bytes of data outstanding. Certainly this range must fall within the transmitted flow control window.

When the transmitter receives a CNTL packet, the *rseq* value contained within should be between **bseq** and **eseq**. Since **eseq** is one greater than the largest sequence number sent by this transmitter, (*rseq*..**eseq**−1) represents the data which has not been completely received by the receiver. This is to say that some of the data in this range, starting with the byte identified by *rseq*, is missing.

The transmitter may retransmit DATA packets covering the range (*rseq*..**eseq**−1) according to the retransmission policies within the transmitter. Some or all of this range may be retransmitted. If the transmitter begins retransmission of data at the point indicated by the *rseq* value and retransmits all of the data from that point, the policy is known as *go-back-n*. This is the approach used in ISO TP4 and TCP in retransmission of lost data. It may be easier for the transmitter to retransmit more than the amount required to cover the range, and hence some duplicate data may be sent.

When spans information is present, the transmitter has available all the knowledge necessary to conduct *selective retransmission*. Since the *spans* field is a set of pairs of sequence numbers that represent the beginning and ending of a contiguous group of data received, we can refer to each span as a pair $(a, b)$.

Let **hseq** be a variable kept at the receiver which represents the sequence number one greater than the highest sequence number received. The value of **hseq** is therefore the receiver's "high water mark" for unacknowledged data. Let the $i^{th}$ span be the pair $(a_i, b_i)$, so that the spans list in the spans field is such a pair for $i$ equal 1 to *nspan*. Since $a_1 = rseq$ and $b_{nspan} = $ **hseq**, the receiver fills in the spans information as follows: $(rseq, b_1), (a_2, b_2), \ldots, (a_{nspan}, $ **hseq**$)$.

The transmitter converts the spans information into the gaps in the data for which retransmission is necessary. The gaps of missing data are derived from the spans thus: $(rseq..a_1-1), (b_1..a_2-1), \ldots (b_{nspan}..$**eseq**$-1)$. Using a selective retransmission policy, the transmitter will use these ranges of missing data to send DATA packets containing data necessary to fill these gaps. Example 4.4 illustrates this point.

### Example 4.4

Consider the situation at the transmitter where **bseq** = 10, **eseq** = 40, and a CNTL packet has just arrived with *rseq* = 15, *nspan* = 2, *spans*$_1$ = (20, 25), and *spans*$_2$ = (30,

35). Figure 4.16 shows these values. If selective retransmission is used, three DATA packets[3] would be constructed as follows:

> DATA Packet 1: *seq* = 15, *data* = (15..19)
> DATA Packet 2: *seq* = 25, *data* = (25..29)
> DATA Packet 3: *seq* = 35, *data* = (35..39)

Note that, when a selective retransmission policy is in use, a receiver can impose a go-back-*n* retransmission explicitly by issuing a CNTL packet with one span: $spans_1$ = (**hseq**, **hseq**). The transmitter selectively retransmits the range (*rseq*..**hseq**−1), which is effectively the same as going back to *rseq*.

To aid in recovering from errors at the earliest possible moment, the transmitter may direct the receiver to generate a CNTL packet each time a gap appears in the data stream. The transmitter does this by setting the FASTNAK bit in the *options* field of the data-bearing packets it sends out on its outgoing data stream. The receiver is instructed to issue a CNTL packet as soon as a gap in the data stream is detected. Such an aggressive negative acknowledgement policy is useful when out-of-order packets are either impossible or extremely unlikely, as on single segment LANs; in such an environment gaps in the data stream strongly suggest that the missing data has been lost (as opposed to delayed).

### Example 4.5

Consider three incoming DATA packets, the first containing *data* = (20..29), the second containing *data* = (30..39), and the third containing *data* = (50..59). If the FASTNAK bit is set in these packets, a CNTL packet will be issued as soon as the third packet is received and processed. This CNTL packet will contain *rseq* = 40 to indicate that 39 was the sequence number of the last correctly received byte of data.

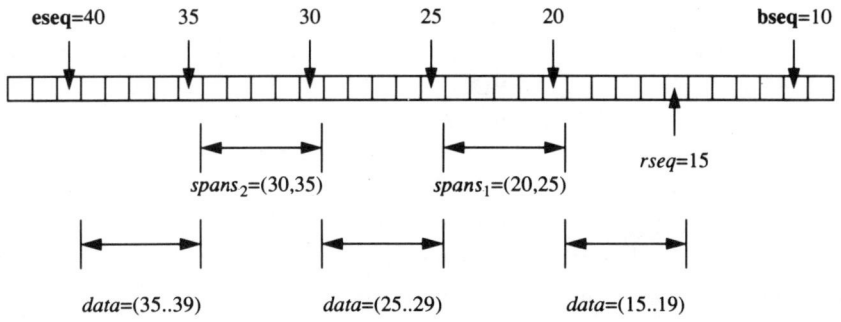

**Figure 4.16 — Selective Retransmission from Example 4.4**

[3] Strictly speaking, selective retransmission requires retransmitting *only* that data which has been lost. It may be more efficient, however, when retransmitting data, to cover as many gaps as possible with each DATA packet. In this example, a single DATA packet would be sufficient under such a strategy.

The transmitter can choose to turn off retransmission by setting the NOERR bit in the *options* field of the Header of a packet sent to the receiver. The NOERR bit, if set, indicates *no-error mode* in which the receiver is instructed to ignore data stream errors and not request any retransmissions. This does not imply that there are no CNTL packets sent back to the transmitter; flow control and other status information are still communicated via CNTL packets. Rather, error control actions at both the transmitter and receiver are modified so that the protocol proceeds even in the presence of lost data.

In no-error mode, the transmitter sends data via data-bearing packets in accordance with the flow and rate control imposed on it. During the transmission of this data, the transmitter will occasionally send a packet with the SREQ or DREQ bit set to request a CNTL packet, which will carry updated flow control information. The transmitter advances its window according to the *alloc* and *dseq* values in the returned CNTL packets, and thus new data may be transmitted.

The transmitter can send data up to but not exceeding its flow control allocation. When it has exhausted its allocation, it is forced to request a CNTL packet by setting the SREQ bit in an outgoing packet. When requested, a CNTL packet containing status information, including a new *alloc* value, is issued from the receiver. Since the receiver is instructed via the NOERR bit not to request retransmissions, it sets the *dseq* and *rseq* values to the value of **hseq**, one past the highest sequence number received. When the transmitter receives this CNTL packet, it moves its flow control window according to the values of *alloc* and *dseq*, and releases all transmit buffers containing data whose sequence numbers are less than the *dseq* value. Hence, in no-error mode, the *dseq* value is set to reflect data received at the remote XTP host but not necessarily delivered to the XTP user.

An interesting scenario occurs when all of the data-bearing packets transmitted are in fact lost and, along with the data, the SREQ bit set in the last packet is also not received. If the transmitter has sent all the data its flow control window allows, the transmitter must wait for the receiver to advance the allocation. If the receiver only issues a CNTL packet when requested, it awaits a packet with the SREQ bit set. In this case the transmitter will time out waiting for the returned CNTL packet and must send a CNTL packet with the SREQ bit set. When the receiver receives this CNTL packet, it issues a CNTL packet, but it can not advance the window since it does not realize that data has been sent. Recall that the *seq* field of any outgoing packet reflects the highest sequence number of the data sent on the outgoing data stream. The receiver must note that the *seq* value is higher than the **hseq** value held internally, and adjust the **hseq** value to be the same as the *seq* value. It can then issue the CNTL packet with a new *alloc* value and with the *dseq* and *rseq* fields set to the newly adjusted **hseq** value.

## 4.7.3 Timers

There are three timers used with an association to aid in error detection and recovery procedures. The WTIMER (wait timer) is a countdown timer whose initial value is the amount of time a context will wait for a CNTL packet response after a packet with the SREQ set has been sent. The CTIMER (connection timer) is also a countdown timer; this long-duration timer signals inactivity on the association. The WTIMER protects against waiting indefinitely for a response to a status request; the CTIMER protects against waiting indefinitely for progress when an association has been damaged. The third timer, CTIMEOUT, plays two roles. It is the *dally timer* that is used to ensure that a released context is not inadvertently reactivated by a late emerging FIRST packet. CTIMEOUT also bounds the amount of time that an XTP endpoint will attempt a synchronizing handshake with the corresponding endpoint before aborting the association.

In addition to these timers, two context variables, **retry_count** and **rtt**, play important roles in error recovery. The **retry_count** variable is used in conjunction with the CTIMEOUT timer to provide an upper bound on the number of times that XTP will retry a message exchange. The **rtt** variable contains the estimate of the roundtrip time across the network to the remote peer context. Its value is obtained from time values exchanged in CNTL packets over the lifetime of the association.

When a context sends a packet with the SREQ bit set, it loads the WTIMER with a value that reflects the amount of time that the context is willing to wait on a response. This value is derived from the average amount of time a packet requires to traverse the path between the endpoints of the association. Twice this end-to-end latency, plus any protocol processing time required at the destination endpoint, is called the *roundtrip time*. The **rtt** variable holds the current roundtrip time estimate, which is a smoothed average of observations during the lifetime of the association.

If the WTIMER expires before the requested CNTL packet arrives, the context making the status request must assume that the request was lost. The context then initiates a synchronizing handshake (see Section 4.7.4). The synchronizing handshake procedure ensures that either the two endpoints successfully exchange up-to-date status information or the context is aborted. The duration of the handshake attempt is bounded by the values found in the user-settable CTIMEOUT timer and **retry_count** variable.

The roundtrip time **rtt** is initialized to some default value at the activation of the context. Any time a CNTL packet is sent from this context, the *time* field contains a timestamp reflecting the current time at this context. At the remote endpoint, the protocol state machine copies the *time* values from incoming CNTL packets into the *techo* field of outgoing CNTL packets. The *techo* value in an incoming CNTL packet is used for estimating the **rtt** for this association. The rules concerning use of the *techo* field (see Section 5.4.3) ensure that any incoming CNTL packet with a nonzero value in its *techo* field is a valid value for updating the roundtrip time.

The value used to load the WTIMER is a roundtrip time that is smoothed over multiple **rtt** observations. The XTP Definition defines two variables, **SRTT** and **RTTV**, to be the Smoothed RoundTrip Time and the RoundTrip Time Variance, respectively. **SRTT** is initialized to the default **rtt** value from the context default values; **RTTV** is initially 0. For each new **rtt** observance,

$$\textbf{SRTT} = \textbf{SRTT} + (\textbf{rtt} - \textbf{SRTT})/8$$
$$\textbf{RTTV} = \textbf{RTTV} + (\text{abs}(\textbf{rtt} - \textbf{SRTT}) - \textbf{RTTV})/4$$

The WTIMER is set to the smoothed roundtrip time value plus twice the variance in the roundtrip time observances:

   WTIMER = **SRTT** + 2 * **RTTV**

The CTIMER signals inactivity on the association. Thus the value with which it is loaded must be sufficiently large that its expiration will signal with high probability the demise of either the path or the destination endpoint. The XTP Definition states that the CTIMER must not have a value larger than 3600 seconds. This restriction stems from the close relationship between the CTIMER and the requirements for properly aging *key* values to protect against aliasing problems. The actual value for CTIMER is implementation dependent.

If the CTIMER is loaded with a value of zero, it is disabled. The **retry_count** mechanism is disabled if the **retry_count** variable is assigned a value of zero. At least one of the two mechanisms, CTIMER or the **retry_count**, must be enabled in any implementation, and both may be enabled.

When enabled, the CTIMER is loaded with the implementation-dependent timeout value and counts down until it expires. When the CTIMER expires, the XTP implementation checks a packet counter for this association. If one or more packets have been received since the CTIMER was last loaded, the association is considered active. If not, the context is forced to initiate a synchronizing handshake. In either case, CTIMER is reloaded and begins counting down once more.

The CTIMEOUT timer has two roles. As we will see in the next section, it plays an important role in the synchronizing handshake. In addition, during association termination, CTIMEOUT serves as the dally timer used to keep a context in a "zombie" state long enough to ensure that a lost FIRST packet will not accidently cause a false association to be established. If there is any possibility that a FIRST packet may still exist in the network, the context issuing the END bit must remain in the zombie state until this possibility passes. Consider for example a scenario where a FIRST packet is sent with the SREQ bit set, and the CNTL packet sent in response has the END bit set, as may happen for a transaction. If the initiating context does not receive the CNTL packet, it retransmits the FIRST packet. If the corresponding context did in fact receive the FIRST packet and then issued a CNTL packet with the END bit set, the corresponding context would be deactivated. The receipt of the retransmitted FIRST packet will cause a new association to be established. By keeping the context identifier (the *key* value used in outgoing packets) for at least CTIMEOUT seconds, the context issuing the END bit will recognize the second FIRST packet as a retransmission and hence will take the proper action: retransmit the CNTL packet. This dally timer need be used only if (1) the context receiving the FIRST packet issues the END bit, and (2) there has been no synchronizing handshake, as described below. Otherwise, this problem can not arise.

## 4.7.4 Synchronizing Handshake

The aspect of the error control procedures which synchronizes the endpoints of an association is called the *synchronizing handshake*. When CNTL packets are delayed or reordered by the network, they convey old or inaccurate state information. Such a CNTL packet may actually countermand a more up-to-date one, and consequently the information within the CNTL packet may fail to have the effect expected by the context which sent the CNTL packet. The synchronizing handshake establishes a point of synchronization in the exchange of protocol information between the endpoints. In particular, a synchronizing handshake is required whenever a WTIMER expiration indicates no response to an outstanding status request (SREQ).

Each context must maintain a monotonically increasing counter used for *sync* values. The algorithm for determining *sync* values must ensure that every DATA packet with the SREQ bit set contains a new *sync* value. A simple algorithm for meeting this requirement is to increment the *sync* value by 1 whenever a data-bearing packet is output.

The value of the *sync* counter at the sender is placed into the *sync* field of every outgoing packet. When an SREQ or DREQ bit is set, the *sync* value placed in that packet is remembered by the sending context in a context variable, **saved_sync**. At the destination context, the largest *sync* value received is placed in the *echo* field of each outgoing CNTL packet. If a CNTL packet is received at the sender with an *echo* value that matches either **saved_sync** or the current *sync* value, a synchronizing handshake has occurred.

The algorithm for performing a synchronizing handshake is as follows:

1. Enable the CTIMEOUT timer and the **retry_count** variable.

2. Set an exponential backoff constant, **K**, to 1.

3. Send a CNTL packet with the SREQ bit set.

4. If a CNTL packet arrives at any time carrying a nonzero *techo* field with an *echo* value matching the current value of the *sync* counter or the **saved_sync** value, a synchronizing handshake has been successfully completed.

5. If packets are received in the interval **K**\*WTIMER but there are no matches for the *sync* counter or **saved_sync**, then the CTIMEOUT timer is reloaded, **K** is doubled, and the algorithm goes to Step 3. The value of **retry_count** is reinitialized.

6. If no packets are received after **K**\*WTIMER seconds, then **retry_count** is decremented, **K** is doubled, and the algorithm goes to Step 3.

7. If at any point during the algorithm either **retry_count** reaches 0 or CTIMEOUT expires, the context is aborted.

A successful synchronizing handshake ensures that the sender knows the current state of the remote endpoint. Control information can thus be updated and data retransmitted accordingly. The use of CNTL packets to perform a synchronizing handshake avoids the problem of repeatedly retransmitted data further loading an already congested network.

## 4.7.5 Time-to-Live

Each packet contains a 4-byte time-to-live (*ttl*) field that is used to restrict the lifetime of the packet in the network. A packet that becomes lost or has been held indefinitely may appear after the information contained within it is no longer useful. Certain error recovery procedures depend upon the assumption that packets lost for a certain amount of time will remain lost. The *ttl* mechanism is the means by which this network-wide guarantee can be met.

The *ttl* field contains a value that represents the maximum lifetime of the packet in units of 100 nanoseconds. The value used should reflect the estimated propagation time between the endpoints of the association. As the packet is forwarded from one intermediate node to another, the *ttl* value in that packet is decremented by an estimation of the amount of time that the packet spent in the node. If a node decrements the *ttl* value and that value becomes zero or less, the packet is discarded.

The time-to-live procedure may be turned off by setting the value of the *ttl* field to zero at the originating context. If a node receives a packet with a *ttl* value of exactly zero, the node does not decrement the value, but rather processes the packet normally.

## 4.7.6 Error Notification

An important aspect of the error control procedures is the ability to detect errors and subsequently initiate various procedures transparent to the XTP user to recover from these errors. However, some errors are not transparently recoverable, and hence the association or path can not be built or maintained. The use of DIAG packets is designed to provide notification by one XTP implementation to a remote XTP implementation of such error conditions. In all situations, the protocol will eventually recover from error conditions even if DIAG packets are not utilized. However, DIAG packets are used to provide error notification in a more timely and informative manner.

A DIAG packet is issued in response to an incoming packet that could not be properly processed. Any intermediate node or endpoint may issue a DIAG packet since such errors may occur at any node along the path. Table 4.4 shows the possible values for the *code* field of the DIAG packet (Table 6.2 elaborates further). An XTP implementation receiving a DIAG packet will take some action according to these *code* values, possibly including notification of the XTP user since the conditions causing DIAG packet generation may be unrecoverable without XTP user intervention.

The initiating context may receive a DIAG packet during association establishment. A DIAG packet containing *code* = 2 indicates that the destination host could not or would not activate a context to be used as the destination endpoint for the association. For example, this may happen when an **input** command at the destination host does not precede the **output** command at the initiating host, or the NOFLOW indication is rejected. The *code* value in the DIAG packet is 3 when there is difficulty finding the proper destination host. This *code* = 3 DIAG packet is generated by the switch that could not locate the destination host. It is possible that the destination host exists but

| Value of *code* field | Message Category |
|:---:|:---|
| 1 | Invalid context |
| 2 | Context refused |
| 3 | Unknown destination |
| 4 | Dead host |
| 5 | Invalid route |
| 6 | Redirect; use a different switch |
| 7 | Can not route/forward |
| 8 | No resource |
| 9 | Protocol error |
| 10 | MTU size error, can not forward FIRST packet |

**Table 4.4 — DIAG Packet *code* Values**

the switch serving it knows that host has failed; the DIAG packet contains *code* = 4 in this case. If a switch can not process the Address Segment, or some unspecified protocol error occurs during association establishment, the DIAG packet received by the initiating context contains a *code* value of 9. A switch may not forward the FIRST packet because the *maxdata* field in the Address Segment indicates that the transmitter may send packets whose size exceeds the maximum transmission size of the subnetwork attached to the switch; in this case, the switch sends the initiating endpoint a DIAG packet with *code* value 10.

After an association and the path used by that association are established, a context may receive a DIAG packet indicating one of several error conditions. A DIAG packet with *code* = 1 indicates that the destination context no longer exists. A DIAG packet with *code* = 4 signals that the destination host has apparently failed. The *code* value is 5 if a switch does not recognize the *route* value in the incoming packet, or if the path is in the midst of path release procedures. When a switch on the path refuses to forward a packet on that path, it sends a DIAG packet with *code* = 6 or *code* = 7, depending upon the status of the router. A DIAG packet with *code* = 8 signals the lack of some resource required to build or maintain the association or path. An invalid request for retransmission also causes the generation of a DIAG packet with *code* = 9.

During association release, one context may become quiescent while packets remain outstanding. If such an outstanding packet arrives at a host after the context has been released, the host issues a DIAG packet with *code* = 1 since the context is no longer valid. As noted above, the failure to process a packet causes a DIAG packet to be generated with the *code* value indicating the nature of the failure.

The atomic entity within the workings of XTP, and indeed any transport layer protocol, is the packet. A *packet* is a bounded-length protocol data unit that contains all of the mechanisms for transferring data and state information from one endpoint of an association, through all of the intermediate switches, to the other endpoint or group of endpoints.[1] The *fields* within the packets provide these mechanisms; how these fields are assigned and interpreted, and under what conditions packets are transferred, define the protocol.

We have seen how the protocol procedure rules use the various packet formats and the information contained within their structures to provide reliable and efficient transfer of data. In this chapter, we examine each field in the various XTP packet formats, providing the syntax for the information contained therein. As well as being a syntax presentation, this discussion motivates the design and layout of these fundamental building blocks of XTP.

## 5.1   Introduction

There are three segments to an XTP packet: the packet *Header*, the packet *Trailer*, and a *Middle Segment*. Figure 5.1 shows the XTP packet and its constituent segments. The Header and Trailer are both fixed format with big-endian byte order and widths of 40 and 4 bytes, respectively. The Header contains some information about what kind of packet it heads, and this information determines the actions necessary for parsing the Middle Segment. The various fields in the Header and Trailer carry state information most often necessary for any packet format. The Middle Segment, then, carries format-specific information, which can be additional state information, address information, user data, or protocol data.

In XTP both the Header and Trailer are fixed syntax and fixed length. Also, the Header, Trailer, and Middle Segment are all constructed to be aligned on 4-byte boundaries. This doctrine of fixed syntax, fixed length, and 4-byte alignment greatly eases the task of creating a packet to send and parsing it once received.

---

[1] **In this discussion, we will refer to the receiver set in the singular for simplicity, although it should be noted that in XTP almost everything that can involve the single receiver can also involve a group of receivers under multicast. Chapters 4 and 8 include discussion on multicast and group communication issues.**

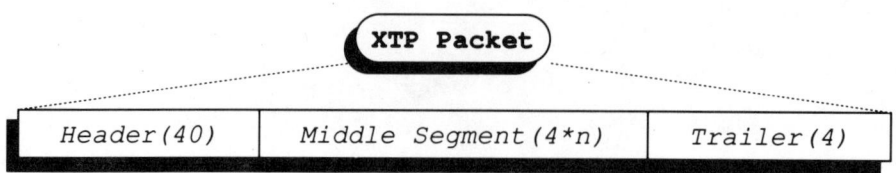

**Figure 5.1 — General XTP Packet Structure**

## 5.1.1 Notation Convention

Throughout this text we adhere to conventions concerning the naming and typeface of the various components of the packets. We also make certain assumptions about the data layout, which are stated below for the sake of precision. These conventions remain mostly faithful to the conventions stated in the XTP Definition.

- The bits in a field are numbered right to left from least significant to most significant, starting with 0, unless otherwise stated.
- Likewise, the bytes of a field are numbered right-to-left from least significant to most significant, unless otherwise stated.
- Bytes are assumed to be transmitted in a left-to-right order. Within the bytes, the bits are transmitted in a left-to-right order as well.
- The values contained in a field are assumed to be unsigned integers unless otherwise stated. Integers are assumed to be 4 bytes wide.
- A field name and the value associated with that field are given in italic font (e.g., *key* field and the *key* value).
- Single bits or bit groups within a field are identified by their bit position (e.g., the most significant bit of the *key* field is bit number 31).
- The number of bytes in a field is given by the number in parentheses (e.g., "key(4)" means that the *key* field is 4 bytes wide).
- The number of bits in a field is given by the number following the field name and a colon (e.g., "pformat:5" means that the *pformat* subfield is 5 bits wide).
- Bits are named using all capital letters in courier font (e.g., the BTAG bit from the *options* field in the Header).
- The terms "set" and "clear" will be used to indicate that a particular bit is given the value of 1 or 0 respectively.

## 5.1.2 Segments

A *segment* is a portion of a packet that can be grouped into one identifiable unit and suggests a high-level format for its contents. A segment may be recursively defined in terms of other segments, as shown in Figure 5.2.

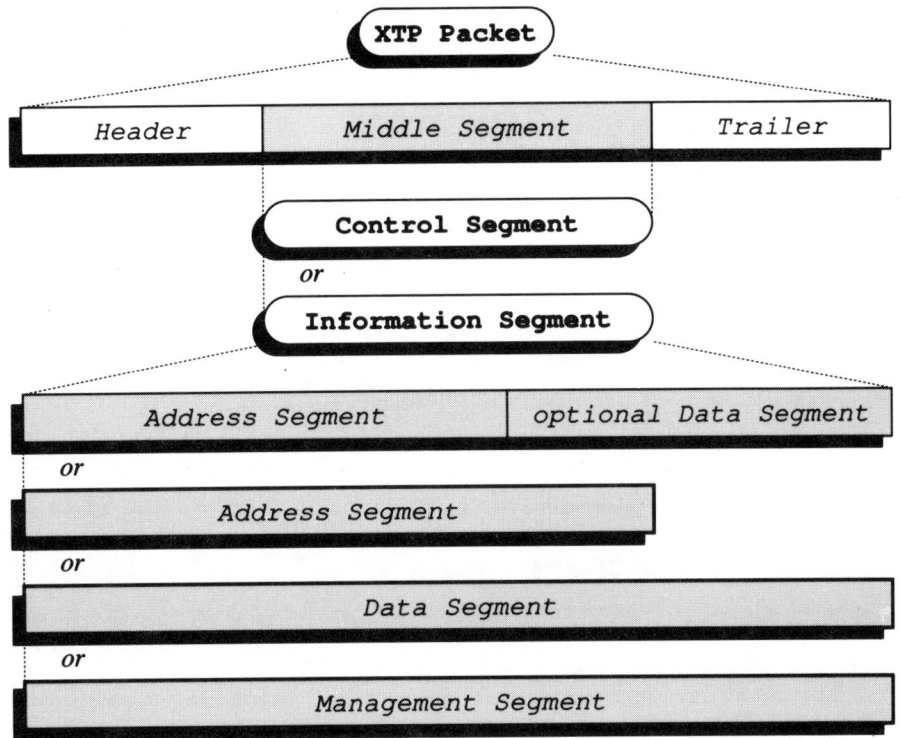

**Figure 5.2 — Composite Segments within the XTP Packet Structure**

An XTP packet has three main segments: the Header, the Trailer, and the Middle Segment. The packet is so partitioned to make it clear that the information contained in each of the segments is related by function; the information in the Header pertains primarily to the identification of the packet, the information in the Trailer pertains to the correctness and validity of the packet, and the information in the Middle Segment pertains to the "cargo" of the packet. The Header and Trailer are fixed format and syntax, which presents obvious advantages in parsing these segments. The Middle Segment, however, must be variable to allow it to encompass the various uses of a packet. Therefore, the Middle Segment consists of one of two segment formats, the Control Segment format or the Information Segment format. The Information Segment also consists of one or more segments. Figure 5.2 shows an XTP packet with its composite segments.

The Control Segment provides the mechanisms to communicate any necessary state information from one protocol state machine to another. Such information includes data reception status, rate and flow control parameters, context and route identifiers, and values used to synchronize state machines. The state machines exchanging this information may be at endpoints of an association or within the switches between the endpoints. The format of the Control Segment is fixed, although not all packets that employ the Control Segment place a meaningful value in each of the fields or utilize all of the fields. Even though the format is fixed, the length is variable since one of the fields has variable length.

The Information Segment provides mechanisms for communication of user or protocol data, rather than protocol state information. If the data is provided by the user as payload, it remains uninspected and uninterpreted from end to end. If the data is protocol-provided, such as diagnostic or managerial information, it may be both examined by the protocol as well as given to the user. Also included within this segment is a mechanism for providing addressing information. The Information Segment is therefore composed of subsegments for each special purpose.

User data is placed in a format called a Data Segment. Addressing is likewise placed in a format called an Address Segment. Three variations of the Information Segment format are combinations of these two subsegments: an Address Segment along with a Data Segment, an Address Segment alone, and a Data Segment alone. The fourth variation of the Information Segment is the Management Segment, used specifically for the protocol-provided data exchange; it never contains an Address Segment or a user-provided Data Segment.

## 5.2   XTP Header

All XTP packets contain a common group of fields called the packet Header. Figure 5.3 shows the breakdown of the Header into its ten 4-byte fields. The *route* field associates this packet with a cut-through path within each switch between the endpoints. A *time-to-live* (*ttl*) field indicates the packet's expected worst-case delivery time, after which the packet will be discarded. The packet's format, as well as other command information, is contained in the *command* (*cmd*) field. This field is used to identify the packet by format so that the packet information can be parsed properly. The *key* field is used to identify this packet and associate it with a particular context. The *synchronize* (*sync*) field is used to associate status requests with the status responses. The *sequence*

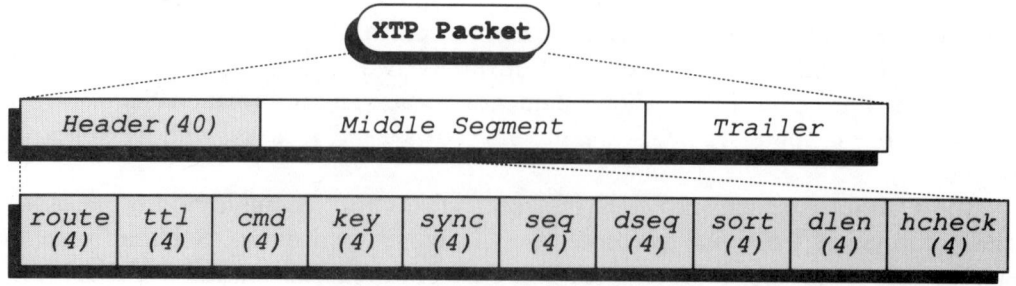

**Figure 5.3 — XTP Header Fields**

*number* (*seq*) field identifies where the data fits within the data stream. The *delivered sequence number* (*dseq*) field indicates how much data has been received and delivered to the XTP user. The eighth field is the *sort* field; it communicates the packet's priority for use within endpoints and switches, and at the destination XTP user. The length of the Middle Segment, excluding alignment bytes, is given next in the *data length* (*dlen*) field. Finally, the *header checksum* (*hcheck*) field contains the checksum over the Header.

## 5.2.1 Route Field (*route*)

When a FIRST packet establishes an association, it threads a path through a set of switches between the endpoints of the association. If this association happens to have endpoints on the same local network, then there are no intermediate switches, and the path is trivial. However, since the general network topology includes several local networks interconnected via switches, an XTP packet must be able to thread its way through this mesh to its destination. Once threaded, the path remains in place since over the lifetime of an association there may be many packets traveling in both directions. The *route* field is the primary mechanism in an XTP packet used to establish and identify the path between endpoints.

XTP uses a technique called *cut-through switching*, where the FIRST packet "cuts" a path between endpoints by leaving a trail of references at each intermediate node (switch) along the path. A *route* value is generated for the FIRST packet at the initiating context. This value uniquely identifies the host exit port used by this context for sending this and all subsequent packets. By using the addressing information within the FIRST packet's Address Segment, the packet is delivered to the first switch. This switch notes the received packet's *route* value, and associates that value with both the initiating host's MAC address and a new *route* value that the switch itself generates as its unique exit port identifier. The packet, now containing the new *route* value, is forwarded to the next switch, and the procedure is repeated. At the destination host the final *route* value is noted for use in sending packets back along the reverse path.

A *route* value is a 32-bit unsigned integer with the most significant bit (MSB) always cleared. The MSB of the route value is set to denote a *return route* value. If the destination host has packets to send to the initiating host, it uses a *return route* value as follows. Since the destination context has noted the *route* value of the packets it received, it sends packets in the reverse direction using a *return route* value consisting of the low order 31 bits of the *route* value and with the MSB set. The packet is sent to the first switch in the return path, which recognizes that the *return route* value is related to the *route* value it generated in the forward path direction. This switch finds the address and *route* value of the next switch, and sends the packet to that switch with that switch's *return route* value. This is continued until the packet reaches the initiating host via the return path. The *return route* procedure is explored more thoroughly in Chapter 6; for now, we offer the following example.

**Example 5.1**

Consider the two hosts and the two switches as shown in Figure 5.4. The initiating context in Host A generates *route* value $R_A$ in sending the FIRST packet to Switch B enroute to Host D. Switch B associates this *route* value with the MAC address of Host A, and then generates a new *route* value, $R_B$, which is a unique exit port identifier within Switch B. Switch C does likewise, generating $R_C$. The path from Host A to Host D, then, is the ordered sequence of *route* values $(R_A, R_B, R_C)$. Note that any packet sent from Host A to Host D can use this path by simply putting the value $R_A$ in its *route* field. Once the packet is received by Host D, it is given to the proper destination context using the *key* value.

If the path in the forward direction is designated as $R$, then let us designate the path in the return direction as $R'$, i.e., the return path is the ordered sequence of return route values $(R'_C, R'_B, R'_A)$. Any packets generated by the destination context in Host D to be delivered to the context in Host A uses the return route value for Switch C, which is $R'_C$.

*Route* values must be aged before they can be reused so that a packet is not delivered to the host associated with an old *route* value. The XTP Definition suggests that the *route* values be the concatenation of an *index* and an *instance*, in a manner similar to the scheme suggested in the next section for *key* values. A path is not necessarily torn down when an association is discontinued in order to allow the efficiency of having a host use an existing path for a new association, instead of forcing the threading of a new path for each association. The ROUTE packet is designed to remove the path information when a path is no longer in use, after which the *route* value is aged until there is no possibility of confusion.

## 5.2.2 Time-to-Live Field (*ttl*)

The 4-byte *ttl* field contains a value that indicates the amount of time that this packet is to remain valid while in the network. As a packet traverses a network, it may become

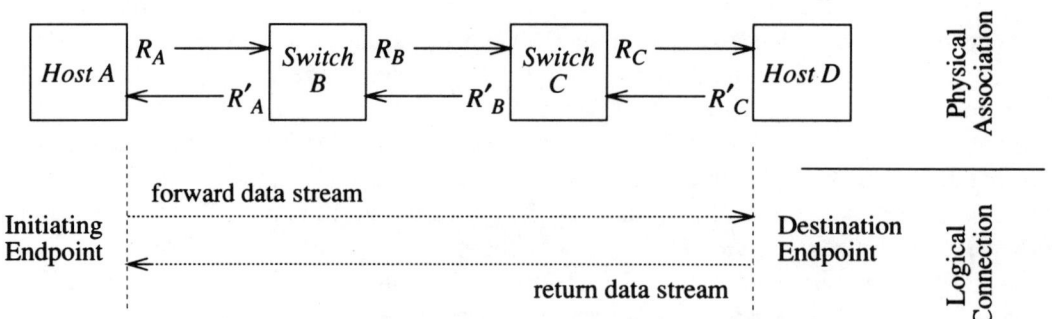

**Figure 5.4 — A Path Created Via *route* Values**

lost or misdirected. It is important that the packet not reappear arbitrarily far into the future when it may confuse an XTP end-system with identifiers thought to have been properly aged and discarded. Therefore an expiration mechanism, namely the *ttl* field, is used to remove extraordinarily old packets.

The value in the *ttl* field is a signed integer representing some number of 100 nanosecond clock ticks. This value is decremented at every intermediate node along the path by an amount reflecting the amount of time it took to process the packet. Each time the packet is processed, the processing time, the time spent waiting in queues, and the network propagation time are added together and decremented from the value in the *ttl* field. If the exact amount of time to decrement is not known, some approximation of the processing time is used.

The algorithm for discarding a packet dictates that every intermediate node check the *ttl* field first. If this value is greater than zero, then the packet is processed and the decrement is made before forwarding the packet. If the value after decrement is zero or less, the packet is discarded. If, however, the value of the *ttl* field is equal to zero upon arrival, then the intermediate node recognizes that this is a special case and does not perform the decrement. The special case of a *ttl* value of zero assigned by the packet's originator indicates that the packet is not subject to aging.

## 5.2.3 Command Field (*cmd*)

The *cmd* field encodes four kinds of information within three subfields: (1) the various protocol options chosen by the association endpoint that generates the packet, (2) the number of bytes of offset before the beginning of user data (if any is present), (3) the format for the remainder of this packet, and (4) the version number of the XTP protocol used by the XTP implementation generating the packet. Figure 5.5 shows the three subfields of *cmd*: the *options* subfield, the *offset* subfield, and the *ptype* subfield.

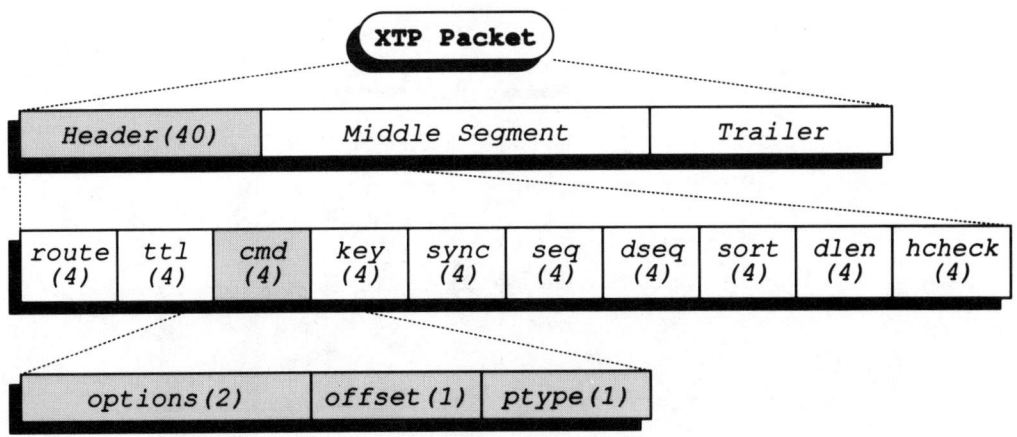

**Figure 5.5 — Command Subfields in the XTP Header**

## Protocol Options Subfield (*options*)

The *options* subfield is a bit field 2 bytes wide with 14 bits defined. These options control many service features of the protocol. Each option may be independently set, although some options preclude others. Some options are termed "modes" since they indicate that the association will be governed by a specific policy. Others are used to indicate a request for the generation of a CNTL packet, to indicate the stage of a graceful disconnect, and to mark certain points in the data stream. Figure 5.6 shows these bits and how they are arranged in the *options* subfield.

The NOCHECK bit (for NO CHECKsum), when set, disables the XTP checksum over the entire Middle Segment. The data checksum field *dcheck* in the Trailer, therefore, does not contain a valid value when NOCHECK is set. The NOCHECK bit may be set at any time during the association since its effects are localized to a single packet.

There are 4 mode bits which indicate that certain conditions are to apply for this data transfer. The NOERR bit indicates that "NO-ERRor mode" is in effect. When set, it turns off certain error recovery procedures at the receiver. The MULTI bit indicates the use of "MULTIcast mode." This bit informs each member of the association that it is not the sole recipient of the information in this packet, and that multicast heuristics and policy are in effect. The RES bit indicates "REServation mode." Reservation mode requires the receiver to throttle the transmitter such that the transmitter never sends more data than will fit in the buffer space reserved at the receiver specifically for this association. This feature prevents overrun of the XTP buffer space at the receiver by requiring a conservative flow control policy. The NOFLOW bit indicates "NO-FLOW mode;" the transmitter can ignore flow control constraints on its outgoing data stream.

Packets may be prioritized by placing a priority value in the appropriate field in the Header; the SORT bit indicates that the value in the *sort* field is valid and is to be interpreted as a packet's priority. Packets are SORTed, or ordered, according to this value. Packets with the SORT bit clear are said to be "unsorted," and are always handled after sorted packets.

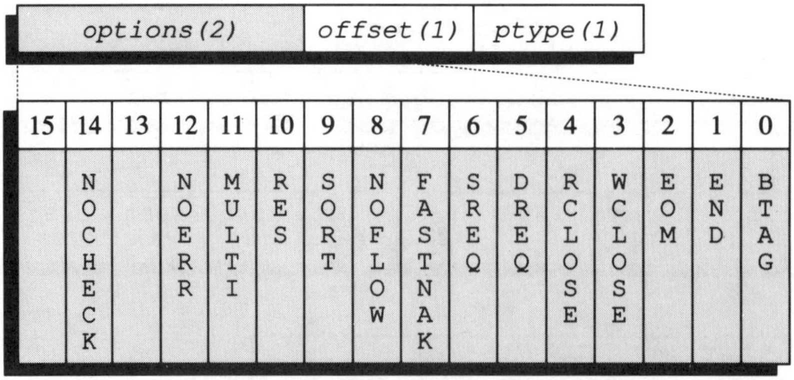

Figure 5.6 — Bits within the *options* Subfield

The FASTNAK bit indicates that a receiver should generate a FAST Negative ACKnowledgement immediately if out-of-sequence data is detected. This is an aggressive strategy designed for those networks that either never or very seldom reorder packets, and hence out-of-sequence data implies that some data has been lost. The value of this bit is ignored when the NOERR bit is set since it does not make sense to have an aggressive retransmission scheme when retransmissions are suppressed.

The SREQ and DREQ bits are used to request the generation of a CNTL packet from an association endpoint. The SREQ bit is the immediate Status REQuest and requires the host receiving a packet with SREQ set to provide an immediate report of its status by issuing a CNTL packet. The DREQ bit likewise requires the receiving host to respond, but only after any data currently enqueued at the receiving endpoint is actually delivered to the XTP user. The issuing of a CNTL packet is thus delayed until the Delivered status REQuest can be honored.

Setting the WCLOSE and RCLOSE bits indicates that the issuing context is closing either the WRITER process, the READER process, or both (recall the WRITER and READER process abstractions from Chapter 2). The WCLOSE bit, for WRITER CLOSEd, means that the side of the context writing the data stream as output to the network is closing operation. Likewise, the RCLOSE bit, for READER CLOSEd, signifies that the side of the context that is reading from the network is closing operation. A context that has both WRITER and READER processes closed has shut off all user data exchange functions and can not respond to packets with new data.

The EOM bit marks a particular point in the data stream as the End Of Message. A message is an arbitrarily long amount of data, and the last byte of user data in the Data Segment of the Information Segment of a data-bearing packet with the EOM bit set is thus marked as the last byte in the message. This mark is indicated to the XTP user. The association, of course, can transfer an arbitrary number of messages during its lifetime.

Carried in the last packet being sent by one endpoint of the association, the END bit signifies the END of the association; that is, the context setting the END bit is being released. At this point the association is considered terminated. The WCLOSE, RCLOSE, and END bits work in concert, according to the handshaking procedures we have seen in Chapter 4, to provide a range of association termination semantics.

When set, the BTAG bit (for Beginning TAG) indicates that the first 8 bytes of user data in the Data Segment of a packet are "tagged." This tagging is not interpreted by XTP; the user is simply notified of the fact that the data is tagged, and it is the responsibility of the user to know how to interpret tagged data.

## User Data Offset Subfield (*offset*)

The *offset* subfield indicates the number of bytes of padding that come before the user data when data is present in an Information Segment. Certain machine architectures can not easily do byte addressing of memory, and when user data does not begin on a natural 4- or 8-byte boundary, an additional data copy is required. Also, some underlying networks require packets of at least a minimum size. The *offset* field can be used to extend a packet to meet this minimum size requirement, or for an alignment that enables efficient data copying. The *offset* field specifies those bytes in a Middle Segment which are padding and may be discarded. The valid range of values in the *offset* field is 0 to 255.

## Packet Type Subfield (*ptype*)

The *ptype* subfield contains two pieces of information, as shown in Figure 5.7. The *pformat* subfield specifies the format of this XTP packet. This subfield is the low-order five bits of the field. The next two higher-order bits specify the XTP protocol version number.

There are nine formats for XTP packets, two of which specify that the Middle Segment be a Control Segment; the remaining seven specify that the Middle Segment be an Information Segment. Table 5.1 shows the formats that correspond to the various values of the pformat subfield. The packets containing the Control Segment have odd *pformat* values, and those containing the Information Segment have even *pformat* values. We have seen how some of these packet formats are used in the protocol procedures of Chapter 4, and in Chapter 6 we will present each of these formats in detail. Briefly, the DATA packet is used to exchange user data. The CNTL packet facilitates protocol status exchanges between endpoints. The FIRST packet is used to initiate the association; it may carry data as well. The PATH packet rethreads a new path between endpoints of an existing association when the old path becomes unusable or undesirable. The DIAG packet permits fault notifications. The MAINT and MGMT packets are as yet undefined, but will be used to disseminate network maintenance and management information in future versions of the protocol. The ROUTE packet is used to release a path, and the RCNTL packet is used to help maintain the path through status and parameter exchanges between intermediate nodes.

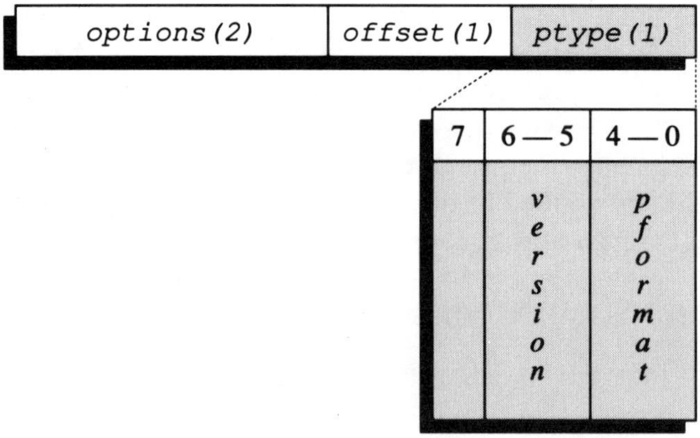

**Figure 5.7 — Subfields In the *ptype* Field**

| Packet Format | Segment Format | pformat subfield value | |
|---|---|---|---|
| | | Decimal | Hex |
| DATA | Information Segment (Data Segment) | 0 | 0x00 |
| CNTL | Control Segment | 1 | 0x01 |
| FIRST | Information Segment (Address Segment or Address and Data Segments) | 2 | 0x02 |
| PATH | Information Segment (Address Segment) | 6 | 0x06 |
| DIAG | Information Segment (Management Segment) | 8 | 0x08 |
| MAINT | (undefined) | 10 | 0x0A |
| MGMT | (undefined) | 14 | 0x0E |
| ROUTE | Information Segment (Management Segment) | 18 | 0x12 |
| RCNTL | Control Segment | 19 | 0x13 |

**Table 5.1 — Packet Formats**

The fifth and sixth bits of the *ptype* subfield are used to identify the version number of XTP being used. The version number will be useful in determining backward compatibility for future releases and evolutions of XTP. For now, no protocol processing depends upon the version number.

## 5.2.4 Key Field (*key*)

When an XTP user directs the creation of an association, the underlying XTP implementation instantiates a context that will serve as the initiating endpoint of the association. A new *key* value is generated that uniquely identifies this context among all contexts active within this host. This *key* value, carried in the *key* field of the FIRST packet, indicates to the receiver of the FIRST packet the *key* field value for all returning packets for this association. Specifically, the *key* value in returning packets will be a slightly modified form of the original *key* value. This slightly modified *key* value, placed in all returning packets, is called a *return key*, and the originating host knows how to associate packets containing it with the proper context. A *key* value is 32 bits long, with the most significant bit (MSB) always cleared; the *return key* has the same value in the low-order 31 bits, but the MSB is set.

The receiving host activates a waiting context for the association upon receipt of the FIRST packet. A new *key* value is generated for this context so that it can be uniquely identified among all contexts within this host, as was done for the context in the initiating host. This value, in the form of a *return key*, may be sent to the originating host to indicate that all subsequent packets to this receiver can use this *return key* value in their *key* fields. The process of a receiver communicating its key to the transmitter is called a *key exchange* as explained in Chapter 4.

It is essential that *key* values be unique within a host since they identify active contexts. An inactive *key* value must be aged a proper amount of time to ensure that the context to which it previously referred has been deactivated. Aging an inactive *key* value at least twice the maximum lifetime of a packet before reuse is considered adequate (see the Delta-t discussion in Section 3.2).

The XTP Definition suggests that a *key* be the concatenation of two values, an *index* value and an *instance* counter value in order to ensure uniqueness of *key* values. The index selects the context by indexing into the context memory space. The instance counter is incremented for each instantiation of that context.

## 5.2.5 Synchronize Field (*sync*)

The *synchronize* field (*sync*) has two functions. First, it is used to carry a unique value in the forward direction which, when that value is returned in the *echo* field of a CNTL packet, suggests that the sending and receiving protocol state machines are in synchronization. This field, along with the *echo* field, is used to perform the synchronizing handshake described in Section 4.7.4.

The second function of the *sync* field within a packet is to help disambiguate the sequence number associated with this packet. As described below, the sequence number field is 32 bits wide; under continuous transmission at 1 gigabit per second this sequence space is exhausted after only 4 seconds. The *sync* values, like the sequence numbers, are defined to be monotonically increasing, but they wrap much less frequently, so a wrap in the sequence number space can be detected by also examining the *sync* value.

The *sync* value, as mentioned, is defined to be monotonically increasing. More specifically, the *sync* value at an endpoint must be advanced for each data-bearing packet with SREQ set, including retransmissions. If the *sync* value advances one per data-bearing packet, then the value represents a packet count. A clock time (whose encoding is implementation-dependent) may also be used.

## 5.2.6 Sequence Number Field (*seq*)

The *sequence number* field (*seq*) is the mechanism by which bytes within a data stream are correctly ordered and identified. A data stream is an arbitrarily long sequence of addressing information and user data that is propagated from one association endpoint to another. Each byte in the data stream is "counted" and, consequently, is assigned a *sequence number* to uniquely identify that byte in the data stream and to ensure proper sequencing. The range of numbers used as sequence numbers constitutes a *sequence number space*, and each byte that has a sequence number to identify it is said to *consume* some of that space. The *seq* field is 32 bits wide, so the sequence number space representable in XTP is 0 to $2^{32}-1$. If the data stream consumes the sequence number $2^{32}-1$, then the next sequence number is 0.

The *seq* field has two purposes, one for use with FIRST and DATA packets, and one for use in CNTL and PATH packets. One use of the value within the *seq* field is for identifying the first byte of the countable information carried in a FIRST or DATA packet. If the packet is a FIRST packet, then the *seq* value is the sequence number of the first byte of the Address Segment. If the packet is a DATA packet, the value in the *seq* field is the sequence number of the first byte of user data (i.e., it does not include the padding bytes indicated by the *offset* field). Also, the bytes counted in the sequence space do not include the bytes that must be added at the end of the Middle Segment to ensure the Trailer begins on the next 4-byte boundary. (In any relevant discussion or figures, these bytes will be called *alignment* bytes. Note that there are never more than 3 alignment bytes.) Figure 5.8 shows the part of a packet that is covered by the sequence numbers. The value of the *seq* field and the length of the Middle Segment (provided by the *dlen* field in the Header) determine a mapping of bytes to sequence numbers for every countable byte in the packet.

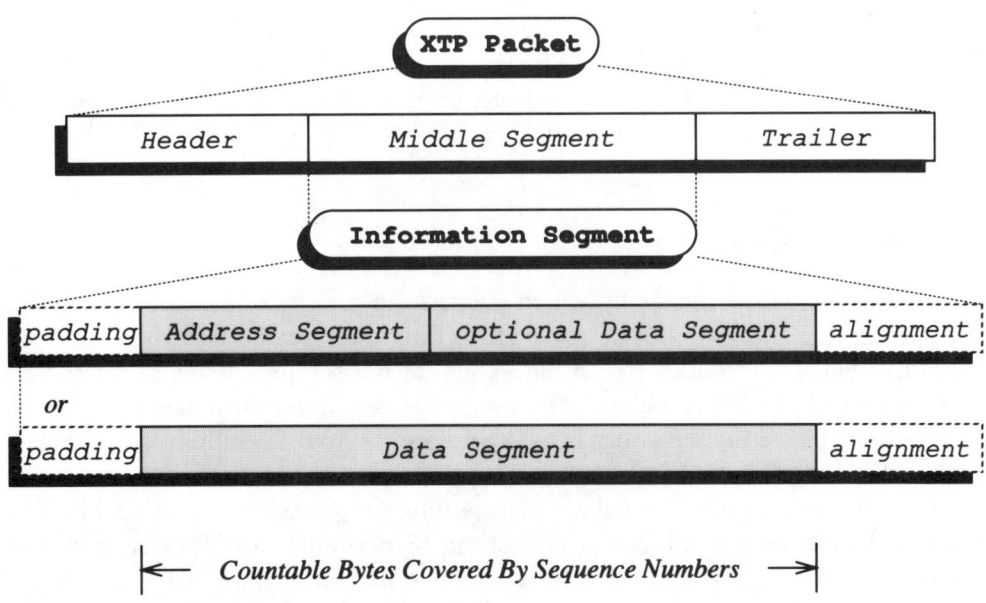

**Figure 5.8 — Bytes Consuming Sequence Number Space in an XTP Packet**

For CNTL packets, the *seq* field value is used to identify the next byte expected on the incoming data stream. The *seq* value in a CNTL packet informs the context receiving the CNTL packet of the highest sequence number received at the context issuing the CNTL packet. Recall that the *seq* field figures prominently in the discussion on data transfer and error control procedures in Chapter 4.

The *seq* field value is interpreted for a PATH packet in the same way as it is for a CNTL packet, and thus refers to the next expected sequence number on this data stream. PATH packets do not consume sequence numbers. Even though the PATH packet contains an Address Segment, its Address Segment does not directly affect the data stream. PATH packets are used to rethread a new path between the endpoints of an association; the *seq* value is useful in preserving data stream information during the rethreading of a path. No other packet formats use or interpret the *seq* field since they do not carry or identify countable bytes for a data stream.

## 5.2.7 Delivered Sequence Number Field (*dseq*)

The *dseq* field indicates the last byte of user data that was delivered to the receiving XTP user. The value contained in the *dseq* field is actually one greater than this last byte's sequence number; hence the value is really the sequence number of the *next* byte expected to be delivered to the XTP user. The XTP receiver uses *dseq* to indicate to the transmitter what data it can free from its buffer space without fear that this data will ever be requested for retransmission.

The *dseq* field has another interpretation as well. When no data has been received on the incoming data stream, the FIRST packet can dictate what initial sequence number should be used on the return data stream. As long as no data arrives at the initiating context, the *dseq* field of outgoing packets will continue to carry the proposed starting sequence number for the return data stream.

## 5.2.8 Sort Field (*sort*)

The *sort* field provides a means by which packets are prioritized so that some packets receive preferential treatment. The *sort* field is only interpreted when the SORT bit in the *options* field is set. Packets with the SORT bit not set are always processed after those packets with the SORT bit set. The *sort* value is a 32-bit unsigned integer, where smaller values denote higher priority. As there are $2^{32}$ (over 4 billion) priority levels available, the *sort* field provides an extensive prioritization capability.

The XTP user sets the *sort* value when issuing output commands to XTP. These output commands are queued in first-in first-out (FIFO) order. As they are processed, the context assumes the *sort* value of the current command being processed. All packets generated as a consequence of the current **output** command have the *sort* value of that command placed in their *sort* fields. The XTP implementation chooses the context having packets with the highest priority (lowest integer *sort* value) to process next.

Packets are thereby ordered as they are presented to the MAC layer. Packets are processed in *sort* value order in all switches along the path and, upon reception at the destination endpoint, are again processed according to the *sort* value. The *sort* value associated with each packet is made available to the XTP user when that packet's data is delivered so that the *sort* value can be used (if desired) in an end-to-end scheduling scheme.

## 5.2.9 Data Length Field (*dlen*)

The *data length* field is a 32-bit unsigned integer field whose value indicates the number of bytes present in the Middle Segment. The *dlen* value includes any bytes specified by the *offset* field, but not alignment bytes, so the actual length of meaningful information within the Middle Segment is *dlen – offset* rounded down to a multiple of four. Since the meaningful information within the Middle Segment is not constrained to end on a 4-byte boundary, but the Trailer must begin on a 4-byte boundary, there may be 0, 1, 2, or 3 additional alignment bytes between the end of meaningful bytes in the Middle Segment and the beginning of the Trailer.

## 5.2.10 Header Checksum Field (*hcheck*)

The *hcheck* field contains the result of a mandatory checksum calculation over most of the Header fields. The *route* field and the *ttl* field are potentially modified at each switch along the path, and therefore are not included in this checksum. The checksum algorithm is described in Section 4.7.1.

# 5.3    XTP Trailer

The packet Trailer, like the packet Header, is a component of all XTP packets. Unlike the Header, however, the Trailer consists of a single field. Whereas the Header information pertains mostly to the format and parsing of the packet, the Trailer information is concerned with the packet processing that is best performed on the packet only after the Middle Segment is seen, namely the data integrity check. When a packet is generated, the checksum can be calculated as the packet is being streamed out onto the network and then appended to the end of the packet. When a packet is received, the checksumming procedure is performed as the packet is arriving, and then checked against the value in the Trailer. Figure 5.9 shows the XTP Trailer, which consists solely of the 4-byte *data checksum* (*dcheck*) field.

When the Middle Segment is an Information Segment with user data, the bytes used for padding are included in the checksum even though these bytes are disregarded otherwise. If the NOCHECK bit in the *options* field of the Header is set, then the value contained in the *dcheck* field remains uninterpreted.

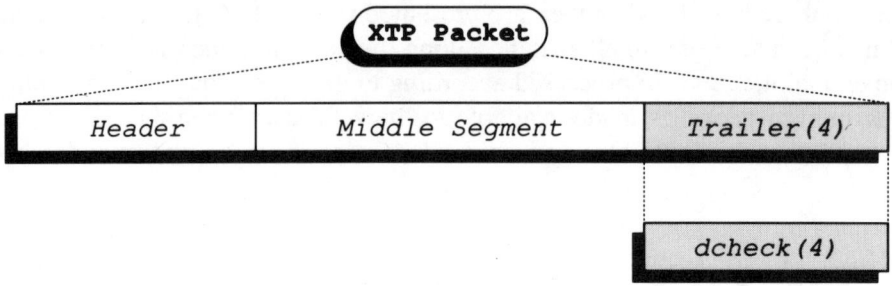

**Figure 5.9 — XTP Trailer Field**

# 5.4   Control Segment

The fields within the Control Segment represent the mechanisms that CNTL and
RCNTL packets employ to communicate protocol state information between protocol
state machines. Figure 5.10 shows the structure of the Control Segment. The *rate* and
*burst* fields carry the values that govern the rate control algorithms. The *echo* field
(along with the *sync* field of the Header) provides a method for synchronizing two state
machines. The *time* and *techo* fields are used for establishing roundtrip delays between
end-nodes. The *xkey* and *xroute* fields carry the key and route values used in establishing short handles for identifying contexts and the end-to-end routes between them. The
*alloc*, *rseq*, *nspan*, and *spans* fields carry values for the flow control and error recovery
procedures, providing received data information and retransmission request information. Two 4-byte fields, shown as *rsvd*, are left in reserve.

## 5.4.1 Rate Control Fields (*rate* and *burst*)

The *rate* field is the mechanism by which a node can specify the maximum rate that it
can process data from the transmitter. The transmitter must use this value to throttle its
WRITER process so as not to overrun the downstream nodes with data. The value of
the *rate* field represents the maximum number of bytes per second that the transmitter
can send on average over a period of time. The *rate* value, therefore, dictates a spacing
between bursts of data. Since the protocol operates on packets rather than individual
bytes, this spacing must be translated from bytes per second into a number of packets
per time interval. The *burst* field contains the maximum number of bytes that a node
can handle in any single packet burst. The values in these two fields define the rate
control parameters imposed on the transmitter by explicit values sent back from the
downstream nodes or by default values.

  The transmitter is allowed to transmit the number of bytes in the *burst* field as a
single continuous transmission of one or more packets. Then the transmitter must wait
for a period of time (*burst/rate* seconds) before another such burst of data may be

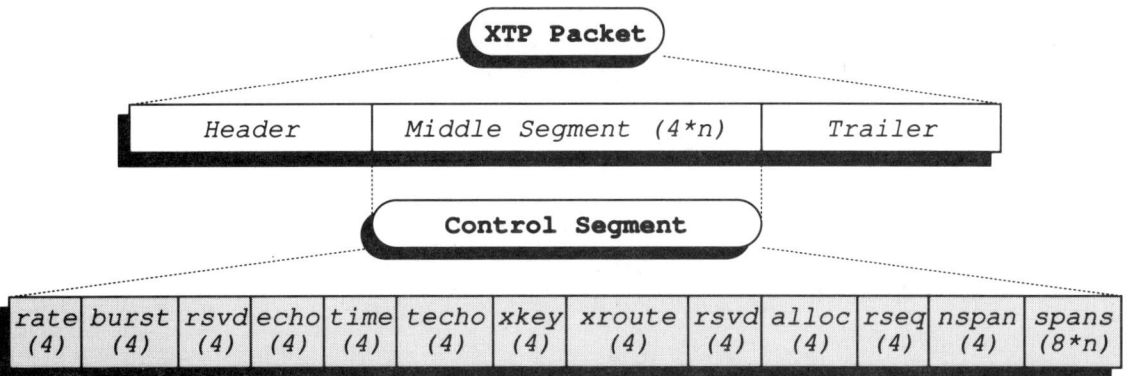

**Figure 5.10 — Control Segment Structure**

transmitted. The rate control algorithm and more detailed discussion of the uses of the *rate* and *burst* values were given in Section 4.6.

## 5.4.2 Synchronize Echo Field (*echo*)

The *echo* field of the Control Segment along with the *sync* field of the Header are used to synchronize protocol state machines by sending and recognizing synchronizing values. Since both endpoints of an association can send and receive packets, any received packet's *sync* value is copied into the *echo* field of the next outgoing CNTL packet. The *echo* field returns the *sync* value back to its originator so that the originator can make certain assumptions about the state of the corresponding protocol machine. When a *sync* value makes such a roundtrip, the endpoints are said to have completed a synchronizing handshake, as was discussed in Section 4.7.4.

## 5.4.3 Time Synchronization Fields (*time* and *techo*)

The *time* and *techo* fields are somewhat similar to the synchronizing fields *sync* and *echo* in that a value is sent in one field and then is returned via the other. The current value of the time at a sending host is placed into the *time* field of each outgoing CNTL packet, as with *sync* values. When a CNTL packet with SREQ bit set is received by the receiving context, it must copy the value of the *time* field into the *techo* field of the next outgoing CNTL packet. This must be the same outgoing CNTL packet used for carrying the *echo* value. When a sending context receives a CNTL packet as a response to the set SREQ, the value of the *techo* field is subtracted from the current time to give an estimated roundtrip time for packets. Since the *techo* value is only interpreted by the XTP implementations that place a value into the *time* field in the first place, there are no assumed units or standard interpretation of this timestamp. This estimated roundtrip time can be used, for example, in error detection procedures.

Either a data-bearing packet or a CNTL packet can have its SREQ bit set, and thereby cause the receiver to generate a CNTL packet. The *techo* field of CNTL packets generated as a result of a data-bearing packet's SREQ must be zero. A transmitter must check the *techo* value before using it to determine the roundtrip time; if the *techo* value is zero, no estimate is made.

The *time/techo* exchange is disabled if the transmitter puts a zero in the *time* field of an outgoing CNTL packet with its SREQ bit set. When this *time* value of zero is received, the receiver places the value zero into the *techo* field of the CNTL packet sent back to the transmitter.

## 5.4.4 Key Exchange Field (*xkey*)

The initiating endpoint (let us call this *C*) gets to choose a unique *key* value for the FIRST packet, which dictates to the receiving endpoint (let us call this *D*) that this *key* value, in the form of a *return key*, is to be in the *key* field of every packet returning to the initiator. Thus, in the *D*-to-*C* direction, a *return key* will always be in use. The *xkey* (exchange key) value is the equivalent of the *return key* for the *C*-to-*D* direction. If *D* places a value other than all zeros in the *xkey* field, then C stops using the original *key* value and begins using this new *xkey* value in the *key* field of all of *C*'s packets. Since the *xkey* value is to be used as a *return* key, it must have its most significant bit set, just as the *return key* values do. As described in Section 4.2.2, using the key exchange can substantially simplify the context lookup required for matching packets to their contexts.

## 5.4.5 Route Exchange Field (*xroute*)

In the same way that the *xkey* field allows the receiver on the forward path to specify what *key* value it would prefer the sender to use, the *xroute* field allows each receiving switch on the forward path to set the *route* value it would like used in packets forwarded to it. Each switch along the return path uses the *return route* value (derived from the *route* value it received) in packets forwarded along this return path. A switch may place a *return route* value in the *xroute* field of a packet traveling the return path, thus indicating to the next switch in the return path what *route* value should be used for packets sent in the forward path. Note that key exchange is always between two end-nodes whereas route exchange takes place on a hop-to-hop basis. After a route exchange, therefore, packets in both directions will carry *return route* values in their *route* fields. The full procedure for exchanging *route* values is given in Section 4.3.2.

## 5.4.6 Allocation Field (*alloc*)

The *alloc* field conveys to the transmitter the highest sequence number that the receiver is able to consume. In this way the receiver can impose flow control upon the transmitter. This value is set according to the amount of buffer space within the receiving XTP implementation. As a receiver frees buffer space, its *alloc* value will increase. A transmitter that has sent data up to and including the sequence number in the *alloc* field of the last CNTL packet seen must wait until a new *alloc* value carried in an incoming CNTL packet allows further data transfer.

When the "reservation mode" bit (RES) from the *options* field of the Header is set, the *alloc* value represents the amount of buffer space exclusively dedicated to this association. An XTP implementation may have some internal buffer space in addition to whatever buffers are provided by the user. In reservation mode the transmitter forbids the receiver from including any internal buffer space not dedicated to this association. The transmitter interprets the *alloc* value whether the RES bit is set or not, but a receiver in reservation mode is restricted to the conservative flow control policy of dedicated buffers.

## 5.4.7 Received Sequence Number Field (*rseq*)

The value in the *rseq* field is one plus the highest sequence number for which all bytes with smaller sequence numbers have been received on this data stream. The receiving side uses the *rseq* value in a CNTL packet to acknowledge receipt into XTP buffer space (but not necessarily XTP user buffer space) of contiguous data on the incoming data stream. The transmitting side uses the *rseq* information, along with other information within the CNTL packet, for retransmitting data on the outgoing data stream. There are three cases for examination: when all sent data has been correctly received, when some sent data is missing, and when no data has yet been sent on a data stream.

If the transmitting side receives a CNTL packet with the *rseq* value equal to the sequence number of the next byte that is enqueued for output at the transmitter, the transmitter can infer that no retransmissions are required since all data has correctly arrived at the destination context. This is the first case. The second case occurs if the *rseq* value from the CNTL packet is less than the sequence number of the next byte that the transmitter expects to send. Then the transmitter can infer that the receiver has not received all of the data sent, and some retransmission may be necessary. It is possible that the receiver receives data in non-contiguous groups. The *rseq* value in the CNTL packet must be set to the sequence number of the next byte expected; so it must be set to one greater than the last byte before the first missing data group. Such a group of missing data is called a *gap* in the receiver's incoming data stream. The *rseq* value and the values from the *spans* field, described in the next section, can inform the transmitter of one or more gaps.

The third case involves the setting of the *rseq* value when no data has arrived on the incoming data stream. Recall that the *dseq* field in the FIRST packet contains the requested starting sequence number for that context's incoming data stream. When the context that sent the FIRST packet has occasion to send a CNTL packet, it must decide what to place in the *rseq* field. If data has been received by this initiating context, the *rseq* value will indicate the next byte expected on this incoming data stream. If no data has been received on the incoming data stream, the *rseq* value is the same as the *dseq* value from the FIRST packet since this value is the starting sequence number requested for the incoming data stream.

## 5.4.8 Selective Retransmission Fields (*nspan* and *spans*)

The *nspan* field indicates how many 8-byte groups are present in the *spans* field. The 8-byte groups represent beginning and ending sequence numbers for received data in the incoming data stream. The "span" is a contiguous group of data; the *spans* field tells the transmitter which spans of data have been received after the first gap in the data stream. For each 8-byte group in the *spans* field, the first 4 bytes contain the beginning sequence number of the span, and the second four bytes contain the ending sequence number. The gaps in the data stream are determined from the spans of correctly received data. These gaps provide the necessary information for selectively retransmitting only that data which is necessary to bridge the spans.

Since *rseq* represents the first byte of the first gap, the beginning sequence number in the first span is one greater than the ending sequence number of the first gap. Each pair of spans thereafter identifies a gap in the data stream. If the transmitter's error recovery policy allows selective retransmissions, these gaps are made into individual DATA packets and sent with the appropriate sequence number in their *seq* fields. Whether and how selective retransmission is handled must be determined by each implementation; the *spans* field provides an enabling mechanism within the protocol. Further discussion about the error recovery policies and procedures was given in Section 4.7.

## 5.4.9 The Reserved Fields (*rsvd*)

Like other reserved fields in the packet structures, these *rsvd* fields are held for future use in case the protocol requires expanded, enhanced, or additional field space. They are not interpreted but must be transmitted as all bits cleared.

# 5.5   Information Segment

The Information Segment is the format for the Middle Segment that allows information exchange, as opposed to the Control Segment which facilitates state exchange. The Information Segment provides the mechanisms to allow users to transfer data. It also provides the mechanisms for the exchange of protocol-provided information in the form of condition codes, values, and messages.

There are four forms to the Information Segment: the Data Segment, the Address and Data Segments, the Address Segment alone, and the Management Segment. These forms are shown in Figure 5.11. The Address and Data Segments form is used for the FIRST packet since this packet format can carry user data while it is establishing the association. The second form, Address Segment alone, is used by a PATH packet to rethread a path when the one threaded by the FIRST packet becomes undesirable or unusable. Since a Data Segment is optional in the FIRST packet, the FIRST packet uses this form when it carries no data. The Data Segment is used for DATA packets and carries only user data. Finally, the Management Segment is used by the DIAG and ROUTE packets for communicating certain conditions, such as protocol errors or route release. This information has a special segment form because it is intended primarily for use by the protocol.

Since the Middle Segment must contain a multiple of 4 bytes of information, the Information Segment must ensure that its content meets this requirement. Since user data does not always start on a 4-byte boundary, the variable-size *padding* field allows the protocol to pad the beginning of the Information Segment so that the user data in the Data Segment starts on a 4-byte boundary. The size of the padding, which can range from 0 to 255 bytes, is given by the *offset* field in the Header. This *offset* value can also be used to extend a packet so that it meets the minimum packet size requirements of the underlying data delivery service.

Since the length of the user data may not be a 4-byte multiple, but the Trailer must start on the nearest 4-byte boundary following the end of data, there may be a need for

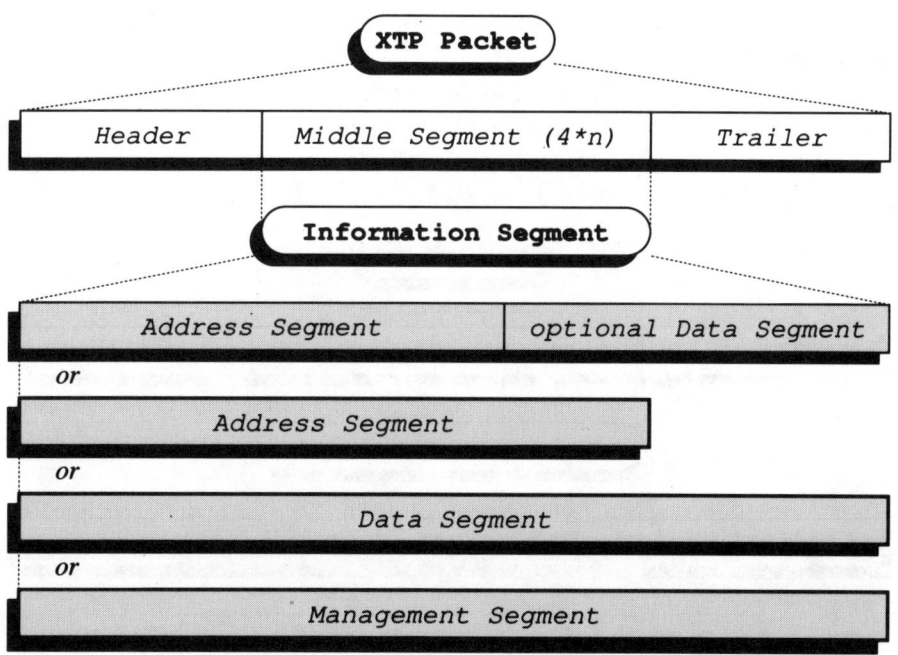

**Figure 5.11 — Information Segment**

additional bytes within the Middle Segment. Recall that these bytes are referred to as alignment bytes.

Each of the four Information Segment forms is made up of one or more of the following segments: the Data Segment, the Address Segment, and the Management Segment. Below we discuss each of these segments and which forms are used by which packet formats.

## 5.5.1 Data Segment

The Data Segment is always present in DATA packets and is optionally present in FIRST packets. No other packet formats can contain a Data Segment. Figure 5.12 shows the field structure of the Data Segment, consisting of the *data* field with an optional *btag* field.

The *data* field is the mechanism for transferring uninterpreted user data. The length of the *data* field is limited only by the maximum frame size of the underlying network. Each byte of the *data* field is counted by the sequence numbers and thus consumes sequence number space. The XTP user may place 8-byte markers in the data stream. This data is called "tagged data" or "tags." While the protocol treats tagged data as normal user data, it indicates to the user at the receiving endpoint where tags appear in the byte stream. If present, tagged data is always carried in the first 8 bytes of the Data Segment and is known as the *btag* field. A *btag* field may appear in any packet with an Information Segment; the presence of a *btag* field is noted by setting the BTAG bit in the *options* subfield in the Header.

Tagged data presents the XTP user with the opportunity to mark the data stream for user-specific purposes such as embedding higher layer control information. Consider an integrated services data transfer where the single data stream must switch between

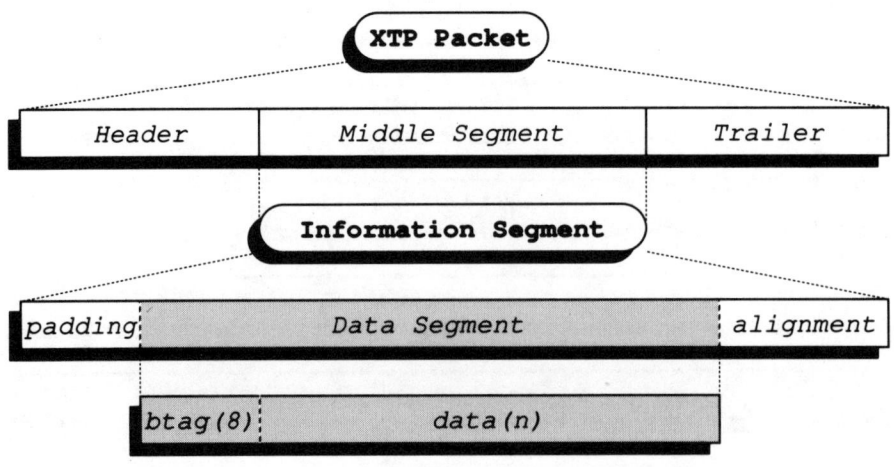

**Figure 5.12 — Information Segment: Data Segment**

video, voice, and data. Each of these types of information can be preceded with a *btag* which identifies the type of the data following. Another example is the use of the tagged data to set major and minor synchronization points as is done in the ISO Session Layer. The actual use of the tagging fields is deliberately left unspecified; their presence is to provide a mechanism for some data policy defined by the user.

An important use of the *btag* field recognized in the XTP Definition is to allow reliable transfer of a zero-length DATA packet. Because of the way sequence numbers are used in XTP, having a *data* field with zero bytes implies that no sequence numbers would be consumed. Since error detection procedures depend upon the consumption of sequence number space, the loss of a zero-length packet would never be detected. The *btag* field is used to force a zero-length DATA packet to consume sequence space. By agreeing on a special value for the *btag* field (the XTP Definition recommends all bits in the *btag* field be set to one), a zero-length DATA packet can be recognized as such. Since *btag* data consumes sequence space, the packet is protected by the error detection procedures in the protocol.

## 5.5.2 Address Segment

The Address Segment holds all of the information necessary to deliver a packet from end-to-end across the network, including location of the destination host and service, and establishment of a path in intermediate nodes between the two endpoints. The Address Segment is included in both FIRST packets and PATH packets. In both cases, the Address Segment enables the packet carrying it to establish both a forward and (as a consequence) a return path through the network.

Instead of creating a new addressing scheme, the Address Segment supports the address formats of several standard and widely used addressing schemes, as well as permitting experimental and special purpose ones. Figure 5.13 shows the Address Segment, with the *descriptor* field and the *address* used to specify and support the format being used.

Since XTP is a transfer layer protocol, the Address Segment must include information necessary for transport as well as network layer addressing. The various formats are included to allow XTP to incorporate the addressing schemes of a number of existing end-to-end protocol suites. Once a path between endpoints is established by a FIRST packet, none of this addressing information appears in subsequent packets unless a new path has to be established. Subsequent packets in the association use only the values carried in the *route* and the *key* fields to reference the path cut by the FIRST packet and identify the destination context.

The Address Segment of the FIRST packet consumes sequence number space since the FIRST packet must always be protected by the error detection procedures. If every FIRST packet were required to carry data, this addressing information would not be required to consume sequence space; however, FIRST packets may or may not carry data. Address Segments in PATH packets are not covered by sequence numbers since the protocol always remains in a stable state regardless of the fate of the PATH packet.

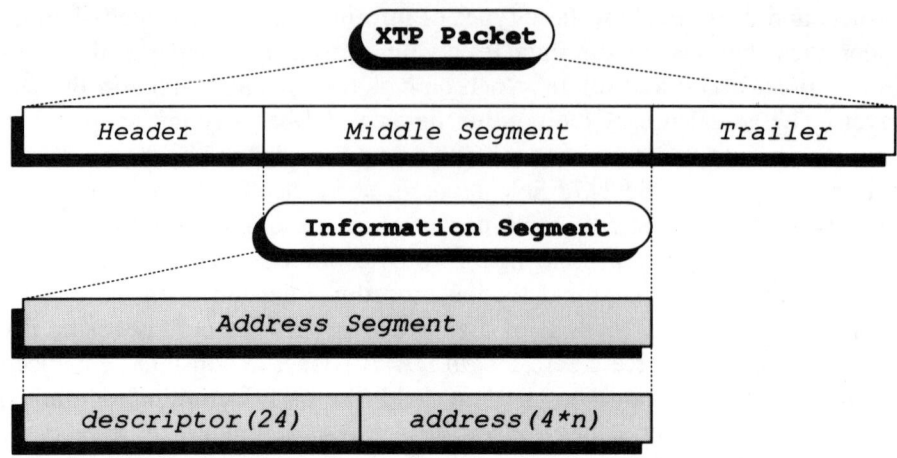

**Figure 5.13 — Information Segment: Address Segment**

## Descriptor Field (*descriptor*)

The *descriptor* field consists of seven subfields, shown in Figure 5.14. This field is used to specify:

- the length of the entire Address Segment
- service options
- the address format carried in the *address* field
- the initial values requested for the rate control parameters *rate* and *burst*
- the maximum protocol data unit size assumed
- the initiating host's MAC address

The Address Segment is variable length in order to accommodate the various address formats. The first subfield of the *descriptor* field, the *alength* field (for Address Seg-

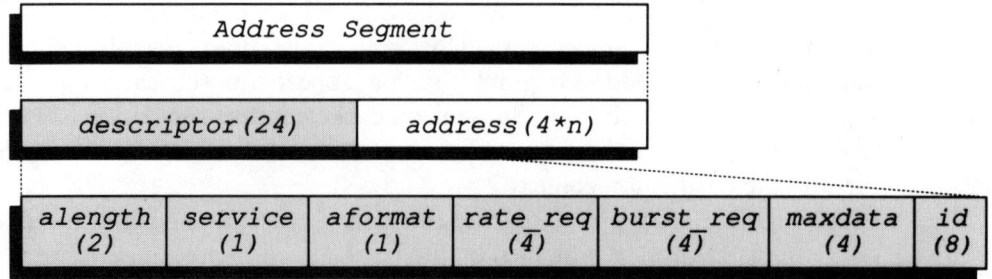

**Figure 5.14 — Address Descriptor Subfields**

ment length), specifies the length of the Address Segment. Like all other segments, the length of the Address Segment must be a multiple of 4 bytes.

The next subfield is the *service* subfield, which specifies two types of service information. The high-order 3 bits indicate the *class-of-service* as given in Table 5.2. The class-of-service indicates to the receiver the profile of the traffic expected for this association. The low-order 5 bits indicate the *quality-of-service* for this association and, although these parameters are currently undefined, they are reserved for future use.

The *aformat* subfield identifies the network address syntax; it dictates how the *address* field is to be parsed. Table 5.3 gives the defined *aformat* values. No other values may be used without authorization from the address assignment authority. Each of these formats will be discussed in more detail in Chapter 7.

The *rate_req* and *burst_req* subfields are used by the initiating context to request that the *rate* and *burst* parameters in the rate control algorithm be set to these respective values for data traveling in the forward direction. The receiver of these values may reject these values and send its own values for rate control in the *rate* and *burst* fields of a CNTL packet.

The *maxdata* subfield indicates the length in bytes of the maximum Information Segment that the initiating context expects to transmit during the lifetime of the association. If an intermediate node can not forward packets whose Information Segment is *maxdata* bytes long, the intermediate node will generate a diagnostic packet containing the maximum transmission unit size that this switch can forward. Since such path information may be kept within host routing tables or other routing databases, an initiating context may have access to an initial estimate of the maximum packet size. If this is the case, the initiating context will know the *maxdata* value, and thus will use the *maxdata* field in the FIRST packet to communicate this information to the receiving context. In this way an association crossing multiple subnetworks can avoid packet loss due to packets being too large for a switch to forward.

| class-of-service bit values | Class-of-Service Specified |
|---|---|
| 0 0 0 | Streams |
| 0 0 1 | Transactions |
| 0 1 0 | Unacknowledged Datagram |
| 0 1 1 | Acknowledged Datagram |
| 1 0 0 | Isochronous Stream |
| 1 0 1 | Bulk Data |

**Table 5.2 — Class-of-Service Specified within the *service* Field**

| *aformat* field value | | Address Syntax |
|---|---|---|
| Decimal | Hex | |
| 0 | 0x00 | No address |
| 1 | 0x01 | Internet Protocol addressing |
| 2 | 0x02 | ISO standard addressing |
| 3 | 0x03 | Xerox Network System addressing |
| 4 | 0x04 | IEEE 802-style source route addressing |
| 5 | 0x05 | MODSIM |
| 6 | 0x06 | MicroSoft NetBIOS |
| 7 | 0x07 | IP-style loose source route addressing |
| 8 | 0x08 | IP-style strict source route addressing |
| 9 | 0x09 | XTP direct (locally-defined) addressing |
| 10 | 0x0A | XTP experimental address type |
| 11 | 0x0B | USAF embedded system addressing |

**Table 5.3 — Address Formats for the Address Segment**

The *id* field carries the sender's MAC address, which may be smaller than the 8 bytes allotted. In this case the MAC address must occupy the low-order bytes, and any more significant bytes must be zero.

### Address Field (*address*)

The *address* field contains the actual addressing information in the format specified by the *aformat* subfield in the *descriptor*. If the *aformat* subfield specifies the value 0, and hence "No address," the *address* field is not present. Addressing information varies from addressing scheme to addressing scheme, but if the *address* field is present, it must identify the address of the source and the addressing information necessary to locate the destination host and service. Each of the formats for the *address* field is given in Chapter 7, complete with a description of how the addressing information is used.

## 5.5.3 Data and Address Segments

Figure 5.15 shows how both the Address and Data Segments can be included in an Information Segment. This is the format for a FIRST packet that carries XTP user data; otherwise the FIRST packet just contains the Address Segment. The only com-

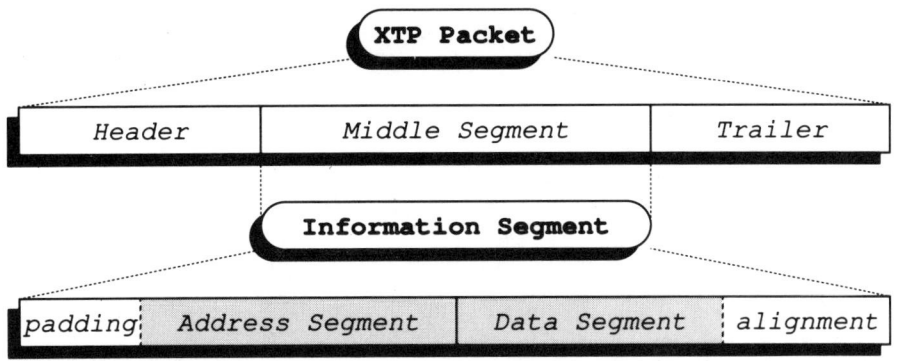

**Figure 5.15 — Information Segment: Address and Data Segments**

plication of having both the Address Segment and Data Segment in the same packet is that the Data Segment may not be a multiple of 4 bytes in length. Consequently there may be padding and alignment bytes to ensure the 4-byte boundary property. The padding precedes the Address Segment, and the alignment follows the Data Segment. Thus, no matter what format the Information Segment has, the padding bytes (if any) always start on the forty-first byte of the packet, and the alignment bytes (if any) always end the Information Segment.

## 5.5.4 Management Segment

The Management Segment is contained within the Information Segment for the DIAG and the ROUTE packets. These packets carry protocol data. When used with the DIAG packet, the information carried informs the receiver of error conditions at the other end of the association, or of the fact that no association can be established at all. As for the ROUTE packet, the protocol information specifies whether a particular path is targeted for release, and when it is released, notifies the nodes along that path. Further explanation of the uses of the DIAG and ROUTE packets is given in Chapter 6. In both cases the protocol issues information in a fixed format: a *code*, a *val* associated with or modifying that code, and a *message*. This information is placed in the fields of the Management Segment, as shown in Figure 5.16.

### Code Field (*code*)

The *code* field holds the condition code that identifies why this packet was generated. As we have seen in Chapter 4, the *code* value specifies the type or category of the situation the packet seeks to describe. For the DIAG packets, all *codes* indicate failed delivery, but the individual code values represent different kinds of failure. For the ROUTE packets, the *code* indicates if the path is being released or if its release is being acknowledged.

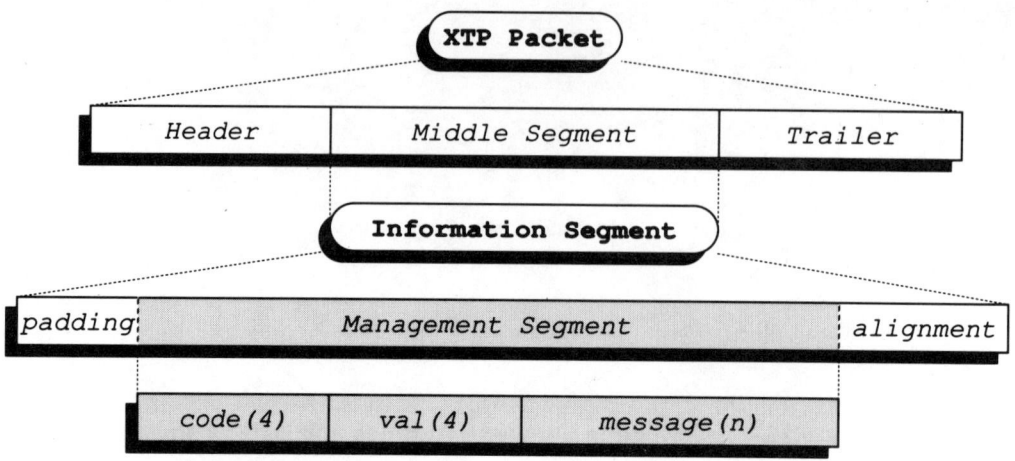

**Figure 5.16 — Information Segment: Management Segment**

## Value Field (*val*)

The *val* field modifies the *code* by including additional information. For DIAG packets, the *val* identifies a class within the failure category by specifying more precisely what failed. There are no *val* values for ROUTE packets.

## Message Field (*message*)

The information contained in the *message* field is not for the interpretation of the protocol but rather for the benefit of the protocol user. This *message* may be delivered to the protocol user as an indication of the conditions which caused the packet to be generated. The protocol is not required to generate an appropriate *message*, and the user is not required to act upon it. The *message* may be followed by alignment bytes, which would be indicated by the alignment field in the Trailer. The syntax of the *message* field (e.g., ASCII characters, bit strings, etc.) is unspecified.

# 6
# Packet Formats

An XTP state machine parses packet information at the highest level based on the *ptype* subfield within the *cmd* field of the packet Header. The nine XTP packet formats support a rich spectrum of protocol information exchanges. More specifically, protocol state machines within an XTP implementation use these packet formats to achieve XTP peer information exchanges that support a variety of user data delivery services.

XTP packets are used in carrying out the several fundamental tasks of the protocol: to establish an association, to transfer user data, to exchange protocol state information, to maintain the path between the endpoints of the association, and to signal error conditions concerning the association. FIRST packets establish the association and optionally carry data; thereafter, data is exchanged using DATA packets. The CNTL packet facilitates state sharing between endpoints of the association. The PATH, ROUTE, and RCNTL packets maintain and eventually terminate the path between the endpoints of the association. The DIAG packet notifies an XTP peer that an error condition has arisen within the association. Two other packet formats, the MAINT and the MGMT formats, are as yet undefined.

In general, this chapter expands on the *ptype* field discussion in Section 5.2.3. Figure 6.1 shows the *ptype* field in the context of a whole XTP packet, and also shows the subfields within the *ptype* field, in particular, the *pformat* subfield. This *pformat* subfield specifies the format for the XTP packet.

This chapter illustrates the field layouts for each of the XTP packet formats. It describes how each packet format is used, under what conditions a packet of a particular format is issued, and what actions are taken upon receipt of a packet of a particular format.

## 6.1 FIRST Packet

The FIRST packet is designed to be used only once per association, namely at association establishment. The FIRST packet's job is to thread a path between two hosts so that all of the state structures necessary for establishing the new association are initialized in each of the intermediate nodes and the endpoints. The FIRST packet carries an Address Segment in order to thread a path through intermediate switching nodes and locate the destination host and service. The FIRST packet may carry user data, as indi-

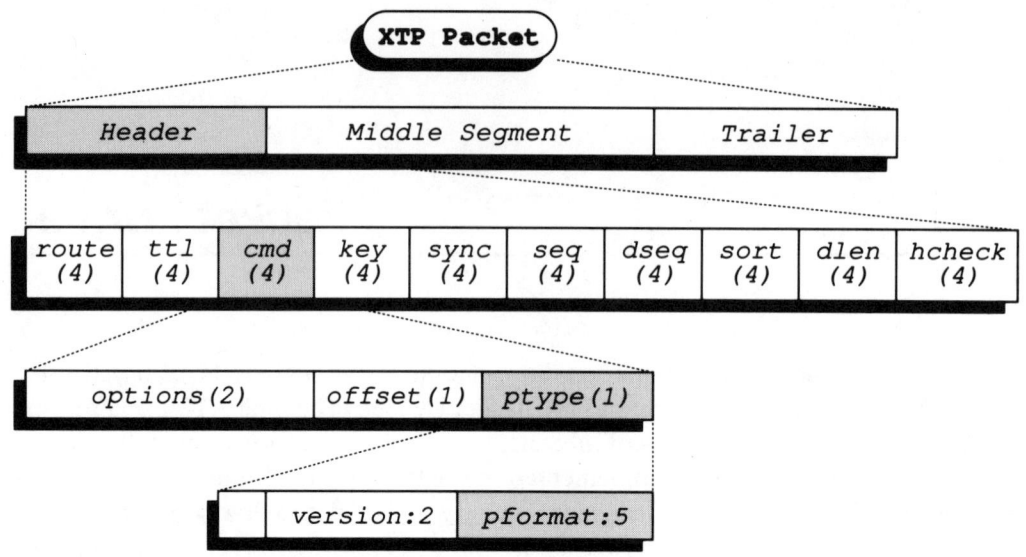

**Figure 6.1 — Breakout of the Packet Format Field**

cated by the optional Data Segment shown in Figure 6.2; if a FIRST packet does not carry user data, its Data Segment is simply not present.

At the destination host, if a context is "listening" on the transfer layer destination address contained within the incoming FIRST packet, then the local XTP state machine activates the listening context. State parameters within the activated context are initialized according to both default values and values carried within the FIRST packet. These parameters include transfer modes, sequence number space starting points, and return information.

The transfer modes set by certain bits in the *options* field in the Header of the FIRST packet include a no-error mode (NOERR), a multicast data transfer mode (MULTI), a buffer reservation mode (RES), and a no-flow mode (NOFLOW). These bits indicate policies that will normally be maintained for the duration of the association. When set, the NOERR bit indicates that the error control procedure will not request retransmission of any lost data-bearing packets. If the MULTI bit is set, then each receiver is one of several simultaneous receivers in a *multicast group*; if not set, the association consists of only two endpoints. With multicast some optimization procedures (such as the key exchange procedure) can not be used, and some error recovery and flow control procedures must be altered to accommodate group communication. If the RES bit is set, the receiving context will operate in reservation mode, wherein flow control is based upon the conservative approach of allowing the transmitter to send only as much data as will fit into the buffers dedicated by the receiving XTP implementation. Finally, if the NOFLOW bit is set, the transmitter indicates to the receiver that flow control information sent back to the transmitter will be ignored. Thus the receiver is prevented from using flow control to throttle the transmitter.

The FIRST packet also carries the starting values in the sequence number space for both the forward and return data streams. The forward data stream begins counting user data bytes with the sequence number held in the *seq* field in the Header. This sequence number corresponds to the first non-padding byte of the Address Segment in the FIRST packet. If used during the association, the return data stream, that is, the simplex data stream from the context that has received the FIRST packet to the context that issued the FIRST packet, must start with the sequence number given in the *dseq* field of the FIRST packet's Header.

The rate request (*rate_req*) and burst request (*burst_req*) fields allow the sender of the FIRST packet to request a rate and burst setting for use in the rate control procedure. Rate control is available to regulate the length of a burst of packets transmitted so that the receiver's resources are not overrun. The *rate_req* and *burst_req* values allow the transmitter to indicate its preferred values for the rate control parameters; how the receiver uses this information is implementation-dependent and hence unspecified by the XTP Definition.

The FIRST packet carries enough information to identify the originating host and service so that CNTL or DATA packets can be sent back to this originating host and service. The source host is identified in the *address* field of the Address Segment, as is the case in the Internet Protocol and ISO Network Layer address formats. Also, the source's MAC address is always recorded in the *id* field in the Address Segment. For transfer layer addressing the receiving context needs the *key* and *route* fields of the FIRST packet's Header in order to send a packet in the return direction. The *return key* and the *return route* values are by definition obtained by setting the most significant bit

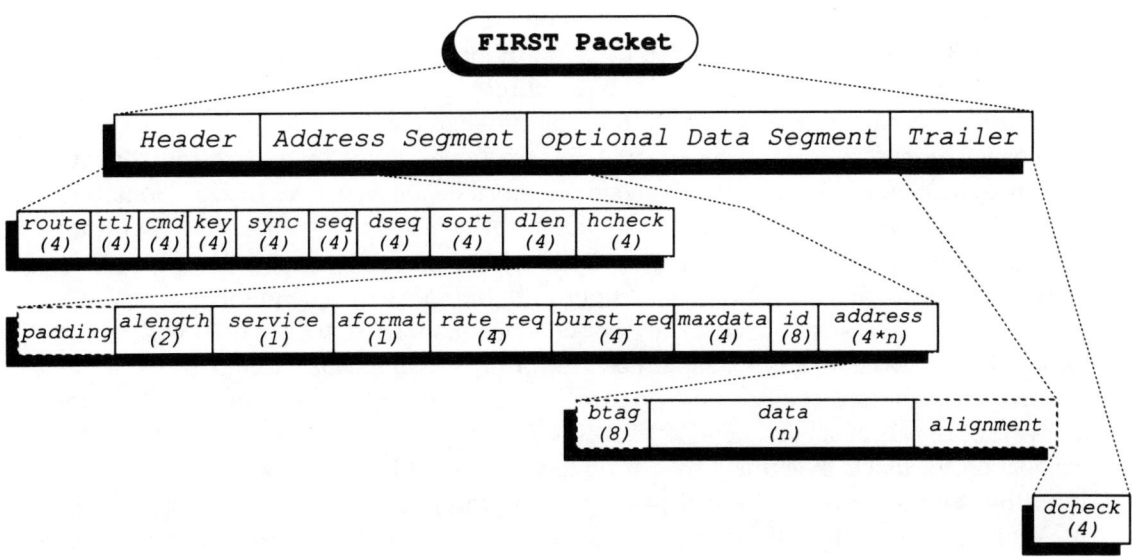

**Figure 6.2 — The FIRST Packet Format**

of the received *key* and *route* values. These values are placed in the *key* and *route* fields of return packets, and the packets follow (in the reverse direction) the path constructed by the FIRST packet to return to the originating host. Upon arrival at the originating host, the packet uniquely identifies its intended context through the *return key* value.

Finally, the FIRST packet may contain user data. In XTP the capabilities for association establishment and data transfer, although orthogonal, are both allowed in the FIRST packet. This gives the XTP user the opportunity to begin sending data before any acknowledgement of the establishment of the association has been given.

In an error-free situation, only a single FIRST packet will be needed for each XTP association. Once an association is established, the duties of the FIRST packet are complete. Subsequent packets will either be data-bearing, control, or managerial packets.

## 6.2   DATA Packet

The DATA packet carries user data subsequent to the association's establishment. Once a context sends a FIRST packet, even before any packet from the remote endpoint of the association has arrived, that initiating context may begin sending DATA packets using the same *key* value as in the FIRST packet. Likewise, the destination context activated as a result of the arrival of a FIRST packet may also immediately begin sending DATA packets on the return path using the *return key* value derived from the *key* value in the FIRST packet. Certainly there is some risk in proceeding with the data transfer before knowing that the association has been established, but the protocol allows the XTP user to make its own decision by providing protocol mechanisms that treat association establishment and data transfer orthogonally.

The DATA packet consists of an Information Segment with only a Data Segment, as shown in Figure 6.3. Each byte of the data contained in the DATA packet is identified by a sequence number. The sequence number of the first byte of data contained within the Data Segment is used as the value of the *seq* field in the Header. Sequence numbers are used to order and identify bytes in the data stream. As DATA packets arrive at the receiver, the data therein is put in buffers in sequence number order. If a DATA packet arrives out of sequence, the sequence number in the *seq* field will dictate exactly how much buffer space should be left for the missing data.

Every packet format carries the protocol options chosen for that association and for that packet in particular. The DATA packet in an association can turn off the checksum calculation for its Data Segment by setting the NOCHECK bit. The packet can be prioritized by setting the SORT bit and placing an appropriate value in the *sort* field. The packet can also tell the receiving context to generate a CNTL packet with retransmission information immediately whenever out-of-sequence data arrives. This is done by setting the FASTNAK bit (as long as the NOERR bit is not also set). The presence of the *btag* field within the *data* field is signaled by setting the BTAG bit.

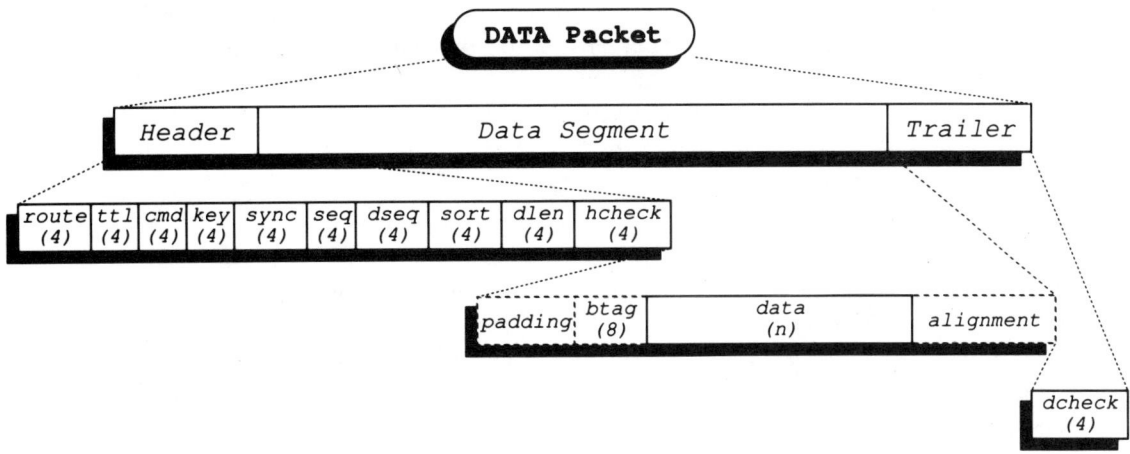

**Figure 6.3 — The DATA Packet Format**

The *btag* feature allows the user to place 8-byte markers, or "tags," into the data stream. Since these tags *are* part of the data stream, they consume sequence numbers and are thereby protected by error control procedures when the user requests an error-controlled data service. As with other user data, XTP does not look at or interpret tagged data (with one exception, described below). Tagged data is intended to support higher layer protocols, and the XTP users must share some common interpretation of what their tagged data means.

The XTP Definition identifies one important role of the *btag* field within the protocol: error-controlled transmission of zero-length DATA packets. Zero-length Data Segments in DATA packets must consume sequence numbers if they are to be protected by error control procedures when reliable transfer services are requested. Hence the XTP Definition dictates that a zero-length Data Segment will be encoded by a Data Segment consisting of a *btag* field containing a special value. The XTP Definition suggests that this special value be that wherein all 64 bits in the *btag* field are set.

Since a message consists of one or more data-bearing packets, the end of the message is marked by the EOM bit in the *options* field of the Header of a data-bearing packet. The data stream likewise consists of one or more messages, and the end of the data in the association is marked by a packet whose END bit (also from the *options* field) is set. The END bit signals the cessation of all packet processing at both ends of the association, and hence the termination of the association itself.

# 6.3  CNTL Packet

A CNTL packet transfers state information between protocol state machines at the endpoints of an association. Since a central XTP design tenet is that the transmitter should drive a transfer, a receiver generates a CNTL packet when requested to do so by the transmitter. In some situations, a receiver may follow policies that cause it to generate unsolicited CNTL packets. These unsolicited CNTL packets may be ignored by the transmitter without disrupting the protocol, although this policy risks the loss of responsiveness to changes in the receiver's status. The transmitter may generate a CNTL packet at any time.

The format of the CNTL packet, shown in Figure 6.4, is designed to allow certain status information and protocol parameter exchanges, optimizations, and synchronizations to be conducted within a single protocol mechanism. Note that two fields, both shown as *rsvd*, have been reserved in the Control Segment.

A transmitter requests its receiver to issue a CNTL packet by setting one or more of 3 bits. A set SREQ bit in the *options* field of the Header of any packet received will cause a CNTL packet to be generated immediately. This CNTL packet carries back to the transmitter the status of the receiver's protocol state machine (e.g., up-to-date flow and rate control parameters). The transmitter can also set the DREQ bit in the *options* field to cause a CNTL packet to be issued, except that the CNTL packet is sent only after all data currently enqueued at the receiver is delivered to the XTP user. The third bit is the FASTNAK bit in the *options* field. When set, this bit instructs the receiver to send a CNTL packet as soon as any data arrives out of sequence. This bit is useful when there is little possibility of the network reordering packets since, in such an environment, out-of-sequence data strongly suggests that the missing data is actually lost.

The *dseq*, *rseq*, *nspan*, and *spans* fields all contribute to conveying the data reception state of the receiver to the transmitter in CNTL packets. The *dseq* value is the sequence number of the next byte to be delivered to the remote XTP user. Located in the Header, *dseq* is found in all packets since the information is useful to XTP peers, regardless of what packet format delivers it. A transmitter releases data buffers for

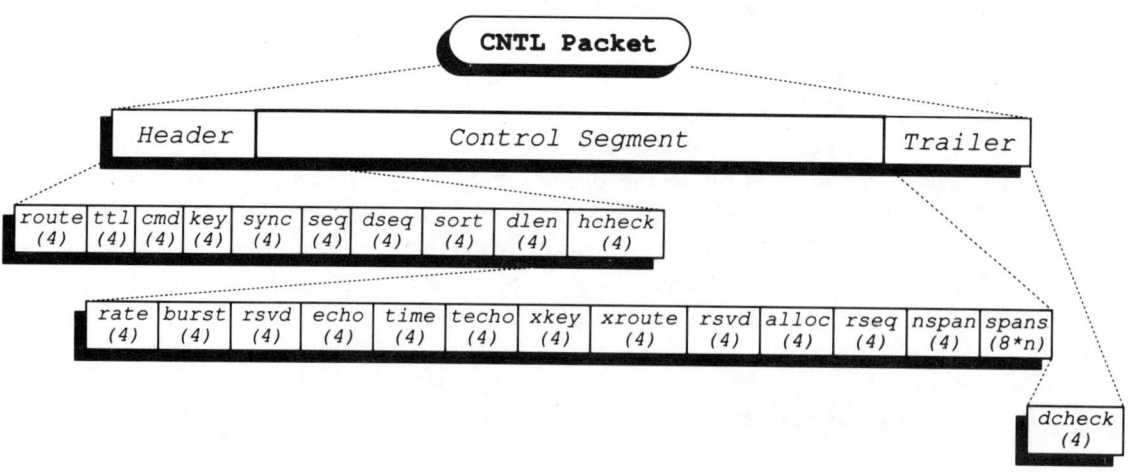

**Figure 6.4 — The CNTL Packet Format**

data whose sequence numbers include values up to the value of *dseq* since this data has been successfully delivered to the remote XTP user. The *rseq* value is the sequence number one greater than the last byte received at the remote context in order and without gaps. Other data may have been received, but *rseq* is the sequence number of the first byte of the first gap in the data. Other missing data information is provided by the *nspan* and *spans* fields. The value in *nspan* indicates how many "spans" will follow, where a span is the beginning/ending sequence number pair that identifies received data. The gaps, implied by the *spans* pairs, are useful for selective retransmission.

The Control Segment also contains rate and flow control parameters. Since the receiver is usually the throttling entity in a data transfer, the receiver sends rate and flow control information to the transmitter via a CNTL packet. This information is contained in the *rate* and *burst* fields for rate control, and the *alloc* field for flow control.

A destination endpoint may provide the initiating endpoint with a *key* and a *route* value that the destination endpoint wishes to have used in subsequent packets sent to it. The *xkey* and *xroute* fields are used for the key and route exchange procedures. When a CNTL packet carries a value in the *xkey* field, the context receiving this value must use the *xkey* value in the *key* field of all subsequent outgoing packets, and likewise for the *xroute* field.

The *sync* field from the Header and the *echo* field from the Control Segment together allow a context to synchronize with another context by sending a unique number in the *sync* field of an outgoing packet and watching for its return in an incoming CNTL packet. The context that generated the *sync* field can then conclude that any packets sent before this synchronizing handshake have either had their effects on the remote context or have been lost. The information in the returned CNTL packet will indicate the up-to-date status of the remote XTP peer at the point of synchronization.

Finally, CNTL packets can be used to estimate roundtrip times for use in time-to-live fields and other protocol algorithms. The *time* field holds the timestamp of the issuing context; when this timestamp value is returned in the *techo* field, the issuing context can estimate the roundtrip time.

## 6.4  PATH Packet

A PATH packet threads a path between two endpoints using the Address Segment information in the same way that a FIRST packet does, except that a PATH packet is issued only if an association already exists and the path in use by that association becomes unusable or undesirable. The new path is built using exactly the same mechanisms used by a FIRST packet, and hence the PATH packet includes an Address Segment like the FIRST packet. Unlike the FIRST packet, however, this packet can not carry data. The PATH packet format is given in Figure 6.5.

When an endpoint deems it necessary to rethread the path, it issues a PATH packet with a new *route* value in the *route* field while all the other fields reflect the current

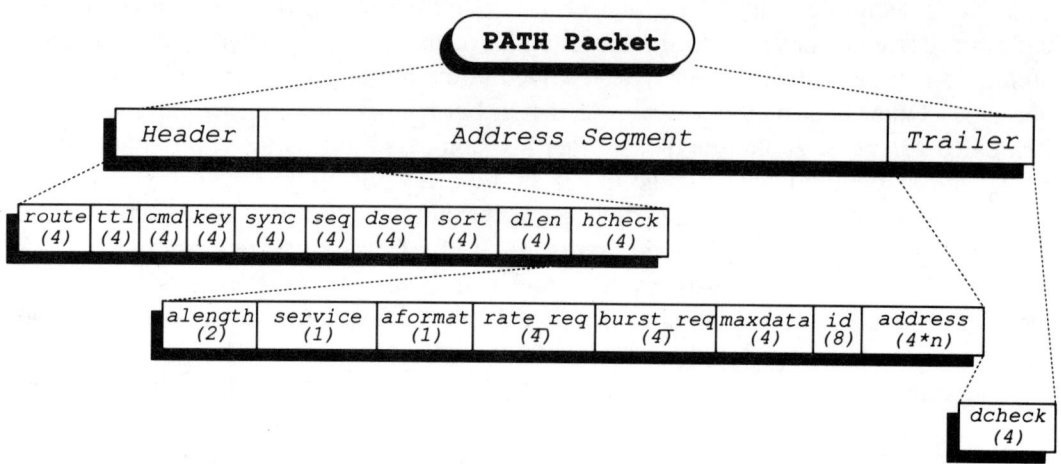

**Figure 6.5 — The PATH Packet Format**

state of the association. This packet will create a new path, if possible, between the association endpoints. All subsequent packets issued from the context which sent the PATH packet will use the new *route* value, and hence a new path. When the destination host receives a PATH packet, the packet is delivered to the context identified by the *key* value. This context records the new *route* value and uses it to form the *return route* value. Any packets sent from this context will contain this *return route* value in order to use the new path threaded by the PATH packet. The old path will eventually be destroyed by other mechanisms.

Notice that the PATH packet can be part of a synchronizing handshake if the SREQ bit is set since every packet carries a *sync* value in its Header. The CNTL packet sent in response to the SREQ will carry in its *echo* field the value received in the *sync* field of the PATH packet. Since path rethreading is a potentially hazardous situation, the synchronizing handshake represents a point in time when both endpoints know the new path has been established. The receiver of the PATH packet can also take this opportunity to send a new *xroute* value in the CNTL packet it issues, providing a *return route* value for use in the forward direction.

Since the PATH packet is not part of the data stream, it does not consume sequence number space. Therefore the loss of a PATH packet can not be detected via gaps in the sequence number space. If the PATH packet is not lost but fails to thread a new path, a DIAG packet is returned.

The PATH packet is also used for joining a multicast group. When an XTP peer wishes to join an in-progress multicast association, and hence become a member of the *receiver set* for that multicast association, that XTP peer issues a PATH packet on the multicast address. (See Chapter 7 for a discussion of XTP multicast addressing, and Chapter 8 for multicast in general.) The PATH packet carries the multicast group address in its Address Segment and a zero *key* value. The XTP Definition specifies that all multicast receivers ignore PATH packets with a *key* value of zero; hence this PATH packet will be received and discarded by every member of the multicast set except the multicast transmitter. This arrangement ensures that joining members do not disturb the state of the currently existing set of multicast receivers.

The multicast transmitter responds to the PATH packet by multicasting a PATH packet to the receiver set. The transmitter's PATH packet contains the information necessary (e.g., the *key* and *route* values) for the joining member to begin receiving on the multicast association. Note that the multicast transmitter can enforce a synchronized join by having the joining member enter the multicast transfer at the sequence number specified by the transmitter in the *seq* field of this outgoing PATH packet.

## 6.5   ROUTE Packet

The ROUTE packet is one of the several packet formats that use the Management Segment as its Middle Segment. The Management Segment, recall from Chapter 5, has three fields: the *code* field, the *val* field, and the *message* field. The *code* identifies the message category, or purpose of the packet. The *val* more specifically identifies this message category or offers some *code*-dependent value. The *message* is designed to be passed to the user for the user's information. This packet format is shown in Figure 6.6.

The purpose of a ROUTE packet is to facilitate the release of an established path after a certain period of inactivity. Since a path can be shared, there is no immediate way for a switch to know that a particular path is no longer needed. Even when the switch sees a packet carrying an association release indication, it can not be sure that

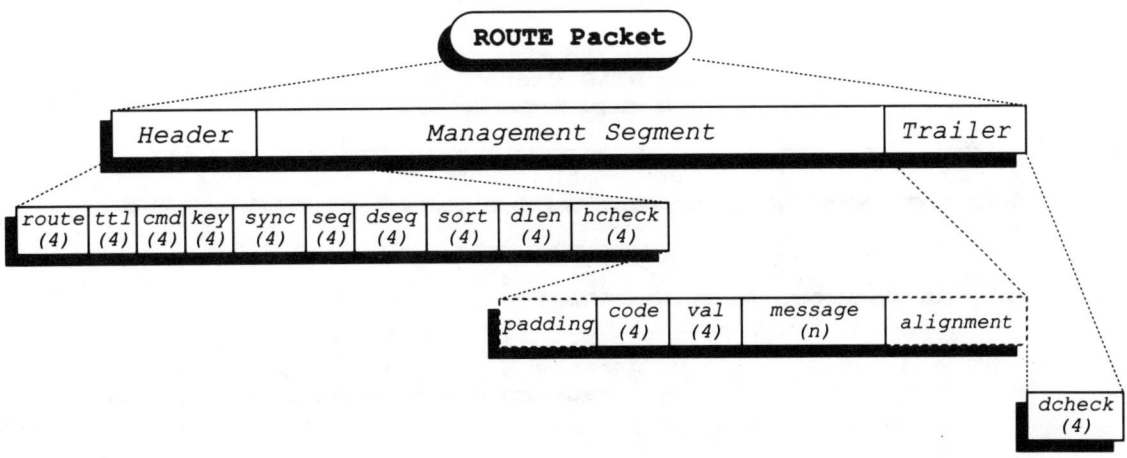

**Figure 6.6 — The ROUTE Packet Format**

| Value of code field | Message Category | Possible *val* field values |
|---|---|---|
| 1 | Release Route | 0 always |
| 2 | Release Acknowledged | 0 always |

**Table 6.1 — ROUTE Packet *code* and *val* Values**

no other associations are using this path.  Consequently, the switches use timeout procedures to identify paths which may be released.

Once a path is determined to be dormant, the nodes must exchange ROUTE packets to first initiate and then acknowledge the path teardown.  The node initiating teardown sends the ROUTE packet with *code* value 1 (see Table 6.1) indicating that the path (and hence each *route* value associated with that path) is being released.  When an endpoint receives such a ROUTE packet, it replies with a second ROUTE packet acknowledging this release.  The *code* for acknowledgement is 2.

# 6.6   DIAG Packet

The DIAG packet signals some error conditions encountered during the processing of a packet.  The information contained within a DIAG packet is designed to give the receiver of the packet some idea of what caused the error condition so that this receiver can make informed decisions about how to proceed.  This information is contained in a Management Segment; the format for the DIAG packet is given in Figure 6.7.

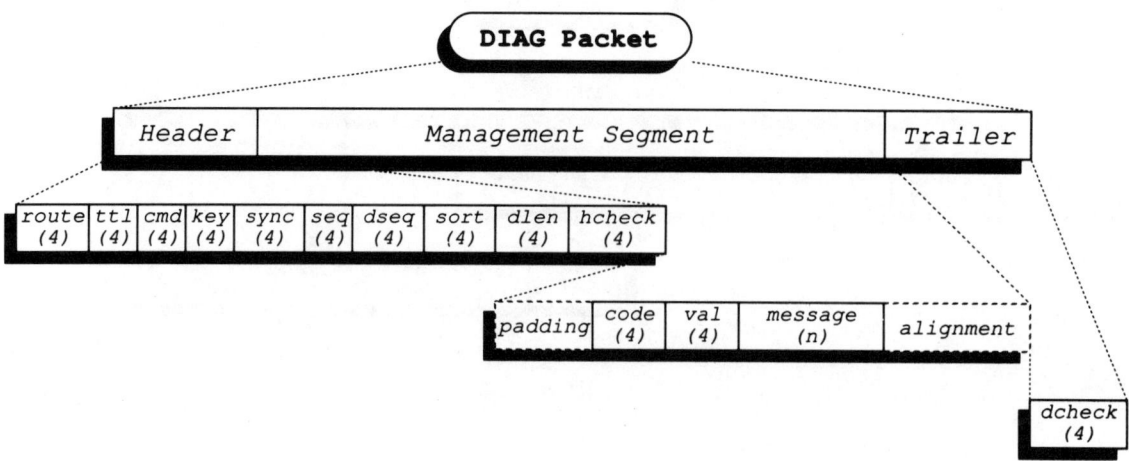

**Figure 6.7 — The DIAG Packet Format**

| Value of *code* field | Message Category | Possible *val* field values |
|:---:|---|---|
| 1 | Invalid context | 0 always |
| 2 | Context refused | 0 — unspecified reason<br>1 — NOFLOW refused<br>2 — no provider for requested *service* |
| 3 | Unknown destination | 0 — unspecified error<br>1 — address format not supported |
| 4 | Dead host | 0 always |
| 5 | Invalid route | 0 always |
| 6 | Redirect;<br>use a different switch | 0 always |
| 7 | Can not route/forward | 0 — unspecified error<br>1 — address format not supported<br>2 — insufficient bandwidth for *rate_req* |
| 8 | No resource | 0 always |
| 9 | Protocol error | 0 — unspecified error<br>1 — malformed Address Segment<br>2 — invalid *route* field of zero<br>3 — invalid retransmission request<br>4 — data segment too big<br>    (*maxdata* error) |
| 10 | MTU size error, can not forward FIRST packet | maximum acceptable MTU size |

**Table 6.2 — DIAG Packet *code* and *val* Values**

The DIAG packet is generated by an XTP protocol machine when that machine discovers one of the error conditions specified in Table 6.2. The generation of the DIAG packet always results from the arrival of a packet that can not be properly processed. The protocol can recover from such a processing failure through error detection techniques such as timeouts, but the use of a DIAG packet allows the sender of the errant packet to be notified of the error on a more timely basis. Consequently, DIAG packets provide an enhancement to the error detection and recovery procedures within the protocol.

Table 6.2 shows *code* field values for the kinds of error conditions that warrant the generation of a DIAG packet, along with the *val* field values that modify the *code* values. The first four *code* values indicate that there is some problem with the destination endpoint. If a host receives a packet but can not match that packet to the appropriate context, a DIAG packet with a *code* value of 1 is sent via the return path. It is possible that a context can not be activated when a FIRST packet arrives due to lack of resources at the destination host, or the receiver refusing some service requirements or requests made by the issuer of the FIRST packet. Under these circumstances, the association is refused with a DIAG packet carrying *code* value 2. The *code* value 3 indicates that the Address Segment of a FIRST or PATH packet did not properly specify a destination host. A *code* value of 4 indicates that the host is not functioning; this DIAG packet would be generated by a switch that knew of the demise of the destination host.

The next four *code* values indicate that there is a problem with the path. If the *route* value is not valid in some switch along the path, that switch will return a DIAG packet with *code* value 5. If a switch becomes unusable, some switch (or possibly a prior switch along the path) will generate a DIAG packet with *code* 6. The host receiving such a DIAG packet may then use a PATH packet to recover from the disabled path. Also, routing tables may be incorrect, and attribute some switch with routing capabilities it may not have (even if the switch once had this capability). The *code* value 7 indicates that a switch can not or does not know how to forward the FIRST (or PATH) packet, and therefore can not participate in the path. A switch may not be able to participate in a path because resource limitations such as lack of buffer space prevent the switch from adequately supporting the new path. The *code* value 8 signals this condition.

The DIAG packet carrying *code* 9 indicates that a protocol error was detected while processing a packet. Besides the catch-all "unspecified error," there are four other *val* values that more specifically identify the error. The Address Segment may be incorrectly formed, and thus some switch along the way, or even the destination host, could not parse the segment. If the *route* value is zero, even though the path includes intermediate hosts (recall that zero is reserved for packets that do not leave the local network), the switch trying to forward the packet will generate a DIAG packet with *val* value 2. If the receiver requests a retransmission of data whose sequence numbers fall outside the range of valid sequence numbers, the transmitter may send the DIAG packet to indicate to the receiver that the two contexts appear not to be synchronized. The *val* value 4 indicates that a received DATA packet contained more data than could be handled at the receiver.

The *code* value 10 indicates that some intermediate node along the path can not forward a FIRST packet because the value of the *maxdata* field of the Address Segment exceeds the maximum transmission unit for the network served by that intermediate node. In this case the packet is discarded and the DIAG packet with *code* 10 and the maximum transmission unit size in the *val* field is issued.

The *code* and *val* values are bound to a well-defined set of diagnostic meanings; no other values may be used. This is required so that the protocol state machine can interpret the DIAG packet in a straightforward manner. The *message* field is not so strictly regulated, however, since it is not designed for parsing by the protocol state machine. Rather, the content of the *message* field is passed to the XTP user or some other monitor for user-level diagnostic logs. The actual message text should pertain to the message category as given in Table 6.2, but is not specified by the XTP Definition.

## 6.7   RCNTL Packet

The RCNTL packet is used to exchange state information concerning a link between nodes on a path, not between endpoints of an association. The RCNTL packet is useful for communicating rate control information and exchanging route information between switches participating in a path. Therefore, as shown in Figure 6.8, the Control Segment is included as the Middle Segment of RCNTL packets. Only the *route*, *ttl*, *cmd*, *sort*, and *hcheck* fields from the Header, the *rate*, *burst*, and *xroute* fields from the Control Segment, and the *dcheck* field in the Trailer are interpreted for a RCNTL packet.

The *cmd* field is needed to indicate which packet format is being used and what options are in effect. The *route* value, of course, is necessary for identifying the path and for delivering the packet to the proper switch. Note that no *key* field is necessary since no contexts are involved in this packet exchange. The *sort* value, when active, ranks the importance of this packet among the other packets competing for processing. The *ttl* field ensures that this packet is valid; the *hcheck* also is required to ensure the integrity of the Header. The rate control information is included in the *rate* and *burst* fields of the Control Segment. Also, the *xroute* field can be used to facilitate a route exchange (as described in Chapter 4) if one has not yet occurred. The Trailer carries the packet validation field *dcheck* to protect against corruption of the control information.

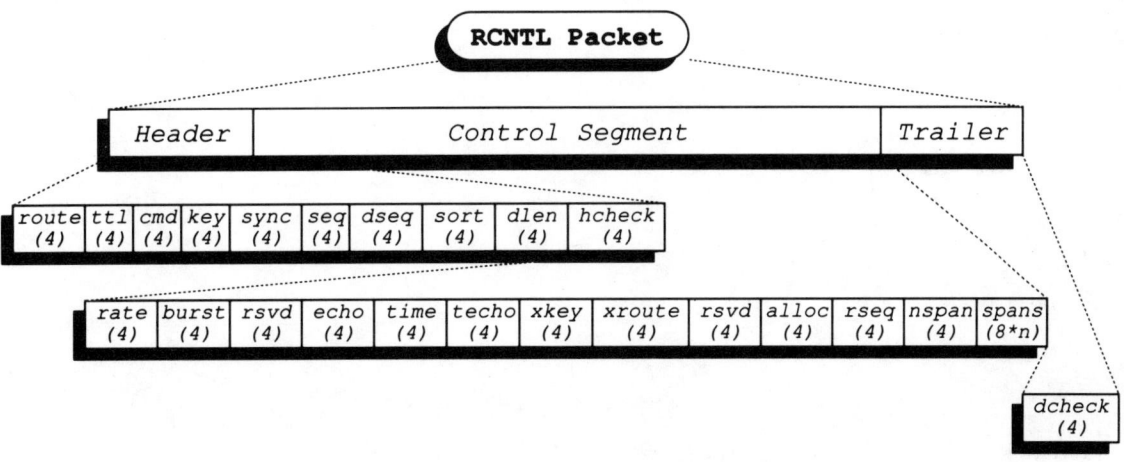

**Figure 6.8 — The RCNTL Packet Format**

# 6.8   MAINT and MGMT Packets

The MAINT and MGMT packet formats are currently undefined. The names serve as placeholders in the protocol for packet formats that will allow network maintenance and network management information exchange.

# 7

# Addressing and Encapsulation

Since XTP is an end-to-end protocol, it must provide sufficient mechanisms for threading the path between the endpoints of an association. End-to-end path establishment requires both global information to steer the path-establishing packet through XTP intermediate nodes and agreement between each XTP implementation and its local data delivery service provider for transmission between successive XTP implementations along the path. Addressing information determines the next link at each intermediate XTP node in the path being established. Encapsulation is the means by which a packet is carried in the local data delivery service between XTP nodes.

Addressing information, which is carried in the Address Segment of a FIRST or PATH packet, is necessary to establish the path between the endpoints of an association. The several fields of an Address Segment indicate both the addressing scheme employed and the particular address for this scheme contained in this Address Segment. Intermediate nodes and the destination host interpret the information within the Address Segment in order to establish a path on which an association may exchange subsequent packets.

Encapsulation specifies how an underlying data delivery service carries the protocol data units of the layer it supports. An XTP implementation hands XTP packets to its underlying data delivery service along with the additional information necessary for delivery to a peer XTP station. This additional information includes the physical address of the destination station on the local network and values identifying XTP as the user of the underlying protocol. In this way, XTP packets are the "data" of the encapsulating data delivery service.

## 7.1  Addressing

Instead of explicitly defining yet another addressing scheme, XTP provides a *parametric addressing* facility. Parametric addressing allows global addresses to be expressed in a number of existing address formats. This novel feature offers a number of advantages. By parameterizing addressing, an XTP implementation may take advantage of routing tables that are built and maintained by auxiliary protocols. Such auxiliary protocols exist for mature addressing schemes and do not have to be reinvented to support XTP. Furthermore, the flexibility of either using a familiar addressing scheme

| *aformat* field value | | Address Syntax |
|---|---|---|
| Decimal | Hex | |
| 0 | 0x00 | No address |
| 1 | 0x01 | Internet Protocol addressing |
| 2 | 0x02 | ISO standard addressing |
| 3 | 0x03 | Xerox Network System addressing |
| 4 | 0x04 | IEEE 802-style source route addressing |
| 5 | 0x05 | MODSIM |
| 6 | 0x06 | MicroSoft NetBIOS |
| 7 | 0x07 | IP-style loose source route addressing |
| 8 | 0x08 | IP-style strict source route addressing |
| 9 | 0x09 | XTP direct (locally-defined) addressing |
| 10 | 0x0A | XTP experimental address type |
| 11 | 0x0B | USAF embedded system addressing |

**Table 7.1 — Address Formats**

or defining one appropriate for a specific XTP communication subsystem allows XTP to be useful in many more environments than would be possible if the addressing scheme were limited to a single format. Finally, parametric addressing enables heterogeneous addressing schemes to coexist within a single XTP implementation.

Table 7.1 shows the addressing schemes supported by XTP.[1] These address formats include the Internet Protocol and the ISO Network Layer addressing. There are several industry-defined formats, such as the Xerox Network System address format and the MicroSoft NetBIOS address format. Also included are project-specific formats, such as the MODSIM and USAF Embedded Systems address formats. Only the formats in Table 7.1 have been defined, and only the Address Assignment Authority—Protocol Engines Inc.—may add to this table.

Figure 7.1 shows the packet structure of a packet containing an Address Segment. The Information Segment in the FIRST and PATH packets contains the Address Segment; in the FIRST packet the Information Segment may contain a Data Segment as well. Within the Address Segment there are two fields: the *descriptor* field and the *address* field. The *descriptor* field contains the specifications for the format of the *address* field; specifically, the *alength* subfield gives the length of the *address* field, and

[1] While XTP supports all of the addressing formats given in Table 7.1, this does not imply that an XTP-based network is plug-in compatible with networks based on protocols whose addressing schemes are shown here.

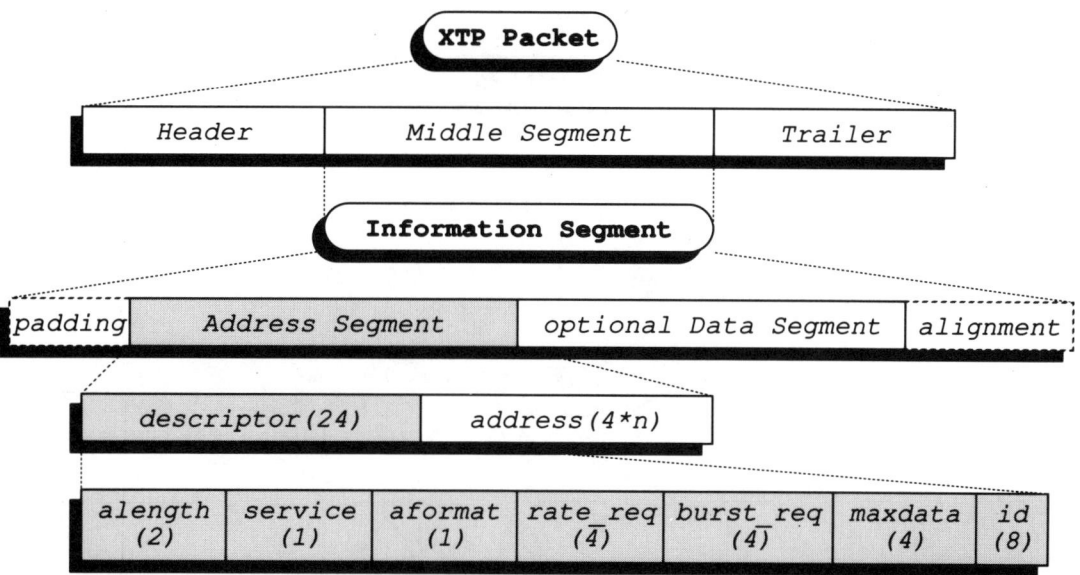

**Figure 7.1 — The Address Segment and Its Fields**

the *aformat* subfield describes the type of addressing information the *address* field contains. This *aformat* field contains a value from Table 7.1. The *address* field contains the actual address being carried. The subfields of the *address* field are determined by the addressing scheme specified by the *aformat* field.

## 7.1.1 Internet Addressing

The Internet Protocol (IP) [DARPA81a] provides a connectionless message service over packet-switched computer communication networks. Blocks of data, called *IP datagrams*, are transmitted from a source host to a destination host. The source and destination host are identified by globally unique fixed-length addresses contained within the header of the IP datagram. The IP datagrams are *routed* from the source host to the destination host via a series of transmissions between IP modules. An IP module will use some routing algorithm to determine the next IP module in the route until the IP datagram is delivered to the destination host.

Internet addresses specify an attachment to a network in such a way that the address specifying this attachment is unique among *all* Internet addresses. The Internet consists of a set of *subnetworks*, and on the subnetwork a set of *local hosts*. Each address is a 4-byte value that is divided into two parts: the *network identification* part and the *local host identification* part. The network identifier is a number which identifies an institution's network, and the local host identifier specifies the host on this network. This arrangement is shown in Figure 7.2.

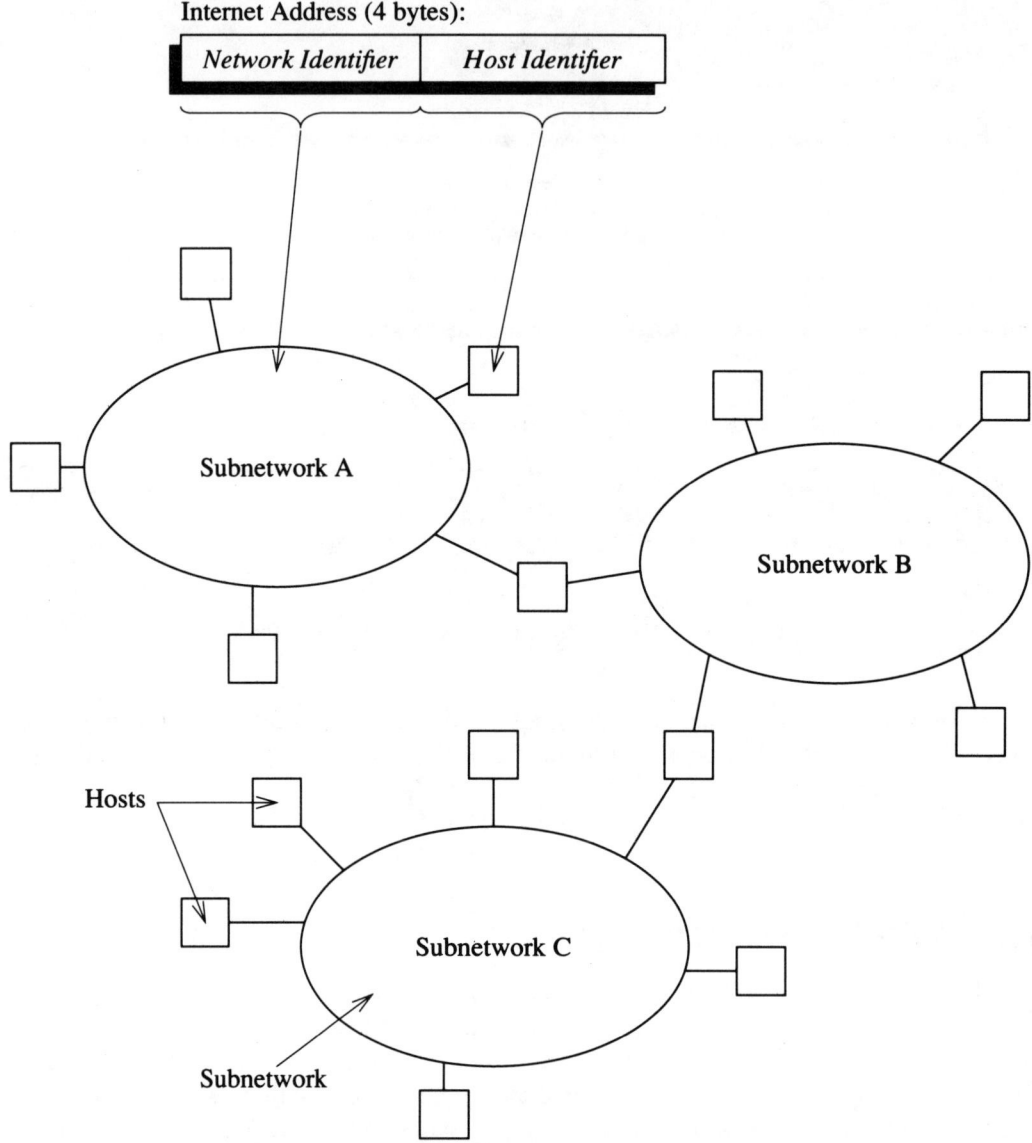

**Figure 7.2 — IP Internetworking Structure**

There are four classes of Internet addresses, Class A through Class D, which provide flexibility in assigning addresses. Each class provides a different allocation of the addressing space, as shown in Figure 7.3. Class A addresses have a large local host identification part, and are thus reserved for networks that have a large number of hosts attached to them. Class C provides address space for those networks with fewer than

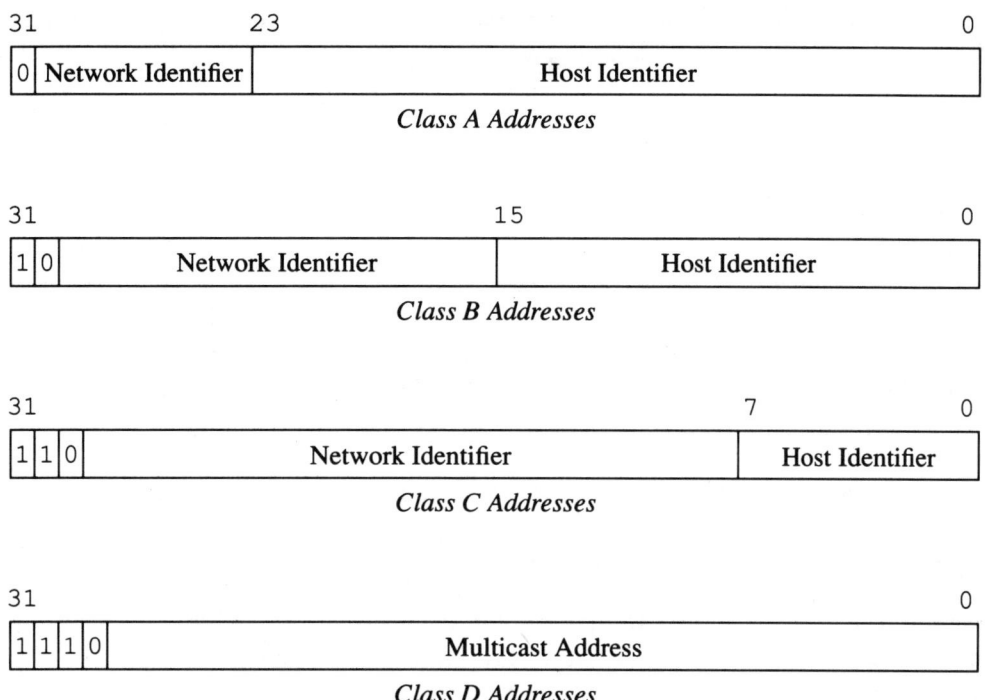

**Figure 7.3 — Internet Address Classes**

256 hosts. Class B provides a middle ground. RFC 1117[2] [ROMA89] lists the "Internet Numbers," which are those network identifiers that have been assigned to institutions. An institution is assigned a network identifier from a class. The class chosen reflects the node population at the institution.

The last class, Class D, is the Internet address format used for multicasting. Class D Internet addressing provides one of the ways for specifying a multicast address in XTP. Section 7.1.7 examines multicast addressing, particularly using Class D Internet addressing, in more detail; Chapter 8 examines multicast in general.

IP datagrams have an optional facility for sender-specified routing. This *source routing* allows an IP-service user who is familiar with the Internet topology to specify the ordered list of nodes that the IP datagram must visit between the source host and the destination host. There are two forms of source routing: *strict source routing* and *loose source routing*. Strict source routing requires that the IP datagram visit only those nodes specified in exactly the order specified in the source route field of the datagram. Loose source routing requires that the IP datagram visit at least those nodes specified, but other intermediate hops may be taken between any two specified nodes.

[2.] **RFCs are "Requests for Comments." These moderated technical reports are written by the Internet community and are made available via several on-line distribution sites.**

XTP parametric addressing formats allow each of the three addressing formats: normal IP addressing, strict source addressing, and loose source addressing.

## Internet Addressing Format

Figure 7.4 shows the fields for *aformat* 0x01, the Internet address format. The *dsthost* field is the Internet address for the destination host; the *srchost* field is the Internet address for the source host. The value in the *dsthost* field uniquely identifies the host to which the packet is addressed. The port number fields, the *dstport* and the *srcport*, specify the destination and source port numbers. These ports are the service access points through which the user receives service. The *ipproto* field corresponds to the tenth byte of an IP packet, the "protocol" field. The information in this field identifies the type of higher-level protocol (e.g., TCP or XTP) using the services of IP; the types of protocols and their assigned values are also given in RFC 1117. The 3-byte *null* field simply ensures that this address format will end on a 4-byte boundary.

## IP-Style Strict Source Route Addressing Format

Along with the fields present in the Internet address format, the IP-style strict source route format, 0x08, contains two extra fields as shown in Figure 7.5. The *pointer* field is used to keep track of a position within the *srcroute* field. The *srcroute* field contains one or more Internet addresses which constitute the route that the XTP packet must take between the initiating host and the destination host. The *pointer* field represents the byte-offset into the *srcroute* field marking the position of the next node in the path.

For strict source routing the following steps are taken at each intermediate node along the path: the node checks to see if the *pointer* value is larger than the size of the *srcroute* field; if it is, routing is to be based only on the destination host address in the *dsthost* field. Otherwise, the node places the next address in the *srcroute* field (that address dereferenced by the pointer value) into the *dsthost* field. The node then moves the address in the *srchost* field into the *srcroute* field (overwriting the value just placed into the *dsthost* field) and writes its own address into the *srchost* field. The pointer is incremented by four, and the packet is sent to its new destination. Hence a source-routed packet begins at the source host with a list of nodes to visit and arrives at its destination host with the list of nodes visited.

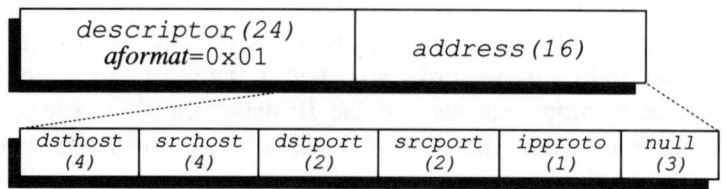

**Figure 7.4 — Format of *address* Field for Internet Protocol Address**

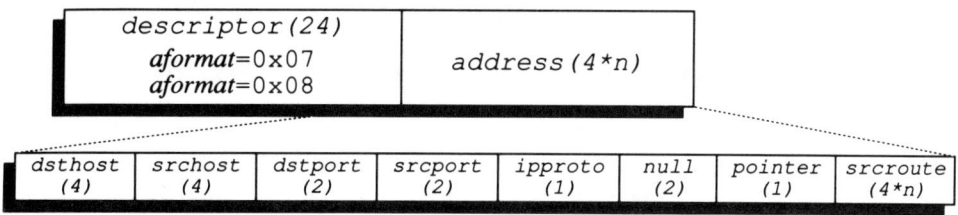

**Figure 7.5 — Format of *address* Field for IP-Style Source Route Addressing**

## IP-Style Loose Source Route Addressing Format

The format for the *address* field using IP-style loose source route addressing, *aformat* $0\times07$, is the same field structure as that for strict source route addressing. The semantics of source routing require that this FIRST packet visit each node along the path indicated by the *srcroute* field. This IP-style loose source route addressing format is so termed since an intermediate node may forward the FIRST packet to a node not in the source route as specified by the *srcroute* field, as long as the FIRST packet is eventually delivered to the node whose address is next in the source route list.

# 7.1.2 ISO Standard Addressing

The document ISO 8348/DAD2 [ISO8348/2], the second addendum to the network service description, defines the addressing scheme for the ISO Network Layer. An ISO network address is used to refer to the network service access point (NSAP) at which the ISO Network Service is made available to a network service user by the network service provider. This NSAP address is the information necessary for the ISO Network Service to identify a particular network service user. Since the network service primitives are conceptual, NSAP addresses must not have any embedded information about the physical location of a node, nor should a network address explicitly contain routing information. Rather, addressing is hierarchically structured based on *addressing domains*. These domains are defined by ISO; administration of the domains and the addressing within them is delegated to *addressing authorities*, which may further subdivide domains and delegate addressing authority.

The structure of an address is given in an *abstract syntax* such that the first part of the address defines how the second part will be interpreted. An address is divided into two parts: the *initial domain part* (IDP) and the *domain specific part* (DSP). The IDP is further divided into two parts: the *authority and format identifier* (AFI) and the *initial domain identifier* (IDI) (Figure 7.6 shows the breakdown). The AFI specifies how the initial domain identifier is interpreted and the syntax used for the domain specific part. The IDI, in turn, indicates the entity allowed to assign values to the DSP—this entity is responsible for allocating values and defining the semantics for the DSP.

Since the formats within several of these fields may be variable, the XTP format for the ISO Standard Addressing scheme allows the maximum size (20 bytes) for both

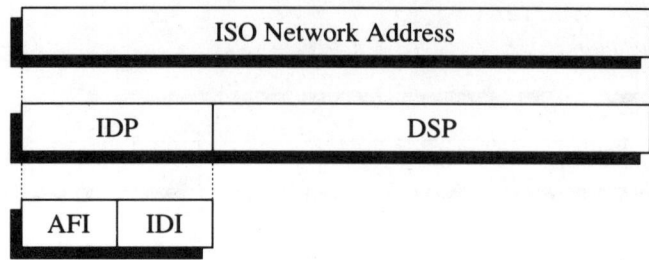

**Figure 7.6 — The Breakdown of an ISO Network Address**

the *dnsap* and *snsap* fields, as given in Figure 7.7. The transport service access point (TSAP) is included in the XTP address format for this scheme to identify the user of the service. The *stsel* field contains the TSAP selecting the service which sent the packet; the *dtsel* field identifies the TSAP of the receiver.

## 7.1.3 Xerox Network System Addressing Format

The Xerox Network System (XNS) Internet Transport Protocols [XERO91] provides the architectural foundation for Xerox's distributed system. Like the DARPA protocols, the fundamental unit of information flow in an XNS network is an *internet packet*. This packet contains control information as well as data; the control information aids in, among other things, the routing of the packet through the internetwork of store-and-forward systems (internetwork routers).

Also, as in the DARPA suite, this internet packet is the protocol data unit for a basic data delivery service: the Internet Datagram Protocol. This protocol provides service to a number of different transport protocols designed to meet specific needs. As such, the internet packet contains the addressing information necessary to facilitate delivery across network boundaries, to specific hosts, and to specific services within the hosts. There are, therefore, three basic pieces of information contained in an XNS address: the network, the host, and the socket, which form a hierarchical address format.

Figure 7.8 shows the XNS address format within an XTP *address* field. The 4-byte *dstnet* field uniquely identifies the destination network within an XNS internetwork.

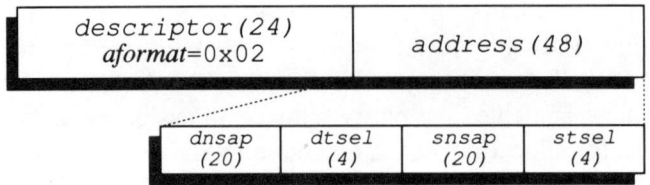

**Figure 7.7 — Format of *address* Field for ISO Network Layer Standard Address**

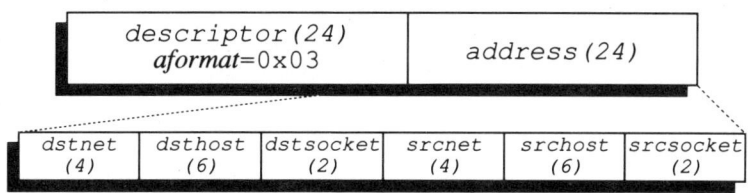

**Figure 7.8 — Format of *address* Field for Xerox Network Service Address**

The 6-byte *dsthost* field identifies a specific host among over four billion possibilities; this value is unique across all XNS processors ever manufactured. The 2-byte *dstsocket* field identifies the destination socket within the operating system of the host; this socket represents the service access point to the application (i.e., the transport protocol) using the service. Likewise, the source information is given in the symmetric 12-byte structure.

Although a destination address specifically identifies the network, host, and socket, in general each of the these three levels in the address hierarchy may take values which are either *unknown*, *all*, or *specific*. For instance, if an address specifically identifies the network, host, and socket, all three fields have *specific* values. However, if a network number is *unknown*, the packet will be sent to all networks connected to the source host. This has the effect of "searching" for a known host among several networks. The implications of allowing the *dsthost* or *dstsocket* field to take *unknown* or *all* values are discussed in Section 7.1.7 on multicast addressing.

## 7.1.4 IEEE 802-Style Source Route Addressing Format

A local area network may be composed of any number of network *segments*, with each segment sharing a common address space of uniform length. As shown in Figure 7.9, two or more segments may be interconnected by a special station called a *bridge*. The bridge contains two or more MAC stations, one on each network segment, each of which operates the MAC protocol specific to that network segment. In the general case for bridged local area networks, each MAC in the bridge examines the frames circulating on one segment and determines whether or not that frame should be forwarded to an adjacent network segment. This scheme implies the existence of address tables and lookup routines within each bridge.

An alternative scheme is *source routing* as defined in [IEEE89] and explained in [DIXO88]. Source routing requires the frame's transmitter to specify the route that the frame is to follow; thus, a source route is an ordered list of segments and bridges that the frame must traverse. Rather than keeping address tables that identify the network segments to which an individual MAC address belongs, the bridge simply examines the source routing field. Each bridge is initialized with its identifying bridge number (say $B$) and the names of the segments that it interconnects (say $X$ and $Y$). When the bridge encounters a frame on segment $X$, it forwards it to segment $Y$ if and only if the

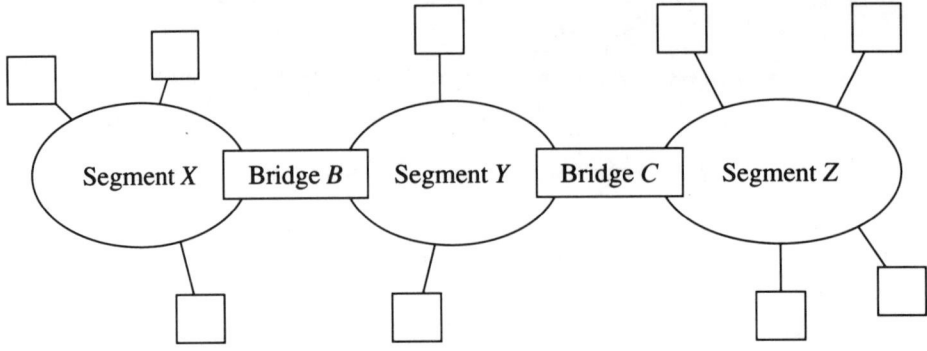

**Figure 7.9 — Bridges and Segments**

segment-bridge-segment identifiers $(X, B, Y)$ appear in the route field. (Special rules are followed to insert broadcast frames, as well as to prevent endlessly circulating frames.) The primary advantage of source routing is that the bridges are simpler; freed from address table lookup and maintenance, bridges make the forwarding decision with only a string-matching operation, thereby making the bridges faster and reducing congestion. The disadvantage is that route discovery and maintenance now become the responsibility of the transmitter.

Addressing format 0x04 allows an XTP address to be specified as a bridge-level source route, as shown in Figure 7.10. The *DestAddr* and *SrcAddr* fields are MAC layer addresses. The first bit of the *SrcAddr* field indicates if there is routing information present. If present, the *RoutingInfo* field consists of a *RouteCntl* field and one or more *RouteDesig* fields. The *RouteCntl* field contains an indication of the number of *RouteDesig* fields which follow. Each *RouteDesig* field contains a *SegNum* and a *BridgeNum* that are unique identifiers for a segment and a bridge on that segment. At each bridge the next *RouteDesig* indicates onto which segment to place the frame, and which bridge on that segment to which the frame should be sent. The *DSAP* and *SSAP* fields are the destination and source service access points, respectively. The *Control* field specifies control information about the packet. Depending on the number of *RouteDesig* fields present, the *Null* field will either be one or three bytes long.

## 7.1.5 Direct Addressing Format

Direct addressing, *aformat* value 0x09, allows a distributed system to define its own addressing format and mapping. It is assumed that, for whatever locally defined addressing scheme is used, the values contained within the *address* field can uniquely identify the destination host and service access point among all other access points within the distributed system. Furthermore, when a distributed system's topology and components are fixed and well known, such as with an embedded system, an address can be formed which specifies only the service access point or the process's identifier.

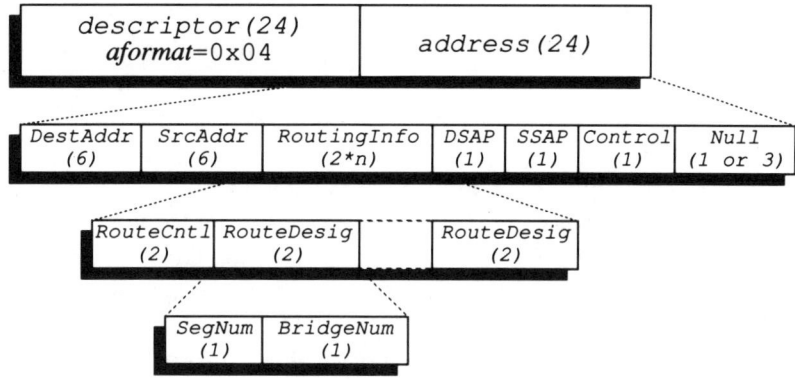

**Figure 7.10 — Format of *address* Field for IEEE 802-Style Source Route Addressing**

Note that, although packets addressed using the direct addressing format may coexist with packets using other formats, all packets with the direct addressing format must share the same address space.

## 7.1.6 Product-Specific and Project-Specific Addressing

Several specific products or projects have requested and have been granted an address *aformat* value from the Address Assignment Authority. These *aformat* values have been included in the list of addressing formats to show the diversity of needs and uses for XTP. Not all of these formats require in-depth discussion here. In particular, the Modular Simulator Project (MODSIM) is a project conducted by Boeing for the U.S. Air Force wherein XTP is specified to link the various modules. Also under Air Force direction is the USAF Embedded Systems work, where XTP will be used in tightly coupled embedded systems. MicroSoft's NetBIOS (Network Basic Input and Output System) was developed for personal computer networking applications as an interface between the PC networking software and the network interface card; the NetBIOS addressing format allows the use of the NetBIOS addresses within XTP.

The XTP Experimental Addressing Format, *aformat* value 0x0A, is reserved for implementors' experimentation. Typically situations arise where a communication system is in use but certain aspects of that system must be tested. This addressing format, like Direct Addressing, is locally defined so that it will not interfere with other standard addressing.

## 7.1.7 Multicast Addressing

When set, the MULTI bit in an XTP packet indicates that the packet belongs to a multicast association. In order to establish a multicast association, the XTP FIRST packet must carry a multicast group address. Several addressing schemes endorsed by XTP define some form of multicast addressing. We refer to *multicast addressing* as the identification of a set of destination nodes, a *logical host group*, using a single global address. This host group represents the set of hosts on which the XTP contexts in a multicast association reside.

RFC 1112 [DEER89] defines the Internet Class D addresses for multicast, as shown in Figure 7.3. These addresses can be used in XTP multicast for host group addressing. On a local area network an XTP implementation must map Class D addresses onto the MAC group addresses. The XTP Definition specifies a mapping between Class D addresses and Ethernet (and, by extension, other MACs such as FDDI and IEEE 802 standards) group addresses. This mapping places the low-order 23 bits of a Class D address into the low-order 23 bits of an Ethernet group address with a fixed prefix, as shown in Figure 7.11.

In order to enable multidestination delivery of packets carrying multicast addresses in an internetwork, the appropriate routing functionality must be constructed within the intermediate switching nodes. Routing tables must incorporate knowledge of logical host groups and coordinate membership changes. As reflected in RFC 1112, work on providing multicast extensions for the Internet Protocol is progressing, but not finalized at this time. RFC 1112 defines, for example, the Internet Group Management Protocol by which hosts report their memberships in logical host groups to the local multicast routers. Definition of these multicast routers is expected to follow. Due to parametric addressing, XTP implementations should be able to benefit directly from the continued advances in incorporating IP datagram multicast into the Internet environment.

Many distributed systems designers using XTP will want to define their own addressing (and, in particular, multicast addressing) schemes. The direct addressing format enables them to do so. Direct addressing schemes that include multicast must devise mechanisms to effect multidestination routing of packets and host group coordination. Small, closed networks—the environment best suited to the direct addressing format—can, however, use solutions that are generally much less complex than those for large internetworks.

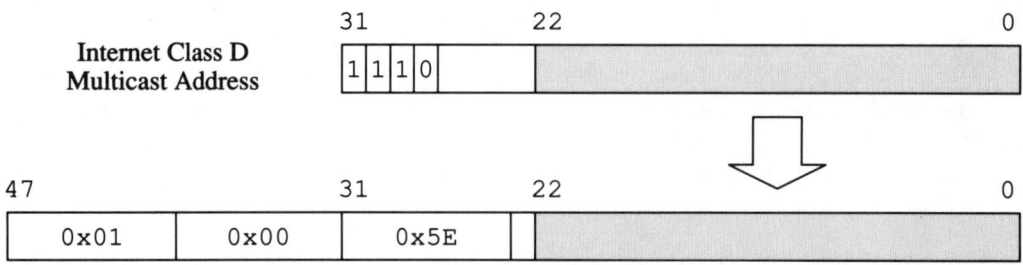

MAC Group Address

**Figure 7.11 — Mapping of Internet Class D Address into an Ethernet Group Address**

## 7.2  Encapsulation

In the general layered model of communication any particular layer will provide services to the layer immediately above it while using the services of the layer immediately below it. A *protocol data unit* (PDU) of some layer $k$ becomes the *service data unit* (SDU) of layer $k-1$. This layer $k$ PDU is the "data" carried within one or more layer $k-1$ PDUs. When layer $k-1$ provides the data delivery service for layer $k$, layer $k-1$ is said to *encapsulate* layer $k$.

XTP requires that its underlying data delivery service provide certain basic services, among them the physical propagation of XTP packets. These XTP packets are the "data" for this data delivery service since the data delivery service encapsulates the XTP packet within its PDU. Note that XTP is not tied to a particular protocol, or even to a protocol from a particular layer, as its data delivery service. Figure 7.12 shows the layer $k$ encapsulation of an XTP packet.

### MAC Layer Encapsulation

Figure 7.13 shows how an XTP packet can be encapsulated within either an FDDI, an Ethernet, or an IEEE 802.5 Token Ring MAC frame. Each of these MAC protocols has a header and a trailer which "frame" the data carried within. Figure 7.13 also shows the possibility of an LLC header or an LLC header with the Sub-Network Access Protocol (SNAP) [IEEE88] extension when LLC demultiplexing and other protocol identification are needed in addition to the MAC framing.

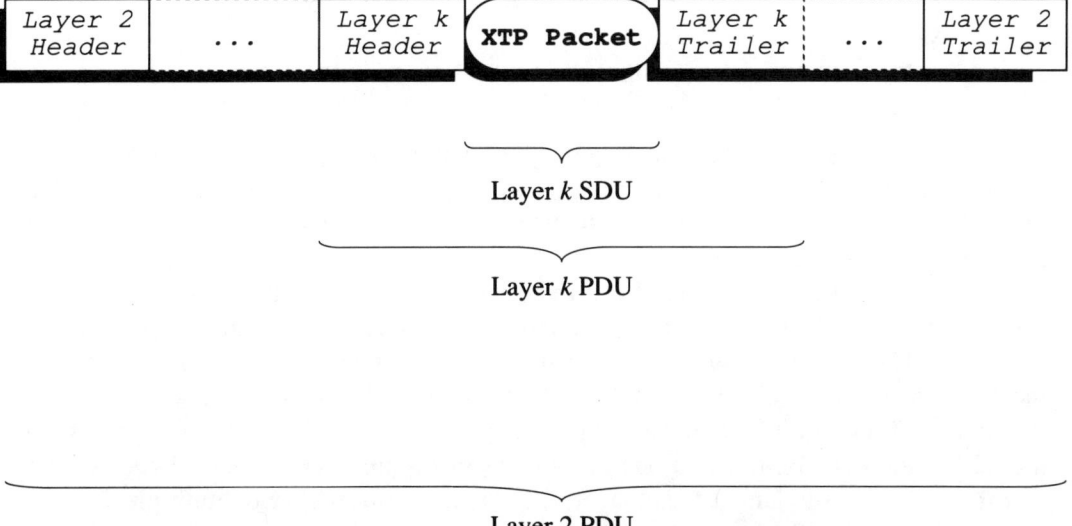

Figure 7.12 — General Encapsulation of an XTP Packet

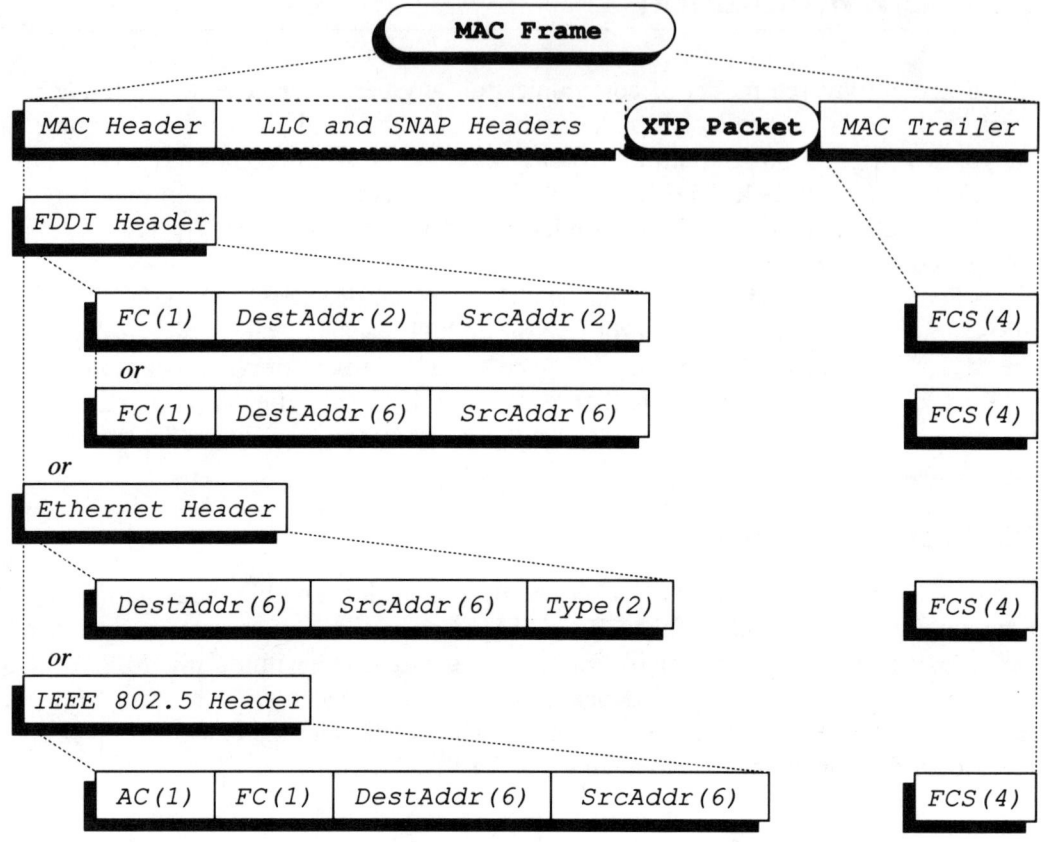

**Figure 7.13 — Encapsulation of XTP in Various MAC Standards**

XTP requires that its encapsulating data delivery service provide XTP access to the source and destination physical addresses. These physical machine addresses are used in XTP look-up algorithms to ensure the proper mapping of packets onto their destination contexts. MAC addresses are the physical addresses in a LAN environment.

The ANSI Fiber Distributed Data Interface (FDDI) [ANSI86] header contains a frame control field (*FC*) and the destination and source addresses (*DestAddr* and *SrcAddr*). The *FC* field contains information about this MAC frame, including rudimentary priority information, the address length, and what kind of data is present in this frame. There are two address lengths supported by FDDI, the 16-bit address and the 48-bit address. Both variations are shown in Figure 7.13. Since FDDI assumes that it will be used by an LLC sublayer, there is no form of service multiplexing present; therefore, the *FC* field only distinguishes between LLC data and MAC control frames. In reality, this assumption restricts FDDI to a single higher-layer user, which may in fact be XTP. The encapsulation of XTP within FDDI follows the guidelines established in RFC 1103 [KATZ89] for the encapsulation of IP datagrams within FDDI.

The encapsulation of XTP within Ethernet [DIGI82], perhaps the most ubiquitous of all MAC protocols, is also shown in Figure 7.13. Here the *DestAddr* and *SrcAddr* fields specify 48-bit addresses. The *Type* field is used to determine the client protocol for which this frame is destined, and thus provides the service demultiplexing for which other MAC protocols require LLC. (The IEEE 802.3 MAC standard [IEEE85a], very similar to Ethernet, differs in that it does not have a *Type* field equivalent and therefore requires the presence of LLC.) XTP has applied for and received from the proper authority, Xerox Corporation, a value for the Ethernet *Type* field which identifies XTP as the protocol using the Ethernet service. This value is 0x817D.

The IEEE 802.5 Token Ring MAC standard [IEEE85b] is also shown in Figure 7.13. The Token Ring header consists of an access control (*AC*) field, a frame control field (*FC*), and the destination and source addresses (*DestAddr* and *SrcAddr*). The *AC* field contains the priority and reservation bits which are used in the priority reservation access mechanism. The *FC* field, like the field in an FDDI frame, indicates whether the data contained within is LLC data or a MAC control frame. The source and destination addresses are 48 bits long.

## IEEE 802.2 Logical Link Encapsulation

The IEEE 802.2 Logical Link Control standard [IEEE84] sublayer provides a service that includes multiplexing various users of the data link layer onto the services of the MAC. These users are identified by an LLC service access point (LSAP). Half of the LSAP address space has been reserved by the IEEE 802 committee for assignment to specific standard network layer protocols. The other half is locally administered. Since these LSAPs are locally administered, there is no guarantee of their global uniqueness within an internetwork.

An XTP packet can be encapsulated in an LLC frame as shown in Figure 7.14. The destination service access point, or *DSAP*, indicates the service to which this frame is destined, namely XTP. The source service access point, or *SSAP*, likewise indicates the service which sent the frame. These service access points must be locally defined LSAP values since XTP has not been assigned a global LSAP value. The *Control* field in the LLC header identifies the particular PDU and specifies various control functions.

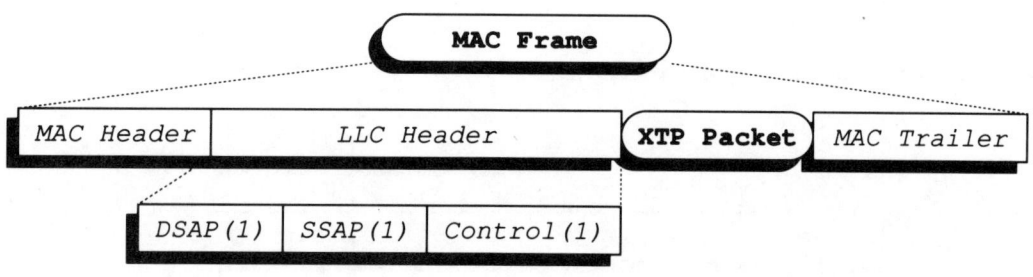

**Figure 7.14 — Encapsulation of XTP in an IEEE 802.2 LLC Frame**

    The Sub-Network Access Protocol specified in [IEEE88] is an extension of the LLC header. The SNAP extension provides a mechanism by which both private and public protocols that have not been assigned an LSAP value by IEEE 802 can be globally identified. There is a particular LSAP (decimal value 170) which indicates that a SNAP header is present. The protocols using SNAP must employ a protocol identifier which enables SNAP to discriminate among these protocols. The protocol identifier is composed of two fields, the *organization code*, which globally identifies an organization, and a *type* field, whose values are administered by the organization.

    XTP follows the guidelines of RFC 1042 [POST88] for using the SNAP header extension. As shown in Figure 7.15, both the *DSAP* and the *SSAP* take the SNAP LSAP value 170. The *Control* field has the decimal value 3, which represents Unnumbered Information. The value of 0 in the *OrgCode* field identifies the organization as Xerox since the *Type* field takes the value 0x817D, which is the same value used in Ethernet's *Type* field to identify XTP.

## IP Encapsulation

An XTP packet may be encapsulated as the data portion of an IP datagram, as shown in Figure 7.16. In this way an XTP packet can traverse the Internet and be delivered to a peer XTP implementation. As specified in RFC 1103, when these IP datagrams are transmitted over FDDI networks, the LLC and SNAP headers are present. The only XTP-specific value which must be placed in the IP header is the value for the *Protocol Type* field; XTP has been assigned protocol type number decimal 36. When a protocol is encapsulated within another protocol that is logically of an equal or higher layer, then the encapsulated protocol is said to be *tunneling* through the encapsulating protocol. Since the Xpress Transfer Protocol is a transfer layer protocol, encapsulation in IP is tunneling.

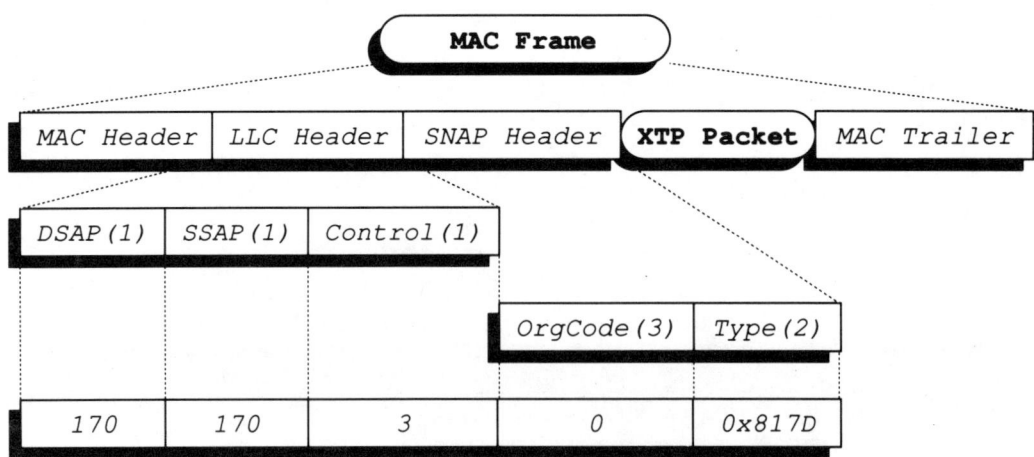

**Figure 7.15 — Encapsulation of XTP in an IEEE 802.2 LLC Frame with SNAP**

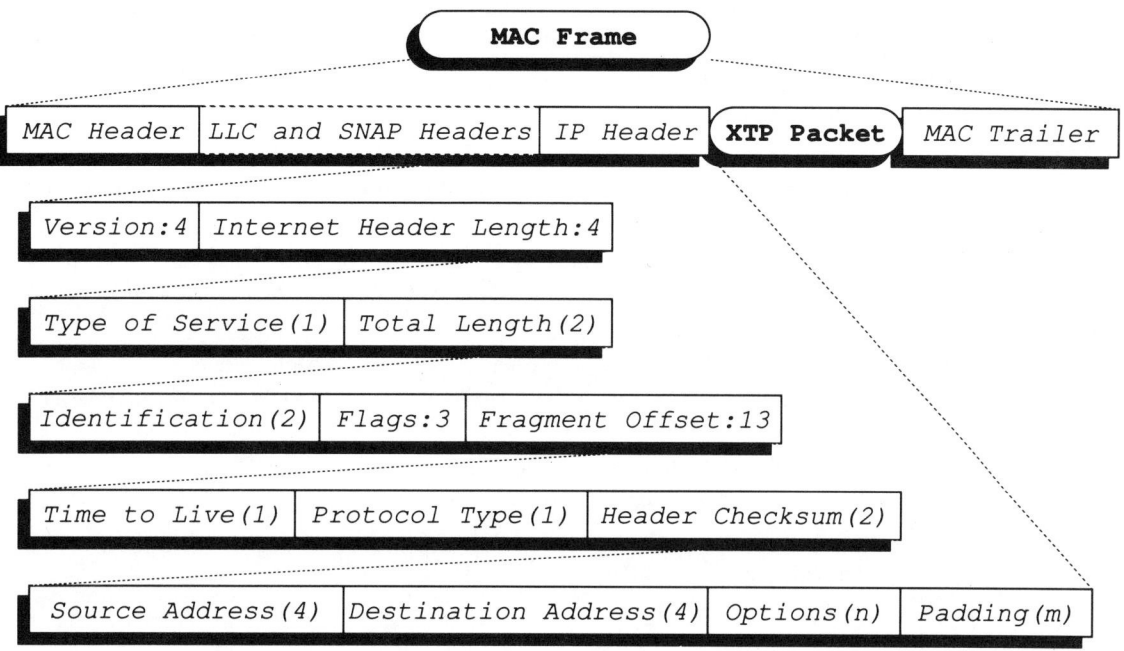

**Figure 7.16 — Encapsulation into an Internet Protocol Datagram**

## References

[ANSI86]      American National Standards Institute, "FDDI Token Ring Media Access Control Standard," *Draft proposed Standard X3T9.5/83–16, Rev. 10,* February 1986.

[DARPA81a]   Postel, J., ed., "Internet Protocol—DARPA Internet Program Protocol Specification," RFC 791, USC/Information Sciences Institute, September 1981.

[DEER89]     Deering, S., "Host Extensions for IP Multicasting," RFC 1112, Network Information Center, SRI International, August 1989.

[DIGI82]     Digital Equipment Corporation, Intel Corporation, and Xerox Corporation, "The Ethernet: A Local Area Network: Data Link Layer and Physical Layer Specifications," Version 2.0, November 1982.

[DIXO88]     Dixon, R. C., and Pitt, D. A., "Addressing, Bridging, and Source Routing," *IEEE Network*, Vol. 2, No. 1, pp. 25–32 (January 1988).

[IEEE84]     Institute of Electrical and Electronics Engineers, "IEEE Standard 802.2 Logical Link Control," 1984.

[IEEE85a]    Institute of Electrical and Electronics Engineers, "IEEE Standard 802.3 Carrier Sense Multiple Access with Collision Detection (CSMA/CD) Access Method and Physical Layer Specifications," 1985.

[IEEE85b]    Institute of Electrical and Electronics Engineers, "IEEE Standard 802.5 Token Ring Access Method and Physical Layer Specifications," 1985.

[IEEE88]      Institute of Electrical and Electronics Engineers, "IEEE Standard 802.1A Overview and Architecture of LAN," *Draft Standard P802.1A*, 1988.

[IEEE89]      Institute of Electrical and Electronics Engineers, "IEEE Standard 802.1D MAC Bridges," *Draft Standard P802.1D*, 1989.

[ISO8348/2]   International Organization for Standardization, "Addendum to the Network Service Definition Covering Network Layer Addressing," *Draft Proposed Addendum 8348/DAD2*, April 1985.

[KATZ89]      Katz, D., "A Proposed Standard for the Transmission of IP Datagrams over FDDI Networks," RFC 1103, Network Information Center, SRI International, June 1989.

[POST88]      Postel, J., and Reynolds, J., "A Standard for the Transmission of IP Datagrams over IEEE 802 Networks," RFC 1042, Network Information Center, SRI International, February 1988.

[ROMA89]      Romano, S., Stahl, M., and Recker, M., "Internet Numbers," RFC 1117, Network Information Center, August 1989.

[XERO91]      Xerox Corporation, "Internet Transport Protocols," Publication XNSS 029191, January 1991.

# 8
# Multicast

This chapter is divided into three sections. The first section overviews communication issues raised by application data streams that fall outside traditional *unicast* (one-to-one) exchanges. The second covers the XTP *multicast* (one-to-many) data transfer service and its implementation heuristics presented in the XTP Definition. The third section presents four applications whose requirements provide concrete examples of the group communication issues introduced in the first section. These applications illustrate the value and limitations of XTP in the overall communications solution for *multiparty data flows* (MDFs).

## 8.1  Group Communication

*Group communication* is a process-level abstraction for data flows within distributed applications that logically involve more than two application processes for each message exchange. Such multiparty exchanges do not fit well into two-party communication models, yet they arise naturally in a number of existing and emerging applications, both in local area and wide area environments. Examples include:

- distributed database applications
- client-multiserver arrangements
- network resource location
- network management
- distribution of digital images
- multimedia applications
- teleconferencing
- electronic mail distribution lists
- industrial automation and process control

The list of applications resulting in MDFs continues to expand due to the explosive growth of distributed systems and the increasing connectivity resulting from advances in LAN/WAN integration, among other factors.

The set of application processes that generate a MDF is called a *process group*. Process groups can be used to encapsulate internal state and hide group members' interactions in order to provide a distributed service with a uniform external interface.

Using such groups, with proper group communication support, simplifies the design and implementation of distributed applications. Homogeneous server groups often represent common processing elements, which are possibly replicated copies of the same sequential process, distributed across machine boundaries to achieve greater parallelism, increased data availability, reduced response time, and increased reliability.

Multiparty data flows are characterized by two parameters: *success criteria* and *topology*. Conventional two-party communication defines fully reliable data delivery as that in which the data arrives in-order, error-free, and duplication-free at the destination process. The reliability concerns for MDFs, the success criteria, are more complex. In the general case they include a semantics for various partial failure modes resulting from dynamic group membership and its relation to message delivery. In addition, application-level requirements that have no unicast analogy may have to be satisfied. An example is message serialization at the destination group.

Topologies for MDFs (shown in Figure 8.1) include: (1) from a single data source to a set of data sinks (point-to-multipoint), (2) from multiple data sources to a single data sink (multipoint-to-point), (3) from multiple data sources to a set of data sinks (multipoint-to-multipoint, with an important special case being *symmetric closed group communication* in which the set of sources and the set of sinks are the same and communication is between group members only), or (4) some other distributed scheme (for example, data sources send to a concentrator node, which then relays the message to the proper set of data sinks). The widespread use of media that offer each network node on the local segment the opportunity to capture each frame (*physical broadcast media*) invites the use of broadcast (one-to-all) and multicast (one-to-many) techniques in the communication subsystem. When identical data needs to be sent to multiple network nodes (*multidestination messages*), there are considerable efficiency and performance gains to be had by exploiting the physical broadcast media, relative to a comparable series of point-to-point transfers. Consequently, multicast primitives have been the focus of much of the research aimed at supporting MDFs.

## 8.1.1 Reliable Group Communication

Developing a notion of reliability for multidestination message delivery begins with defining the semantics for managing dynamic membership within the process group. Each message in a MDF is bound to some set of destinations, called its *receiver set*. Sets of messages, possibly from physically distributed data sources, may be required to reach the same set of group members. Defining the reliability of the service offered by a group communication facility includes consideration of the following factors: when and how the binding of a message to its set of destinations occurs, the registration and modification of *group views* (snapshots of group membership), how a user expresses the set of destinations that are sufficient for the message delivery to be successful, what failure recovery actions (if any) are specified, and whether changes in group membership are coordinated with message delivery to the group.

Consider the approaches to group communication taken in two widely known distributed systems—the V Kernel [CHER88b] and the ISIS project [BIRM91]. The V

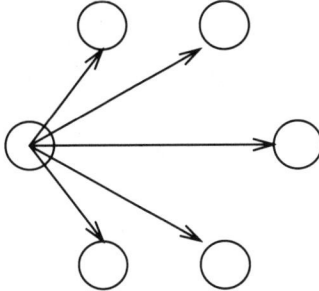

Point-to-Multipoint

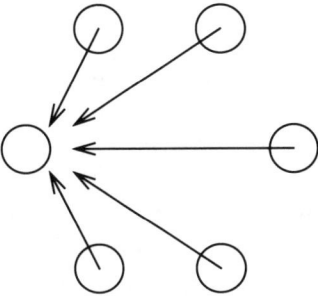

Multipoint-to-Point

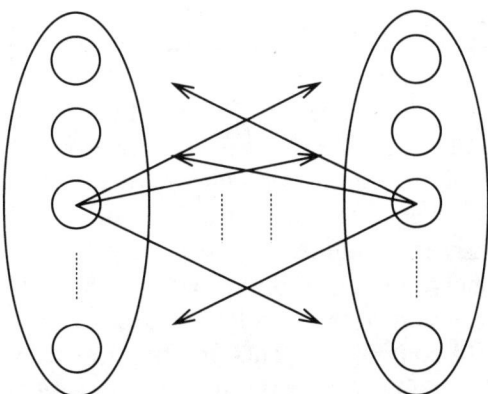

Multipoint-to-Multipoint

**Figure 8.1 — Multiparty Data Flow Topologies**

Kernel began as one of the earliest attempts at designing a software environment to support LAN-based distributed systems. It provides the lightweight mechanisms necessary to support request-response communication between a client and a server group.

The ISIS system, on the other hand, provides much more powerful group communication primitives in order to create an environment in which process groups are the building blocks for the development of distributed programs. In particular, ISIS supports *atomic multicast* (if one process in the destination set receives the message, then all members of the destination will receive it) with ordering guarantees (discussed later in this section).

V Kernel communication primitives use *k-reliable* semantics. That is, the user of the V primitive specifies the need for $k$ replies that must be collected from the receiver set before a timeout. Under $k$-reliable semantics the group view need only be a logical group address, which maps directly to a MAC group address in the underlying LAN.[1] A message is dynamically bound, when launched on the network, to the set of group members currently listening on the group address. Group members are not enumerated, and there is no provision for tracking the changing set, due to factors such as node failures and process migration, of physical servers that make up the logical group.

Within the Versatile Message Transaction Protocol (VMTP) used to support the V Kernel, a multicast transaction is considered successful as soon as the first reply from some member of the destination group arrives. Just as with single servers, a multi-server request fails only if no replies are received. This model relies on the V Kernel communication primitive to provide reliability beyond the first reply. Its advantage is in allowing VMTP to handle client-multiserver transactions with essentially no modification to the client-server protocol mechanisms. Server groups can be substituted for single servers, and individual servers can relocate or fail, all transparent to the client.

The ISIS system is intended to simplify the task of designing distributed software and, in particular, to provide a process group abstraction that encapsulates the difficulties of updating replicated, physically distributed data and state. An important component of this distributed programming environment is the communication primitives. A set of multicast primitives is available to enable atomic delivery to a group with ordering guarantees.

Ordered atomic communication under ISIS has the underlying support of a group management primitive, GBCAST, that transmits information about failures and recoveries to the process group. A recovering component issues a GBCAST to join operational process group members; when a component fails, some other component, possibly a local monitor process, issues a failure GBCAST on behalf of the failed component. GBCAST events are totally ordered with respect to the message-bearing broadcast primitives, and when a component fails, its failure GBCAST is delivered after any other broadcasts from the failed component. This ordering of membership events and message events is achieved in terms of logical orderings implemented in the multicast protocols, not explicit synchronization in terms of wall-clock time.

Message ordering guarantees greatly simplify concurrency control algorithms in many distributed applications. Two ordering properties are *multiple source ordering* and *multiple group ordering*. Multiple source ordering ensures that all messages from different sources are received in the same order at all members of a receiver set. Con-

---

[1] **IEEE 802.2, 802.3, 802.4, 802.5, and ANSI FDDI LAN standards support group addressing at the Medium Access Control Layer.**

sider the case where two messages, M and N, as shown in Figure 8.2, are delivered at group members A, B, C, and D. Suppose message M is placed ahead of message N at all receivers except C, where N is placed first. This violates multiple source ordering. If the sequence {M, N} results in a different state than {N, M}, then process C is not in a state consistent with that of other members of the receiver set.

Multiple group ordering is a more stringent ordering constraint than multiple source ordering. In this case, all processes belonging to the intersection of different groups order messages sent to these groups in a consistent fashion. Figure 8.3 illustrates a violation of multiple group ordering where message M is sent to group $G_1$ and message N is sent to $G_2$. Processes B and C belong to both groups, $G_1$ and $G_2$, and fail to order messages consistently.

The message-bearing multicast primitives in the ISIS system provide message ordering guarantees as well as atomic delivery. The ISIS multicast primitive BCAST(message, label, destinations) ensures that all messages with identical *labels* are ordered in the same way at all common destinations, achieving both multiple source ordering and multiple group ordering.

The absolute ordering provided by the BCAST primitive, which is implemented as a two- or three-phase agreement protocol in the ISIS system [BIRM87], is unnecessarily expensive in some cases. One useful way to relax the absolute ordering requirement is the notion of *causal broadcast*, based on the idea of potential causality introduced by Lamport in [LAMP78]. In this model the flow of information in a distributed system can be used to define a partial order on events occurring in the system.

Consider a computer teleconferencing application. When a participant in the conference receives a message sent to the group, the participant may reply either directly

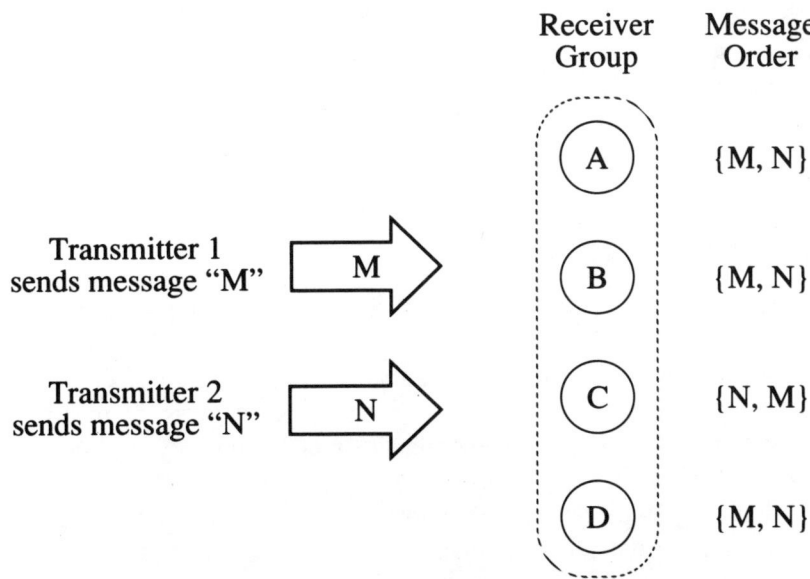

**Figure 8.2 — Violation of Multiple Source Ordering**

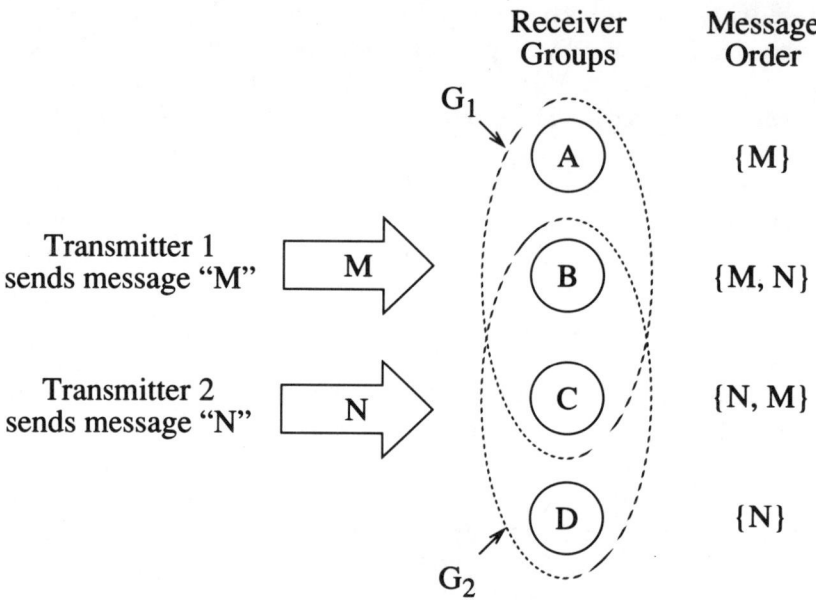

**Figure 8.3 — Violation of Multiple Group Ordering**

to the message's source or to the group. In a follow-up message, F, the speaker may make a point based on all the messages related to F that the speaker has received; these messages are called the "environment" associated with F. For other participants to understand F properly, they must have reference to its environment. A recipient should not see a message without having previously received its environment. This dependent relationship is a causal relationship and defines a partial ordering among all messages submitted to the computer conference [LIAN90]. In the ISIS project's protocol suite implementation, a causal multicast has been reported to be three to five times faster than an absolutely ordered multicast [BIRM91].

## 8.1.2 Group Management

In unicast communication, entities outside of the data transfer protocols must coordinate application processes such that communication is possible. For example, the process that wishes to send a message must know the global address of the destination process, and the receiving process must be waiting for a message to arrive. Group communication, however, introduces another layer of complexity to this coordination, requiring a *group management facility*.

If the destination process in a reliable unicast association is not active, or if it fails during a data exchange, the reliable unicast protocol will detect this failure as a communication failure. That is, there is no need for a separate entity to monitor the "liveness" of the destination process since liveness can be determined as a by-product of a reliable communication with the process. With group communication, however, the situation is different. Individual members failing do not necessarily affect data exchanges since, under some success criteria such as $k$-reliable multicast, data exchanges between active group members can continue.

Thus, independent of the protocol that handles group communication, a group management facility must oversee all operations concerning the membership and status of the group. This includes the creation and deletion of groups, monitoring of members joining and leaving the group, and other functions relating to group status.

The nature of group management depends heavily on the type of communication which the group supports. Consider again the V Kernel environment. For 1-reliable resource location, for example, group members may join and leave the group at any time. For $k$-reliable majority voting applications, the client process must establish the size of the group in order to know what constitutes a majority. Hence, in this group, members may leave, but not join, without notifying some group management authority. In an environment such as ISIS where ordered, atomic group communication is desired, the group management authority (i.e., the BCAST facility) must ensure that all membership changes in a group are ordered with respect to message events involving the group [PALI88].

## 8.2   XTP Multicast

In line with a lightweight protocol design philosophy, the designers of the Xpress Transfer Protocol strove to balance the need for group communication support with the desire to avoid distorting or overburdening the protocol with special case processing for the multiparty case. By extending and modifying unicast association procedures, multicast associations are incorporated into XTP and benefit from almost all of the functionality built into unicast associations.

Protocol mechanisms may be assumed to operate identically for both the multicast and unicast cases except for explicit differences called out in the XTP Definition. One important distinction between a multicast association and a unicast association is that the former is not duplex. While an endpoint of an XTP unicast conversation has a sending and a receiving "side" for duplex communication, in the multicast case endpoints are "one-sided." Receiving endpoints in the one-to-many case can not send data in the reverse direction since *concentration* techniques (management of the fusion of these multiple data streams at the multicast transmitter) are not part of the protocol. Rather, the XTP Definition describes an implementation technique involving context *cloning* that can be used for efficient setup of associations for handling multipoint-to-point data flows.

Algorithms in XTP for multicast communication are independent of the size of the group. Attempts to identify or enumerate the individual members of a multicast group are the responsibility of group management protocols that reside outside of XTP. Multicast contexts know only the group address of the multicast association, and all packets for the association, both data-bearing and control, are sent on the group address. This implies that all members of the multicast group, including the transmitter, "listen" on the same group address. The receivers may "overhear" each other's control packets. This ability of the receivers to monitor the progress of other group members is exploited in two of the heuristics proposed by the XTP Definition, *slotting* and *damping*.

Slotting and damping are two of the four multicast heuristics proposed in the XTP Definition. (The other two are the *bucket algorithm* and *cloning*; all are discussed in Section 8.3.) These four heuristics are not part of the XTP protocol. They are instead suggestions for strategies that the protocol implementor can use to implement and enhance XTP's support for group communications in the implementor's particular target environment.

The heuristics are included with the XTP Definition, but not as part of XTP itself, for two primary reasons. First, the heuristics guide the implementor in supporting features unlike any that the implementor may have previously encountered. Transfer layer multicast, and in particular XTP-style multicast, is novel. Unicast features in XTP, by contrast, are largely new embodiments or combinations of familiar concepts, e.g., components of a sliding window protocol. Second, the heuristics are useful in providing lessons learned from the implementation experience of XTP's designers. Inclusion of the heuristics in the protocol, however, would not leave room for later improvements or new approaches. The heuristics serve as guides and examples, not definitive solutions hard-wired into the specification of the protocol. As group communications research continues, other techniques may add to or replace those mentioned here.

While XTP multicast algorithms are targeted to networks with an underlying broadcast medium, the multicast facility can be adapted to operate, with additional support from the underlying data delivery service, over a point-to-point network. No explicit features of the multicast algorithms prevent the introduction of intermediate switching nodes in the multicast path. In such an environment, however, implicit timing dependencies in implementation heuristics must be examined carefully. In addition, since XTP specifies that all CNTL packets in a multicast association be sent on the group address, excessive traffic at the switching nodes is possible if a large number of CNTL packets are generated.

## 8.2.1 Error Control in Multicast Associations

A XTP multicast association operates under one of two error-control policies. When error control is requested, the service provided delivers data with high probability of success to the receiver set active for the duration of the transfer. (The receiver set is the set of contexts receiving the data from the multicast transmitter.) We refer to this service as *semi-reliable multicast*. When error control is not requested (by setting the NOERR mode bit), an XTP multicast association operates under no-error mode semantics, as described in Section 4.7 for unicast associations. We refer to this as *blast multicast* service.

Semi-reliable multicast takes its name from the fact that, while the association has active flow, rate, and error control mechanisms, the size and composition of the receiver set are unknown to the transmitter. Consequently, when collecting status reports from the receiver set, the transmitter must use timer-driven methods to determine the data transfer status. The transmitter can not detect failed receivers and also risks not being responsive to an active receiver whose CNTL packet does not arrive in a timely fashion. The transmitter in semi-reliable multicast focuses on providing a robust association for all "healthy" receivers, that is, those that do not fail or lag too far behind the group.

The aggressiveness of the semi-reliable multicast transmitter in acting on accumulated status reports from the receiver set determines the robustness of the semi-reliable service. Since the degree of robustness required is heavily influenced by application and implementation considerations, the XTP multicast heuristics include an algorithm, the *bucket algorithm*, for tuning transmitter aggressiveness.

In semi-reliable multicast, the transmitting context will at certain times request the collective status of the receiver set. The transmitter does this by setting the SREQ bit in an out-going packet. The transmitter is not allowed to request status reports from receivers by setting the DREQ bit instead of the SREQ bit. The DREQ option has been disallowed in multicast mode because the transmitter's task of determining the collective status of the receiver set becomes more difficult as the receivers' status reports become scattered over a longer time interval. Thus, in order to maintain as tight a synchrony as possible between the multiple replies expected after each request, the SREQ option must be used. Section 8.2.3 on CNTL packet processing for multicast elaborates further.

Blast multicast follows the no-error mode rules set forth for unicast exchanges. That is, the association has flow and rate control, but not error control. When solicited for status, each multicast receiver issues its CNTL packet with the *rseq* and *dseq* values set to the highest sequence number seen at that receiver. Requests for group status are likely to be less frequent in blast multicast than in semi-reliable multicast.

## 8.2.2 Multicast Association Establishment

Multicast association establishment begins when an XTP user submits an **output** command for a multicast address. An initiating context is activated, and a FIRST packet carrying the group address in its Address Segment is issued. Since XTP multicast is designed for networks with a physical broadcast medium, the destination MAC address for the FIRST packet is a MAC multicast or broadcast address, derived from the group address in the Address Segment. The FIRST packet will be delivered to the set of hosts on the network that have filters active on the group address carried in the FIRST packet. These contexts have requested local activation of filters on the group address because of **input** commands issued on that group address by a set of XTP users some time before the FIRST packet is launched. The FIRST packet of a multicast association has identical properties to that of a unicast association with two exceptions: (1) the MULTI bit is set in the *options* field in the Header and (2) the DREQ bit must not be set. The MULTI bit informs the receivers that a multicast association is being established.

# 8.2.3 Multicast Association Maintenance

The procedures for multicast association maintenance include managing the association identifiers (*key mapping*), the procedure that allows new or recovering receivers to join an in-progress multicast association (*join procedure*), and the procedures at the multicast transmitter for fusing a multiplicity of CNTL packets into a view of the receiver set's current state (*CNTL packet processing*).

## Key Mapping

When the initial context is activated at the transmitting side due to an **output** command, a new *key* value is assigned to that context. This *key* value is included in the *key* field of the FIRST packet and all subsequent DATA and CNTL packets sent from this context. The receivers in the receiver set use the *return key* value as the *key* field value in all CNTL packets sent to the transmitter. This use of the *key* values is precisely that set forth in Chapter 6; however multicast associations never perform the key exchange procedure.

The key exchange procedure is an optimization that only works between pairs of communicants. Recall that under unicast the *xkey* field in a CNTL packet can carry a *return key* value chosen by the receiver. Since multicast implies a set of receivers, there can be no consensus on a proper *return key* value to use as the *xkey* value for this entire set. Consequently, multicast transmitters must ignore the *xkey* field in all incoming CNTL packets, which forces XTP implementations at the hosts of receivers to do full context lookups on incoming multicast packets. The XTP implementation at the multicast transmitter's host, on the other hand, has the benefit of abbreviated lookups since the multicast receivers are using the *return key* procedure.

The absence of the key exchange procedure in multicast has an interesting side-effect. If the transmitter elects to use, say, $K_T$ as its *key* value, then any packets originating at a multicast receiver will carry the *return key* value, $K'_T$. All packets originating at the multicast transmitter carry $K_T$. This fact is useful in that it allows multicast set members, at all times during the association, to distinguish easily between packets issued by the transmitter and those issued by members of the receiving set.

## Join Procedure

The multicast FIRST packet establishes an association between the transmitter and all remote XTP contexts that are currently listening on the group address. At any time during the association, the receiver set may shrink, transparently to the transmitter, due to network or host failures. The procedure by which a new context can join or rejoin the receiver set of an in-progress multicast association, however, is not transparent to the transmitter.

The *join procedure* involves the transmitter participating in an exchange of PATH packets with the joining member. The joining XTP peer must have a context activated in order to join the receiver set. This context issues a PATH packet containing the multicast group address and a value of zero in the *key* field. Issued on the group address, this PATH packet is seen by each receiver in the receiver set as well as by the transmitter; the XTP Definition requires that other receivers not respond to this packet. When the transmitter receives such a PATH packet it responds by issuing a PATH packet containing the multicast group address, but also containing the *key* value for this transmitter context. The new receiver receives this PATH packet and begins to accept packets with this *key* value. Dependent upon the XTP implementation, the XTP user controlling the multicast transmitting context may be able to dictate the points in the data stream at which receivers may enter the group.

## CNTL Packet Processing

When soliciting CNTL packets from the receiver set, the transmitter is required to use only the SREQ bit and never the DREQ bit in the *options* field in the Header. As discussed in Section 8.2.1, this restriction follows from the difficulty of synthesizing the status of the receiver set from the CNTL packets of the individual members of the set.

Semi-reliable semantics dictate that the multicast transmit context be responsive to all active receivers by updating the transmit context's state based on the *worst-case* values of all reported status variables. (Of course, in cases where a receiver lags too far behind and so requests retransmission of data in transmit buffers that have already been released, the transmitter must necessarily ignore the worst-case report.) It is consequently important to determine the "age" of CNTL packets to avoid the inclusion of an "old" CNTL packet in the synthesis.

The use of the SREQ bit ensures that CNTL packets are generated at the multicast receiver as soon as the packet with the SREQ bit set arrives. CNTL packets of the same era are thus issued at the same time. To fully ensure synchrony, the multicast transmitting context performs a synchronizing handshake (explained in Section 4.7.4) with each receiver. That is, each of the transmitter's CNTL packets has as its *sync* field value some counter incremented at least with each data-bearing packet. At each member of the receiving set, the in-coming CNTL packet with the SREQ bit set causes a status report to be generated. This report (i.e., CNTL packet) carries in its *echo* field the *sync* value just received in the transmitter's CNTL packet. In this way the relative age of each CNTL packet that arrives at the multicast transmitter can be determined.

# 8.2.4 Terminating a Multicast Association

Graceful termination semantics for multicast resemble those for the graceful close with forced termination (see Section 4.2.3) since multicast associations never have reverse direction (receivers-to-transmitter) data flow. Accordingly, for a multicast close the transmitter issues a CNTL packet with the WCLOSE, RCLOSE, and SREQ bits set. Upon reception of this CNTL packet, a receiver responds with a CNTL packet having the WCLOSE and RCLOSE bits set. After a period of time during which retransmissions may occur, the transmitter then issues the final CNTL packet with the WCLOSE, RCLOSE, and END bits set. Figure 8.4 shows this close procedure.

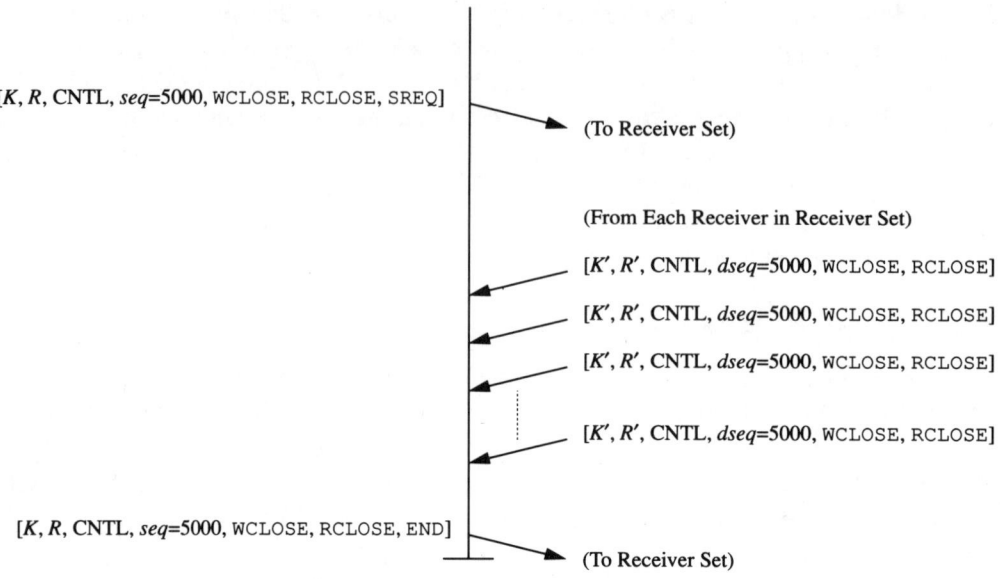

[K, R, CNTL, *seq*=5000, WCLOSE, RCLOSE, SREQ]

(To Receiver Set)

(From Each Receiver in Receiver Set)

[K′, R′, CNTL, *dseq*=5000, WCLOSE, RCLOSE]

[K′, R′, CNTL, *dseq*=5000, WCLOSE, RCLOSE]

[K′, R′, CNTL, *dseq*=5000, WCLOSE, RCLOSE]

[K′, R′, CNTL, *dseq*=5000, WCLOSE, RCLOSE]

[K, R, CNTL, *seq*=5000, WCLOSE, RCLOSE, END]

(To Receiver Set)

**Figure 8.4 — Termination of a Semi-reliable Association**

During the close procedure the multicast transmitter must wait some amount of time for retransmission requests. Since the transmitter has no knowledge of set size, this wait time must be based on a timer. Thus, the set of receivers that gracefully close depends upon how aggressive the transmitting context's algorithm is in determining the timeout value.

For abrupt termination, the transmitter sends a CNTL packet with the END bit set. The transmitting context is released immediately. All receiving contexts that receive this CNTL packet are released as well. If some number of the receivers fail to receive this CNTL packet, they will eventually be released due to the time-outs of the connection activity timers. Multicast receivers should never send CNTL packets with the END bit set since the transmitter can not know if all receivers have released.

# 8.3   XTP Multicast Heuristics

The XTP Definition offers four multicast heuristics: the *bucket algorithm*, *slotting*, *damping*, and *cloning*. These techniques are intended to provide implementors with algorithms and suggestions for using XTP's mechanisms that may improve the efficiency and effectiveness of XTP's group communication support. These heuristics are not actually part of the Xpress Transfer Protocol, and so their use in an XTP implementation is optional. They do, however, represent knowledge gained through XTP implementation experience and are sufficiently universal mechanisms as to deserve inclusion in the XTP Definition document.

## 8.3.1 Bucket Algorithm

The XTP implementor must provide the method by which a multicast transmitter determines (1) how the transmitter synthesizes the information in the stream of CNTL packets returning from the receiver set and (2) the *switch-time interval*, which is the length of time that the transmitter waits before updating its status based on this stream of CNTL packets. In the XTP Definition a heuristic known as the *bucket algorithm* is proposed as one approach. The bucket algorithm dictates that the multicast transmitter sort the returning CNTL packets by age into "buckets" that hold certain state values representing the information contained in CNTL packets of a similar age.

A *bucket* is a data structure kept at the transmitter and is labeled with one of the *sync* values generated by the transmitter. When a multicast transmitter issues a CNTL packet with its SREQ bit set, it labels an empty bucket with the *sync* value placed in the Header of the outgoing CNTL packet. This bucket then serves as the repository for all receiver-generated CNTL packets whose *echo* fields match the label on the bucket. (Notice that this is a synchronizing handshake as described in Section 4.7.4.) The bucket merges the information from each CNTL packet of the same "era" since *sync* values, generated at the transmitter and echoed by the receivers, are essentially values of a logical clock at the transmitter. The values of interest that are collected in the bucket are the *dseq*, *rseq*, *alloc*, and *techo* values carried in the CNTL packets that match the bucket's label.

An XTP transmitter using the bucket algorithm will have a number of buckets ready for use so that the control information from several different eras can be compiled concurrently. Collection into a new bucket is started after a period of time called the *switch-time interval*, when the transmitter issues a packet with the SREQ bit set. Each switch-time interval is based on the current estimated worst-case roundtrip time between the transmitter and its receiver set, this roundtrip estimate having been calculated from the *techo* values in receiver-generated CNTL traffic (see Section 4.7.3). Initially, during a multicast data transfer, the end of a switch-time interval simply marks the instantiation of another bucket from the bucket set. Once all the buckets in the set have been used, however, the information in the oldest bucket (bucket with the lowest *sync* value label) is used to update the transmitter's state at the end of every switch-time interval.

The length of time between when a packet with SREQ set is issued by the transmitter and when the status information resulting from that packet is used to update the transmitter's status is dependent on the number of buckets in the bucket set. The tradeoff is simple: as the collection time gets longer (more buckets), the more certain the transmitter can be that the information in the oldest bucket reflects the status of the entire group, but also the longer the transmitter must wait before it can use that information.

After the transmitting context's state has been updated, the processed bucket is emptied. That is, all values in the bucket's variables are forgotten, and the bucket is available for reuse. At this point, all buckets are effectively aged by making the just-emptied bucket into the "newest" bucket. The newest bucket is initialized by marking it with the *sync* value of the packet with SREQ set being issued by the transmitter on this switch-time interval boundary.

### Example 8.1

Assume a transmitter keeps two buckets. It issues a CNTL packet with its SREQ bit set and a *sync* value of 2. As CNTL packets come back from the receiver set, the status information is collected in a bucket labeled 2. Later, a second CNTL packet with the SREQ bit set is issued by the transmitter, this time with *sync* value 3. (In our example, the transmitter chooses to send its requests for status (SREQs) in CNTL packets.) All CNTL packets coming from the receiver set with an *echo* value of 2 are dumped into the bucket labeled 2; all those with *echo* value 3 are dumped into the bucket labeled with 3. Later another CNTL packet is issued with *sync* value 4. At this time all of the information kept in bucket labeled 2, being the older bucket, is now used to update the transmitter's status, and the bucket is emptied and relabeled with 4, the *sync* value of the outgoing CNTL packet.

Figure 8.5 illustrates these steps in more detail. The diagram depicts selected elements of the transmitter's state—shown here are transmit buffers held for possible retransmissions on the left side, the values of certain variables (*rseq* and *dseq*) in the bucket data structures in the center, and the sequence of packet events on the right. Packets are shown with the values of certain state variables; the FIRST and DATA packets are shown with the sequence number interval of the data they carry.

Figure 8.5 shows a FIRST packet sending the first 100 bytes of data, and a DATA packet sending the next 100 bytes of data, for a multicast association. When the first switch-time interval expires, a CNTL packet is issued with *sync* value 2. This instantiates a bucket with the label 2, as shown in Detail (1). As the first two inbound CNTL packets arrive, their information is placed in the bucket labeled 2 since each packet's *echo* field value matched that bucket's label. At Detail (2) the second switch-time interval expires, and the second CNTL packet is issued by the transmitter. At a later time, the third inbound CNTL packet arrives, and it indicates that some data was missed at some receiver. By Detail (3a) several more DATA packets have been issued and the bucket labeled 3 has information accumulated from more inbound CNTL packets. At the point in time of Detail (3a), the bucket structure is full and some bucket must be emptied in order to create a new one. The oldest bucket, the one labeled with the lowest value, is chosen. Detail (3a) shows the state of the oldest bucket before the application of this bucket's information to the state of the transmit context; Detail (3b) shows the bucket after it is emptied and relabeled.

Between Details (3a) and (3b), two processing steps occur. First, the oldest bucket is emptied and the transmitter's state is updated accordingly. In this step, as shown on the left side of the diagram, the buffer for data with sequence numbers 0 to 99 are released. This results from the bucket having a *dseq* value of 100. Also, as shown on the right side of the diagram, applying the information in this bucket results in the retransmission of data with sequence numbers from 100 to 399. This retransmission occurs because the transmitter has sent all data up to sequence number 399, but the

Transmit Buffers                          Buckets                          Packet Events

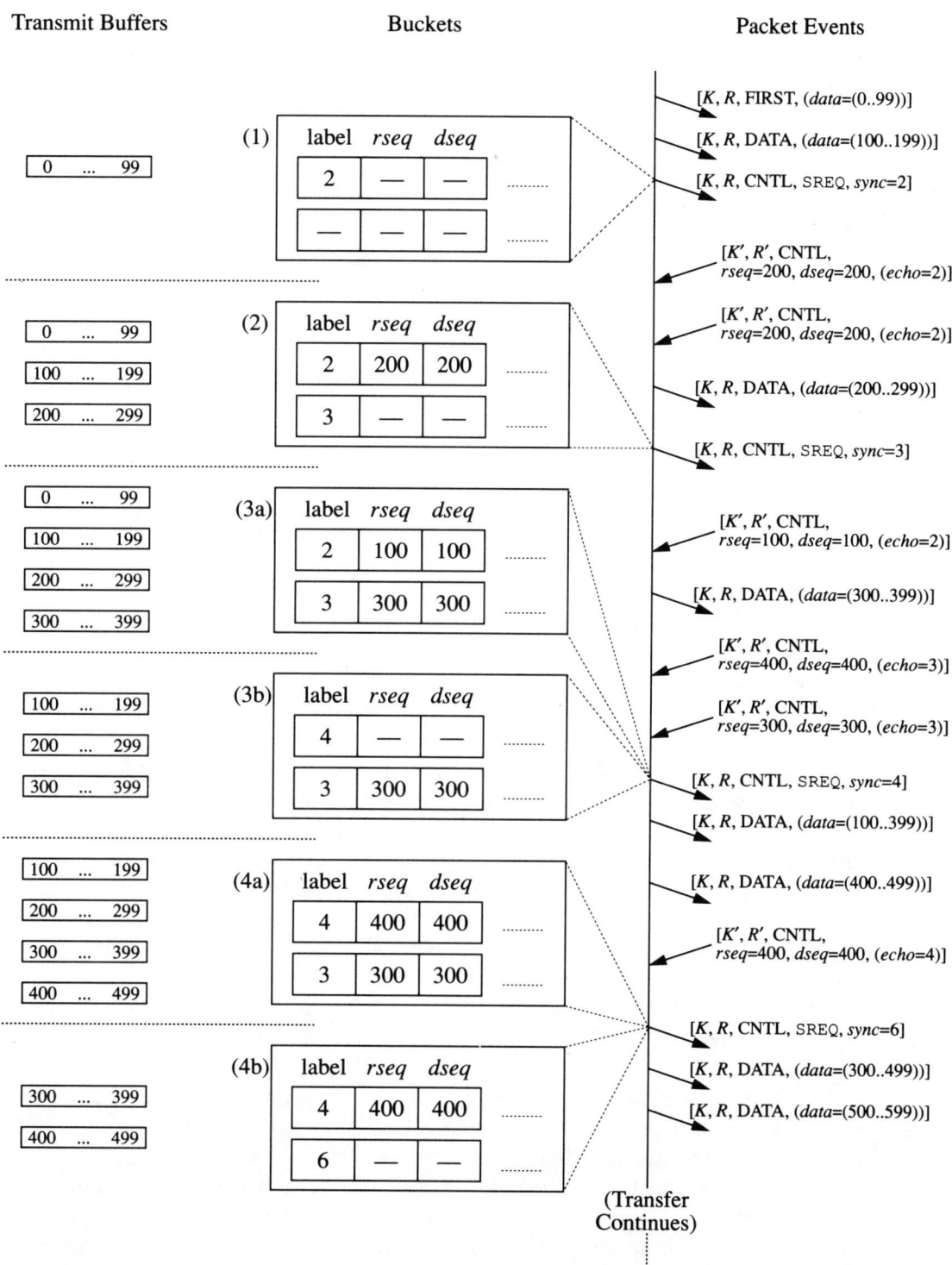

**Figure 8.5 — Bucket Algorithm Example**

*rseq* in the bucket with label 2 is 100. This *rseq* value indicates that only data through sequence number 99 has been contiguously received at some receiver (at least one). Since go-back-*n* is the retransmission policy associated with the bucket algorithm, the transmitter resends all data from 100 to 399.

The second processing step between 3(a) and 3(b) is the reuse of the just-emptied bucket. This bucket is now initialized with the value of the outgoing *sync* value so that it effectively becomes the "newest" bucket. Detail 3(b) shows the new bucket properly initialized.

At the next switch-time interval and all switch-time intervals thereafter, the same sequence of processing steps takes place: empty the oldest bucket, update the transmit context, and initialize the just-emptied bucket as the newest bucket. In Detail (4a) the oldest bucket is that with label 3. In this case the new *dseq* value allows the release of two transmit buffers (from 100 to 299) while the *rseq* value indicates the need for another retransmission.

## 8.3.2 Slotting and Damping

*Slotting* and *damping* are heuristics for reducing the number of CNTL packets necessary to support a multicast association. They are complementary techniques. Since multicast receivers send their CNTL packets on the group address, receivers overhear each other's CNTL packets. Damping refers to the technique of having a receiver refrain from transmitting its CNTL packet if it receives some other CNTL packet that would render the locally generated CNTL packet superfluous. A receiver allows its CNTL packet to be damped if all of the control information being tracked at the transmitter is duplicated in the CNTL packet of another receiver. For instance, if the transmitter is using the bucket algorithm, then a CNTL packet is damped at a receiver when the local *rseq*, *dseq*, and *alloc* values are larger than the corresponding values in the overheard CNTL packet and the *techo* and *echo* values are smaller.

This packet suppression method will significantly reduce the total number of CNTL packets on the network as long as the receiver set generates CNTL packets with enough time variance to allow for damping to take place. That is, there must be enough time to receive and examine other receivers' CNTL packets if damping is to occur. The slotting heuristic addresses this requirement.

Slotting forces receivers to spread their CNTL packets over an interval of time. After having received a request for status, multicast receivers wait a randomly chosen time period (the local *slot time*) before issuing a CNTL packet. This back-off interval allows a receiver to examine other CNTL packets while its own CNTL packet is queued for transmission, thus increasing the likelihood that damping will occur.

Employing slotting and damping trades off increased processing at the members of the receiver set for a reduction in the number of CNTL packets that are placed on the network and that must be processed at the transmitter. This trade-off increases in importance in proportion to the product of two factors: group size, and frequency of CNTL packets. This product represents the total number of receiver-generated CNTL packets per time interval. As the product grows, it becomes more critical to protect the transmitter and (possibly) the underlying network from excessive packet traffic and packet processing demands.

Figure 8.6 shows a measurement of the effect of slotting and damping on a small network using a software XTP implementation at the University of Virginia [HART91]. The measurements were performed using Western Digital WD8003E EtherCard Plus interfaces on a standard 10 Mbit/sec Ethernet. Each of the four XTP receivers is located on a different AT-class computer using an Intel 80386 processor running at 25 MHz. The multicast transmitter resides on a 16-MHz 386-based machine.

The experiment involved the transfer of two megabytes of data. Each iteration of the experiment fragmented the data into a fixed packet size, as plotted on the horizontal axis. The vertical axis shows the total number of receiver-generated CNTL packets issued over the entire 2-megabyte transfer. In the experiment the multicast transmitter issued a CNTL packet with the SREQ bit set after each message sent to the group. The lower curve in the graph shows the number of receiver-generated CNTL packets issued as a function of message size with slotting and damping algorithms turned on. The upper curve shows the number of receiver-generated CNTL packets issued under identical conditions, but without slotting and damping.

In this XTP implementation slot times were determined as follows. Each slot is equivalent to 32 ticks of a system clock, or approximately 27 μsec. Each multicast

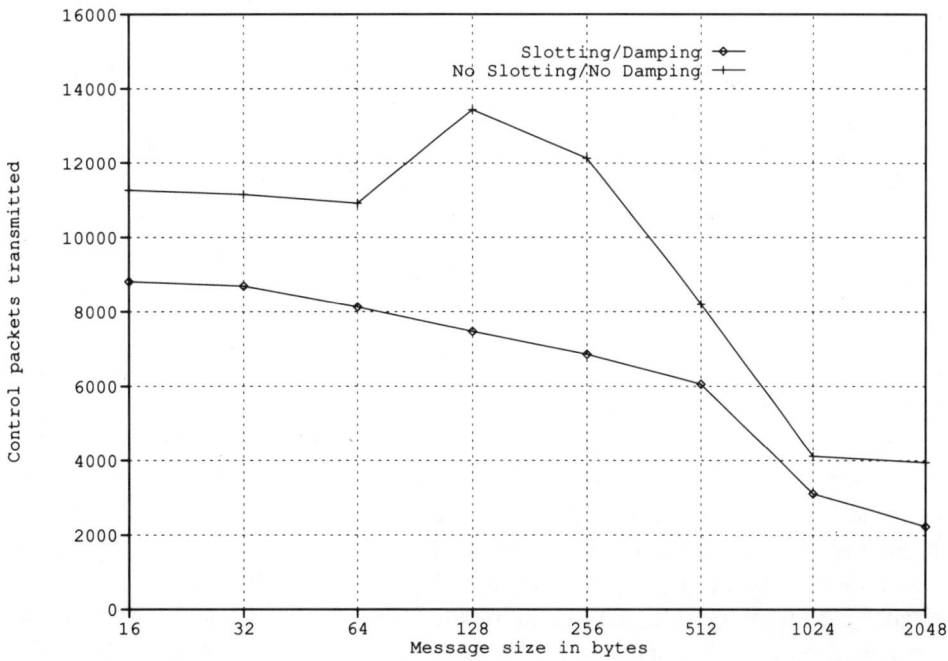

**Figure 8.6 — Experimental Measurement of Slotting and Damping Effectiveness**

receiver seeded a random number generator with a portion of the local station's MAC address and obtained an integer between 1 and 500. This integer represented the number of slots that the receiver held its CNTL packets before transmitting them (if they were not already damped). Thus, in this experiment, slotting introduces a pseudo-random delay in the range of 27 μsec to 13.5 msec.

An important consideration in interpreting these curves is the effect of *overrunning*. If each of the transmitter-generated CNTL packets were to induce a responding CNTL packet from each member of the receiving set, the total number of packets generated would be much larger than that shown in the graph. However, the rate of transfer and the processing capabilities at the receiving nodes is such that members of the receiver set can not respond immediately to each transmitter-generated CNTL packet. Instead, by the time the receivers can issue a responding CNTL packet, some number of additional transmitter-generated CNTL packets have arrived. Since a receiver sets its *echo* value to reflect the highest *sync* value yet received in a CNTL packet, the most recent inbound CNTL packet *overruns* the earlier CNTL packets. That is, for example, before a receiver can generate a CNTL packet with an *echo* value of 234, the transmitter may have sent CNTL packets containing *sync* values (for instance) 240, 247 and 252. Therefore the *echo* value in the outgoing CNTL packet at the receiver will carry the largest of these, hence 252.

In the experiment, then, small message sizes mean that the receivers will experience a high rate of inbound CNTL packets, but little processing overhead per message. Large messages, on the other hand, mean fewer inbound CNTL packets, but greater per-message processing overhead. Figure 8.6 shows that these factors result in a maximum number of receiver-generated CNTL packets at a message size of 128 bytes.

Independent of the overrunning issue, this experiment shows unambiguous evidence of the positive effect of slotting and damping in reducing message traffic. By having the receivers back off over a few millisecond interval, the number of receiver-generated CNTL packets was significantly reduced.

## 8.3.3 Cloning

The term *cloning* refers to the on-demand spawning of slave contexts from a master context. Cloning may be used so that many-to-one, or *concentration*, data flows can be constructed from existing multicast associations. There is no facility within XTP for concentration since it is not clear how to fuse the data streams from multiple transmitters. Instead, the XTP Definition suggests using a heuristic involving cloning for constructing a set of back channels for a multicast association, leaving it to the application to determine how best to fuse these multiple data streams.

Under cloning, the multicast transmitter is able to spawn slave contexts in the Listening state after the multicast association has been established. A slave context is created in response to an incoming FIRST packet, which has been issued by a multicast receiver in the extant multicast association. Once instantiated, the slave contexts act as

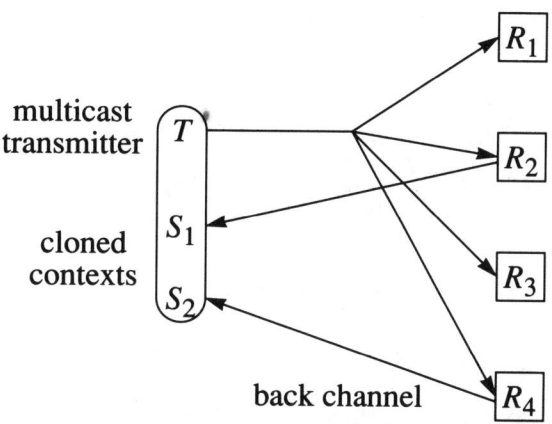

**Figure 8.7 — Multicast Concentration via Cloning**

the receivers for each of the incoming data streams, or back channels. Figure 8.7 shows this relationship. Now full-duplex data flows can commence: the multicast transmitter multicasts to its receiver set, some of whom send data back to the transmitter via the slave contexts.

The exact mechanisms for cloning are implementation-dependent, but any cloning scheme must deal with the following issues. The XTP host implementations must manage context identifiers and other addressing information so that contexts can be spawned, duplicate FIRST packets do not create spurious cloned contexts, and all packets are correctly mapped to their destination contexts. Also, a multicast receiving context with a back channel open must correctly handle multiple data flows. After receiver $R_2$ in Figure 8.7 has set up a back channel that clones slave context $S_1$, receiver $R_2$ must process packets on two separate data streams, that from the original multicast transmitter $T$ and that to $S_1$. This situation is quite different from normal protocol processing in which two communication peers manage one duplex communication between them. Processing at the receiver $R_2$ must ensure that state information from a packet on one data stream does not interfere with correct processing on the other data stream.

Finally, the user interface to an XTP multicast service that allows cloning must handle the grouping of a multicast transmitting context with its set of slave contexts. The XTP multicast service user does not explicitly open the cloned contexts with an **input** command and thus the service user does not have a descriptor for the back channels. The interface then provides for the multiplexing of all of the incoming data streams.

# 8.4   Group Communication Application Examples

This section points out the value and limits of XTP multicast through an evaluation of XTP's role in satisfying the communication needs of a set of prototypical group communication applications. These applications are prototypical in that each is representative of a class of distributed applications. The discussion of these applications focuses on making concrete the envisioned uses of XTP's functionality. Of course, the suggestions given here for using XTP multicast are in no way comprehensive: the protocol will doubtlessly be used in ways that neither we nor the XTP designers ever envisioned.

## Distribution of Periodic Updates

In a wide variety of communications environments, it is desirable to maintain a set of physically distributed processes that periodically receive data from a central source. Consider an industrial automation setting in which a sensor periodically distributes its readings to some set of data processing nodes, or *readers*. Updates are sent frequently enough that readers can tolerate the loss of a small number of updates. If a reader can not obtain an update for some system-dependent time interval on the order of tens of update periods, however, the reader begins failure recovery actions that may seriously disturb normal system functioning. Thus, while individual updates may be lost with impunity, application requirements put a premium on update reliability, or availability, at a coarse-grained level.

One solution is to use transport layer datagrams. Supposing that this transport layer datagram service has a multicast facility, these updates may be distributed in a "fire and forget" fashion. However, with a connectionless service such as this, each update is a separate and independent communication service call. One implication is that no segmentation and reassembly of large updates is provided by the communication service. Furthermore, flow and rate control are not available for the update stream. In an XTP-based network, a no-error mode multicast association could be used instead.

A no-error mode multicast association is well suited to respond to the success criteria of this application. Error control for individual messages is absent while the join procedure allows a new reader node to join the association without disturbing the data distribution. The requirement of continuous availability of the updates means that it is likely to be very undesirable to shut down and restart the multicast association. The join procedure allows for shifting membership in the set of readers; membership changes are transparent to the application data source, and receivers join the conversation concurrent with continued data distribution.

Since proper handling of a no-error mode association results in a minimal amount of CNTL traffic, a small number of intermediate switching nodes in the path from data source to the data sinks would not be problematic for this application class. LANs with a backbone to which a number of small subnetworks are attached with network-layer switching nodes, so-called *federated systems*, are a popular model for avionics, ship-board, and other sensor-rich networked environments. These closed systems often define their own multicast address schemes, which are accommodated in XTP through Direct Addressing.

## Distribution of Real-Time Digital Images

In shipboard or ground-based command-and-control environments, signal processing techniques are applied to raw data from sensors and the processed data distributed across high-performance networks to display workstations for human operators [COHN89], [MARL89]. In a separate application domain, magnetic resonance and other medical imagery play an important role in diagnosis, and the ability to move these images quickly to multiple sites has been the focus of increasing interest [CHIM90].

These applications are characterized by the following requirements: the amount of data to be moved is generally quite large, and the inherent real-time constraints of updating a video display or supporting a real-time conference can result in high throughput needs. In the medical imaging environment message loss on the network may not be tolerable at all, or, at least, errors must be atomic. That is, if an image is partially corrupted, the user should have some indication that the entire image is unus-able. Screen refreshes during interactive video do not generally require a reliable ser-vice. Retransmission of incorrectly received data can, nonetheless, be valuable when delays caused by retransmissions are well below the threshold of the jitter constraints on refreshing displayed images.

Under such scenarios, an error-controlled XTP multicast association fits the needs of the application's data flow quite well. Using the bucket algorithm with the proper parameters (or an implementation-dependent equivalent), the XTP user at the multicast transmitting context can reliably deliver the digital images to the display devices at a rate bounded by the slowest display device. If a display device suffers a failure and the XTP peer on that device can not make progress, the failed peer will eventually be dropped from the conversation. Thus, in the medical imaging case, display devices can be guaranteed to have the desired behavior: either the display is active and all data is correctly received, or the display drops out of the multicast group and the user is noti-fied of communication failure.

With the bucket algorithm, parameters allow tuning to trade greater buffer space requirements at the transmitter for increased probability that a slow receiver will not be dropped from the distribution. In real-time environments such as command-and-control platforms, system designers have knowledge about how system resources need to be allocated to handle peak demands. Also, closed systems can be tuned to expected traffic characteristics. The bucket algorithm allows this type of system-dependent knowledge to be incorporated into the underlying XTP implementation such that sys-tem goals can be met.

As with the Periodic Updates example, the join procedure in XTP multicast is valuable for image distribution. The node distributing images has a semi-reliable association open with its receiving set at all times. A one-to-many data flow need not be halted or restarted, due to malfunctioning receivers dropping behind or due to new receivers joining the conversation. When a failed device recovers, it can rejoin the data distribution, and this procedure is transparent to other XTP users.

In this class of application the real-time constraints in combination with the volume of data to be transmitted make a high-performance, streaming multicast service not merely efficient, but an enabling technology. Using a link-layer multicast datagram service is a crude and limiting solution, due to the lack of desired functionality—rate, flow, and error control are very valuable, if not essential, to these applications. Using unicast transfer layer connections may be infeasible due to throughput requirements. The throughput necessary to deliver this type of application's data using serial unicasts can exceed the maximum bandwidth available.

## Wide-Area Resource Location

Network connectivity is rapidly increasing. High-speed wide area network standards such as broadband ISDN, the proposed National Research and Education Network (a gigabit WAN for the United States, [KAHN90]), and emerging metropolitan area network standards [MOLL88], promise to create future computing environments in which access to resources across wide area networks becomes routine [WULF88]. The lessons learned in developing LAN-based distributed systems should in many cases scale to these MAN/WAN environments. One such lesson has been the value of having a pool of servers to respond to requests on the group address in order to increase data and service availability and fault tolerance.

Recent work [DEER89] proposes to extend the IP protocol suite, including addressing and routing functionality, to provide for the delivery of multidestination IP datagrams in the Internet environment. The Internet Stream Protocol [TOPO91] includes support for long-distance conferencing, which involves management of logical multipoint-to-multipoint data flows. Work is also under way in the OSI community to provide for network layer group communication functionality.

These developments strongly indicate that multicast will be an integral part of future wide area networks. Though the characteristics of these very high-speed, wide area environments is largely an open research question, the goal is to have LAN-like communication. Current research, as indicated above, focuses on the first-order issue of building routers that support group communication.

XTP subsystems will be able to take advantage of the development of wide-area multicasting, as it becomes available, since XTP packets can be encapsulated and passed through wide-area routers. XTP multicast algorithms have no explicit features that would prevent correct operation over a wide-area environment, although new heuristics or modifications to existing heuristics might be expected. For example, aggressive slotting and damping or router intervention could be used to ensure that associations with large receiver sets do not generate an unacceptable number of CNTL packets.

## Multiclient/Multiserver Model

As mentioned in the discussion of the ISIS protocol suite in Section 8.1.1, the problem of providing *reliable atomic broadcast* appears in many distributed system applications, such as distributed databases and replicated program execution. The multiclient/multiserver model is an abstraction that captures the essence of a number of architectures for addressing fault-tolerance concerns [LELA91]. In this model, system elements send requests to a set of processes known as Clients, which then convert these requests into service commands for an appropriate set of processes, the Servers. As shown in Figure 8.8, the Clients and Servers may be co-located on the same machines, and multiple concurrent operations may be in progress at any time.

Interactions between the Clients and the Servers must be coordinated for concurrency control and fault tolerance. What is needed is an atomic reliable broadcast, the precise nature of which depends upon the fault model and degree of processing parallelism in the design. The many solutions to this problem can be characterized as (1) those involving only coordination between the Servers, (2) those involving only coordination between the Clients, and (3) those involving both Clients and Servers.

The multiclient/multiserver scenario is very general. What group communication services would be appropriate depends upon the exact communication needs of the higher-layer protocols chosen to provide the atomic reliable broadcast. One communication pattern that is useful to a number of schemes and that benefits from multicast mechanisms is a *full-duplex multicast transaction*.

A full-duplex multicast transaction involves an initiating process, the Transaction Manager, that wishes to send an application message (a Request) to a server group and then receive some number of arbitrarily large application messages (the Responses). The server group may be known by the Transaction Manager when the Request is launched or discovered as the Responses return. The Transaction Manager has knowledge of the success criteria by which the transaction is managed. Since full-duplex transactions may be a basic communication mechanism, there is considerable emphasis placed on the speed with which a Transaction Manager can complete (that is, determine the success or failure of) each transaction.

As noted in Section 8.3.3, the XTP cloning heuristic coupled with a one-to-many association can implement an efficient full-duplex multicast transaction primitive. A multicast transmitter sets up a multicast association with a receiver set, each of which sends replies via a reverse direction association. If semi-reliable XTP multicast is used, then the Request is flow-, rate-, and error-controlled under semi-reliable semantics as are the Responses in the unicast back channels. The cloning technique allows the set of responding Servers in a transaction to be determined at run-time without prior coordination and without the Transaction Manager having to open a specified number of contexts with explicit **input** commands.

The Multidriver approach [DEMP90] demonstrates how a full-duplex transaction service can be implemented using XTP. In the Multidriver scheme, a transaction-layer coordination protocol is efficiently layered onto XTP using XTP's *btag* channel. By

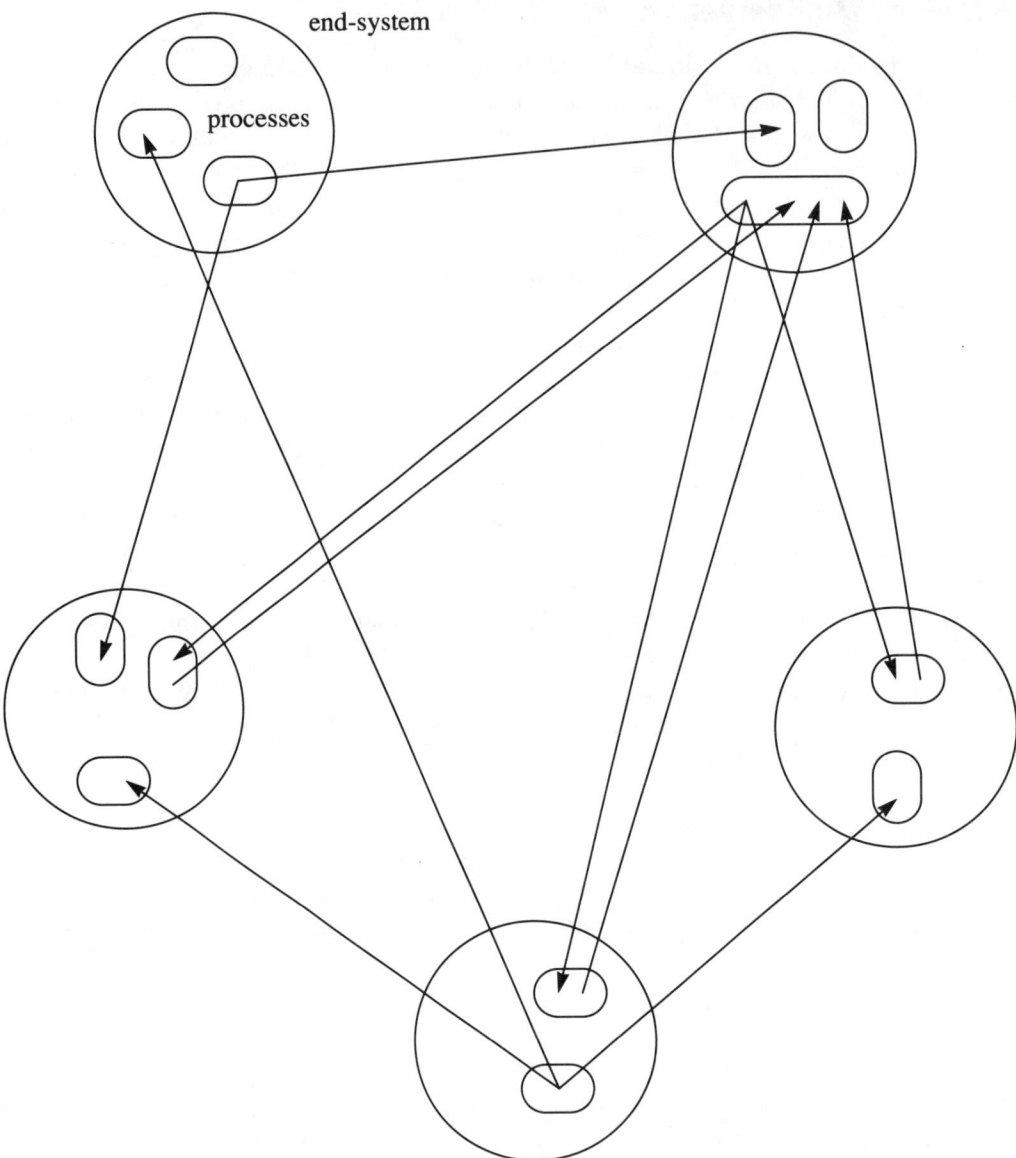

**Figure 8.8 — Multiclient/Multiserver Model**

embedding transaction-layer control information in the btag field of both the forward (one-to-many) association and the reverse (one-to-one) associations, the coordination protocol manages a full-duplex transaction. Control commands and data are
concurrently transmitted, and the success of individual transactions can be predicated
on explicit group views using primitives such as those in [DEMP91]. The Multidriver

approach provides a more powerful group communication facility than the XTP semi-reliable multicast alone since the former builds upon XTP a notion of the explicit group membership.

## References

[BIRM87]      Birman, K., and Joseph, T. A., "Reliable Communication in the Presence of Failures," *ACM Transactions on Computer Systems*, Vol. 5, No. 1, pp. 47–76 (February 1987).

[BIRM91]      Birman, K., and Cooper, R., "The ISIS Project: Real Experience with a Fault Tolerant Programming System," *ACM Operating System Review*, Vol. 25, No. 2, pp. 103–107 (April 1991).

[CHER88b]     Cheriton, D. R., "The V Distributed System," *Communications of the ACM*, Vol. 31, No. 3, pp. 314–333 (March 1988).

[CHIM90]      Chimiack, W., "Radiology Information Systems," Protocol Engines, Inc., Report PEI-90-172, 1990.

[COHN89]      Cohn, M., "Functional Addressing: Another Way of Looking at Multicast," *Transfer*, Vol. 2, No. 6, pp. 13–15 (November/December 1989).

[DEER89]      Deering, S. E., "Host Extensions for IP Multicasting," RFC 1112, Network Information Center, SRI International, August 1989.

[DEMP90]      Dempsey, B. J., Fenton, J. C., and Weaver, A. C., "The Multidriver: A Reliable Multicast Service Using the Xpress Transfer Protocol," *Proceedings of the 15th Conference on Local Computer Networks*, Minneapolis, Minnesota, pp. 351–358 (September 30–October 3, 1990).

[DEMP91]      Dempsey, B. J., "Design and Analysis of a Transport Layer Reliable Multicast," Master's Thesis, The University of Virginia, Department of Computer Science, January 1991.

[HART91]      Hartrick, T. W., "Performance Analysis of a Software Implementation of the Xpress Transfer Protocol," Master's Thesis, The University of Virginia, Department of Computer Science, August 1991.

[KAHN90]      Kahn, R. E., "CNRI Gigabit Testbed Initiative," *Transfer*, Vol. 3, No. 6 (November/December 1990).

[LAMP78]      Lamport, L., "Time, Clocks, and the Ordering of Events in a Distributed System," *Communications of the ACM*, Vol. 21, No. 7, pp. 558–565 (July 1978).

[LELA91]      LeLann, G., and Bres, G., "Reliable Atomic Broadcast in Distributed Systems with Omission Faults," *ACM Operating System Review*, Vol. 25, No. 2, pp. 80–86 (April 1991).

[LIAN90]      Liang, L., Chanson, S. T., and Neufield, G. W., "Process Groups and Group Communications: Classifications and Requirements," *IEEE Computer Magazine*, Vol. 23, No. 2, pp. 56–66 (February 1990).

[MARL89]      Marlow, D. T., "Requirements for a High Performance Transport Protocol for Use on Naval Platforms," Revision 1, Naval Surface Warfare Center, July 1989.

[MOLL88]      Mollenauer, J. F., "Standards for Metropolitan Area Networks," *IEEE Communications Magazine*, Vol. 26, No. 4, pp. 15–19 (April 1988).

[PALI88]      Paliwoda, K., "Transactions Involving Multicast," *Computer Communications*, Vol. 11, No. 6, pp. 313–318 (December 1988).

[TOPO91]      Topolcic, C., "The Internet Stream Protocol (ST)," Presented to ANSI Committee X3S3.3, Report X3S3.3/91–197, Boston, Massachusetts, June 1991.

[WULF88]      Wulf, W. A., "The National Collaboratory—A White Paper," National Science Foundation, December 1988.

# 9
# The Protocol Engine

The charter of the XTP development team was the creation of a protocol rich in functionality yet lightweight in mechanism so that this functionality could be coupled with high performance. To accommodate these design goals, the creators of XTP focused on two main ideas: (1) streamlined protocol processing through the judicious use of orthogonal mechanisms and the avoidance of optional and variable-length control fields that complicate parsing control information, and (2) assurance that the protocol could take full advantage of an implementation using highly parallel VLSI circuits.

It has been recognized that as much as 80% of the processing involved in sustaining data communications is related to non-protocol activities, such as buffer management, host-to-network interfacing, and data copying [NORD89]. Traditional implementations force the protocol to compete for a single host processor with a variety of other entities; host busses used for moving data to and from the network often prove to be a bottleneck due to high latencies and interrupt servicing. Thus, closely associated with the Xpress Transfer Protocol development, but distinctly independent, is the development of a synchronized hybrid multiprocessor complex within which XTP will be able to source and sink the full bandwidth of a 100-plus Mbit/sec medium. This multiprocessor complex is designed to exploit the functional decomposition of XTP protocol procedures and to off-load non-protocol related activities such as buffer management and data movement. This effort is called the Protocol Engine Project.

## 9.1   The Goal of the Protocol Engine Project

The primary design goal of the Protocol Engine (PE) is to provide at the user level the data rates of the medium. To do this, the PE must process time-critical and interrupt-intensive tasks on-board, thereby relieving the host of these real-time demands of the network. The PE must be designed such that the processing of packets occurs as the packet "flows" into the host from the network; that is, packet processing must be completed within the arrival time of a packet. Analysis [CHES91b] indicates that the "real-time" packet processing goal can be met even for small (60-byte) packets arriving from an FDDI network.

To achieve such "real-time" packet processing, the PE consists of specialized chips that provide basic packet processing capabilities and that are connected through high-

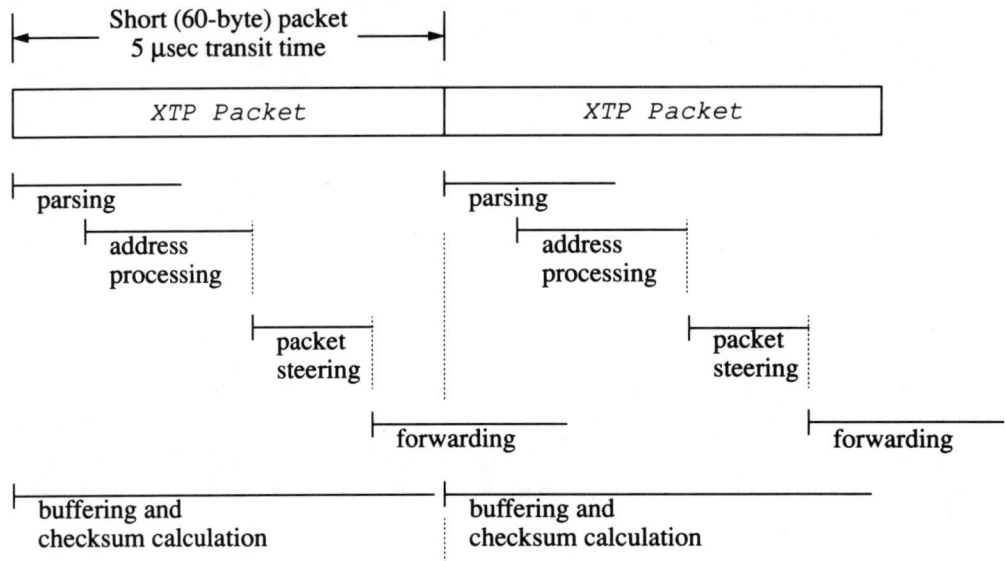

**Figure 9.1 — The PE Packet Processing Timeline for Short XTP Packets**

speed data paths. The chips represent a functional decomposition of all the processing necessary to carry data to and from the network, including both protocol processing as well as non-protocol communication activities. Each chip internally reflects the "flow-through" architecture; the processing particular to a chip is done as the packet moves through pipelined stages. Figure 9.1 illustrates the way in which various actions performed on a packet can be overlapped and executed in parallel.

Inside each individual chip, an on-chip core processor employs a multithread approach that handles accepting, processing, and dispatching data in pipelined stages. Internal buffering delays are limited to the time spent in hardware FIFOs, which can be bounded to stay within the real-time processing requirements. Projections [SCHW90] of the processing power of the PE estimate the throughput at a sustainable 200 Mbit/sec for chip clock rates of 25 MHz.

The PE "accelerates" the protocol in the sense that it provides high-speed data movement and hardware-based packet processing. Since protocol processing is only one component of the processing handled by the PE, the Protocol Engine concept is not inherently tied to the Xpress Transfer Protocol alone. That is, due to the generality of its design, the PE can be used to accelerate protocols other than XTP.

## 9.2   The Protocol Engine Architecture

The PE1000 Series Protocol Engine Chipset is a set of highly parallel VLSI subsystems suitable for implementing XTP and, due to the generality of its design, other protocols as well [CHIN92]. There are various configurations of these chips, any one of which is termed a Protocol Engine. Certain components of the PE1000 chips are programmable, providing the performance advantages of specialized hardwired circuits while retaining the flexibility of a programmable approach.

There are four different chips in the PE1000 series, the MAC Port (MPORT), the Host Port (HPORT), the Buffer Controller (BCTL), and an optional Control Processor (CP). Each of these chips is composed of programmable finite state machines, specialized sequencers, and bus interface logic. These chips are organized around two busses, the Data Bus (DBus) and the Control Bus (CBus). These busses allow inter-component communication via separate channels, thus reducing the interference between control information exchange and data streaming during protocol processing. Various memory modules are attached to these chips to provide control information storage (such as contexts), buffers for data, and microcode instructions.

Figure 9.2 shows the system block diagram for each of the components of a PE. The MPORT provides an intelligent MAC layer interface, including checksumming, header parsing, context identification, and address resolution. The HPORT provides an intelligent direct memory access (DMA) engine with a synchronous bus interface to the host, including byte swapping if needed. The BCTL provides buffer management and arbitrates the access to it via the DBus. The CP is a programmable processor which provides specific protocol processing functions, such as connection management.

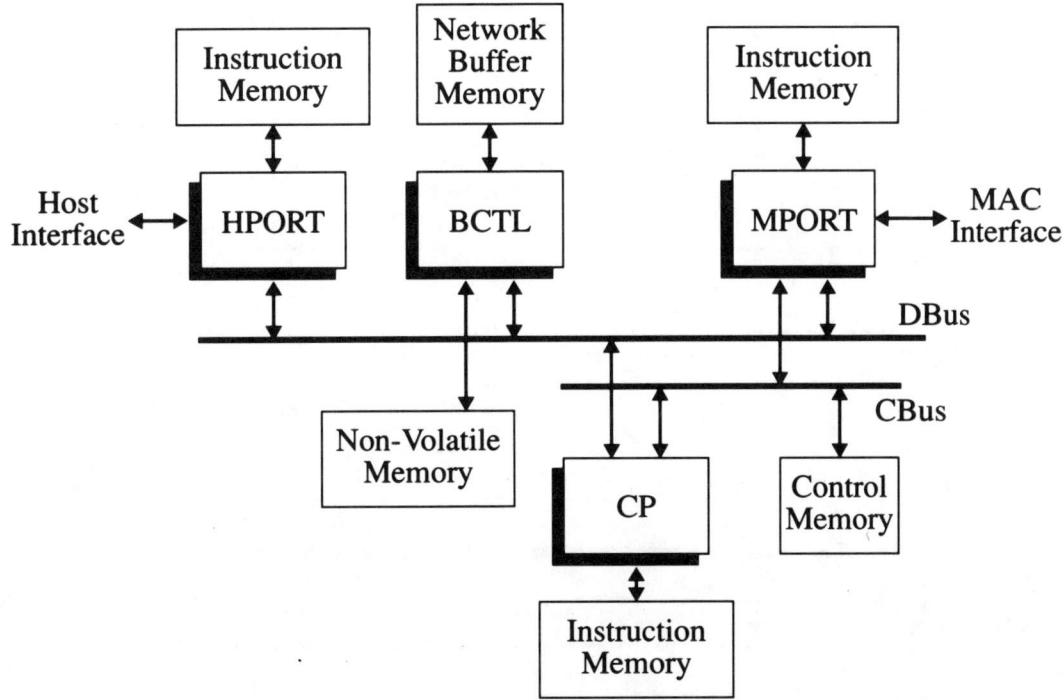

**Figure 9.2 — System Block Diagram for the Protocol Engine**

## MAC Port (MPORT)

The MPORT chip connects the PE to a MAC implementation (generally a MAC chipset). The MPORT transfers packets between the MAC device and the Network Buffer Memory, performing various protocol processing as the packet passes through the chip.

The MPORT is composed of six functional blocks used to process packets coming from or going to the MAC chipset. These six functional blocks are the MAC Interface, the Receive Engine, the Transmit Engine, the DBus Interface Unit, the Packet Processor Module, and the CBus Interface Unit. The MPORT and its functional blocks are shown in Figure 9.3.

The MAC Interface connects the PE to the MAC device via a control block interface. The implementation details are somewhat MAC-specific. The Receive Engine examines an incoming XTP packet and decides if this packet should be kept or discarded. As the packet passes through the Receive Engine, the checksums are fully validated, certain information is extracted from the packet's header, and the packet is demultiplexed according to its context. The parts of the header that are extracted are delivered to a buffer for transmission on the CBus at the same time that the whole packet is placed on the DBus. The Transmit Engine conversely passes a packet from the DBus through a Transmit FIFO out to the MAC Interface. This Transmit FIFO is

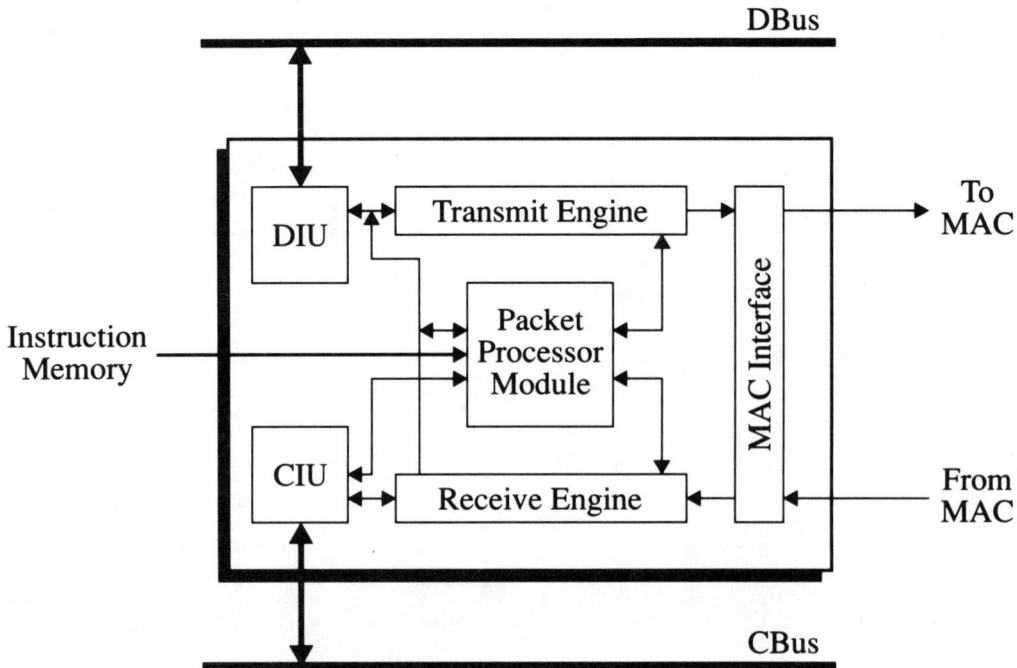

**Figure 9.3 — The Functional Blocks of the MPORT**

used to absorb bus latencies incurred from the different data rates between the DBus and the network.

The DBus Interface Unit (DIU) and the CBus Interface Unit (CIU) provide the MPORT with access to these two busses. During receive operations, the DIU reads data from the Receive FIFO in the Receive Engine; during transmit operations, the DIU writes data to the Transmit FIFO in the Transmit Engine. The CIU provides access to the Control Memory for storing the extracted header information.

The Packet Processor Module (PPM) is a powerful on-chip RISC processor designed to respond to real-time events from the network. It has a four-thread architecture to allow fast context switches while it processes information from the Receive Engine. By using this information, the PPM accesses Control Memory via the CBus to determine the packet's context.

## Host Port (HPORT)

Like the MPORT, the HPORT uses specialized processing units and an on-chip RISC processor for high-speed protocol processing in a flow-through manner. The HPORT provides high-speed DMA transfers between the host bus and its internal FIFOs and accesses the Network Buffer Memory to send and retrieve packets. In addition to controlling the DMA operations at a projected 200 Mbit/sec rate, the HPORT performs packetization on the data from the host and then generates checksum values for each of the packets.

The HPORT processes data as it flows between the Network Buffer Memory and the host memory. On data destined for the network, the HPORT provides packet header and trailer generation, checksum insertion, sequence number insertion, byte swapping, word alignment, and padding. On data destined for the user, the HPORT separates the protocol and data fields from the packet and delivers them both to the separate parts of the user memory.

Figure 9.4 shows the functional blocks of the HPORT. These blocks include the HBus and the DBus Interface Units, the Receive and Transmit FIFOs, the Checksum Generator, the HBus and the DBus DMA Engines, and the Packet Processor Module. When a transmit command is given, the Packet Processor Module (PPM) uses certain information from the command to prepare the HBus and DBus DMA Engines for operation. The HBus DMA Engine transfers the data from the host memory into the Transmit FIFO. The data is simultaneously sent to the Checksum Generator. The PPM packetizes the data; as the DBus DMA Engine begins to transfer the packet to the Network Buffer Memory, the PPM and the Checksum Generator insert sequencing and checksum information into the packet.

The MPORT initiates the HPORT's receive operation when packets are received from the network and are placed into the Network Buffer Memory. The DBus DMA Engine retrieves the packet and places it into the Receive FIFO. The PPM separates the data from the protocol information so that the HBus DMA Engine can place the various information directly into the desired locations in host memory.

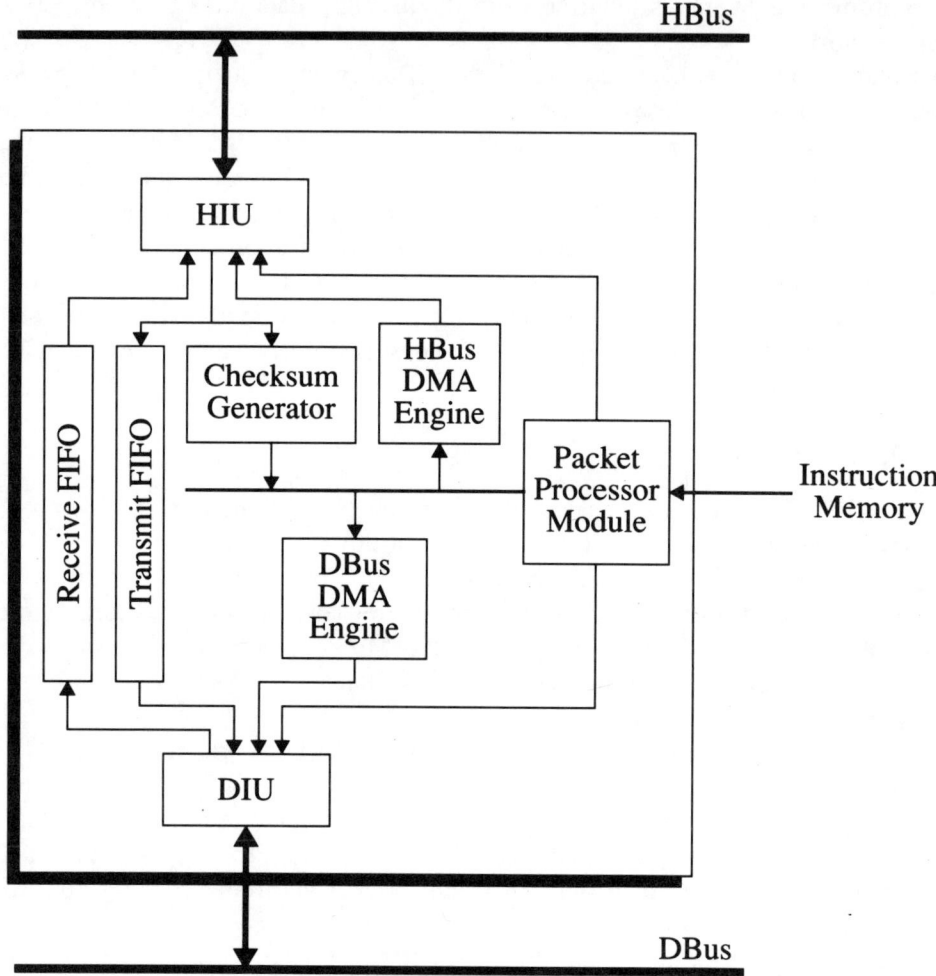

**Figure 9.4 — The Functional Blocks of the HPORT**

## Buffer Controller (BCTL)

The BCTL is a programmable memory controller used to provide a seamless interface for data transfer between the DBus and the various memory modules, namely the Network Buffer Memory and the Non-Volatile Memory. The BCTL arbitrates mastership of the DBus. At the DBus interface the BCTL converts the signals from the DBus to allow direct access to the Network Buffer Memory, and maintains high data transfer rates by interleaving the two banks of DRAM which comprise the Network Buffer Memory. Instructions for the BCTL as well as for the other port chips may be stored in the Non-Volatile Memory, where they are retrieved and distributed by the BCTL at system boot time.

There are seven functional blocks within the BCTL, as shown in Figure 9.5. These include the DBus Interface Unit, the DBus Arbiter, the DRAM Controller, the DRAM Transceivers, the Configuration Registers, the Non-Volatile Memory Controller, and Test Logic. The DBus Arbiter dictates DBus ownership among the various DBus masters, which may be the DIU of any port chip, including the BCTL itself. Data and addresses flowing from the DBus enter through the DIU, then pass through the DRAM Transceivers and the DRAM Controller, then out to the DRAM. The DRAM Controller provides the required signals for read, write, and refresh operations. The Configuration Registers govern the actions of the DRAM Controller and the Non-Volatile Memory Controller, allowing these controllers to be customized for the environment. The Test Logic supports an IEEE standard Test Interface for robust board-level testing and the location of faults in the DRAM.

## Control Processor (CP)

The CP provides high-level protocol processing, such as association and path management procedures. While each of the other port chips performs the same generic packet processing functions, the CP is primarily concerned with protocol-specific processing. Current designs for the CP include a microprogrammable RISC processor for performing the protocol processing, as well as interface modules for connecting the CP to the CBus and the DBus. Since the protocol processing may instead be done within the host, the CP is an optional component of the PE; clearly, a PE with the CP attached will provide a significant performance enhancement.

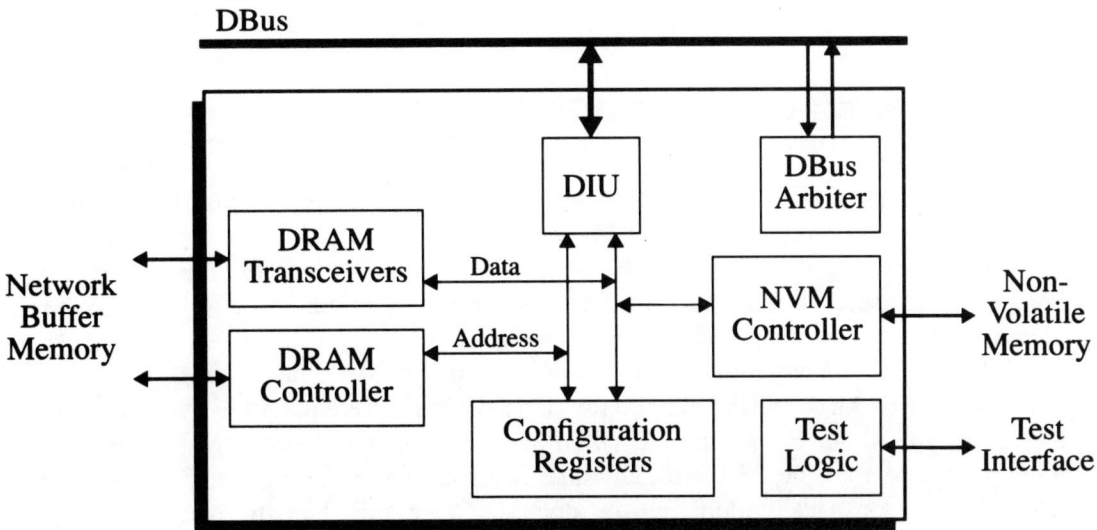

**Figure 9.5 — The Functional Blocks of the BCTL**

## Busses

There are two main busses within the Protocol Engine, the Control Bus (CBus) and the Data Bus (DBus). The CBus is used to allow the MPORT and the CP access to the Control Memory, where frame control information is stored. The DBus connects all of the port chips since each chip performs some processing function on the flow of data either from the host or from the network.

The HPORT and the host's backplane bus are connected by another type of bus, called the Host Bus (HBus). This bus is optimized to interface to typical backplane busses, such as the VME or SBus industry standards.

The Instruction Memory is connected to the HPORT or MPORT chip via an Instruction Bus (IBus), through which a port chip accesses an instruction stream for its on-chip RISC processor.

## Memory

The Network Buffer Memory consists of two banks of dynamic RAM interleaved to reduce access time. The Network Buffer Memory is used as the main repository of data both destined for and received from the network. In addition, the Network Buffer Memory may be used to store context-related information for each association.

Control Memory is used for storing frame control information and various data structures including address lookup tables, connection context blocks, and other control blocks. The standard Control Memory in the PE1000 series is designed to support up to 1000 active connections.

The Instruction Memory consists of fast static RAMs (SRAMs) used by the on-chip RISC processor for program storage. The Instruction Memory is loaded at boot time by the BCTL using the Non-Volatile Memory.

# 9.3   Extended Configurations

The basic design of the PE, especially the busses, allows up to five port chips within the chipset. At least one each of the MPORT, HPORT, and BCTL chips must be present. The remaining slots may be filled with a CP or multiple MPORTs or HPORTs or both. Adding these various chips to the basic PE provides configuration possibilities including bridging, routing, and host multiplexing.

Adding a second MPORT to the PE allows a second MAC device to be connected to the host. This MAC device may be the same type or different. If the two MACs are the same type, as in FDDI, the PE could serve the dual redundant MAC for fault-tolerance purposes. The PE board may also be used as a bridge or router between the two subnetworks; packets delivered on one MAC are stored in the Network Buffer Memory until they are forwarded to the network served by the other MAC. A third MPORT can be added (if no CP is present) to make it possible to implement any combination of the above configurations.

Multiple HPORTs allow the PE board to be attached to multiple data sinks or sources, such as sensors or mass storage devices, or even another host. In this case data from the network is demultiplexed from the DBus through the appropriate HPORT and into the attached sink, or it is multiplexed from the multiple HPORTs onto the DBus and eventually to the network.

# 9.4   Availability

It is anticipated that the PE1000 chipset, configured with an MPORT for a commercial FDDI chipset and an HPORT for a VME bus, will be available in 1992. More information on this product and its timetable is available from Protocol Engines Inc.

### References

[CHES91b]      Chesson, G., "The Protocol Engine Chipset," Extended Abstract, Protocol Engines Inc. Report PEI-91-52, 1991.

[CHIN92]       Chin, H. W., Edholm, P., and Schwaderer, D., "Implementing PE-1000 Based Internetworking Nodes," Protocol Engines Inc. Report PEI-92-49, 1992.

[NORD89]       Nordmark, E., and Cheriton, D. R., "Experiences from VMTP: How to achieve low response time," *Proceedings of the IFIP Workshop on Protocols for High-Speed Networks*, Zurich (May 9–11, 1989).

[SCHW90]       Schwaderer, W. D., "XTP in VLSI: Protocol Decomposition for ASIC Implementation," *Proceedings of the 15th Conference on Local Computer Networks*, Minneapolis, Minnesota, pp. 249–252 (September 30–October 3, 1990).

# Index

780